Life Is to Be Celebrated
Messages for the 21st Century

ALSO BY ROBERT LEE HILL

PROSE

All You Need Is (More) Love . . .
and 101 Other Musings, Essays, and Sundry Pieces

Life's Too Short for Anything But Love . . .
and 101 Other Musings, Essays, and Sundry Pieces

The Color of Sabbath:
Proclamations & Prayers for New Beginnings

Empowering Congregations:
Successful Strategies for 21st Century Leadership
(with Denton L. Roberts)

We Make the Road by Walking:
Proclamations & Prayers

Made Whole by Broken Bread

POETRY

Hard to Tell: A Congregation of Poems, 1990 – 2003

Life Is to Be Celebrated

Selected Sermons Messages for the 21st Century

Robert Lee Hill

CAROLINE STREET PRESS

Kansas City

Published by Caroline Street Press
Kansas City, Missouri

Cover design and book interior by Jason McIntyre
Cover photography by Levon Weaver

Unless otherwise noted, all scripture quotations are taken from the New Revised Standard Version of the Bible, copyright 1989, Division of Christian Education of the National Council of the Churches of Christ in the United States of America. Any divergence in text reflects the author's translation.

Hill, Robert Lee
Life Is To Be Celebrated: Selected Sermons: Messages for the 21st Century

ISBN: 978-0-578-98765-1

IN MEMORIAM:

DENTON LOWELL ROBERTS, JR.
GERALDINE HILL ROBERTS
KELLY MILLER SMITH, SR.
FRED BRADDOCK CRADDOCK
GARDNER CALVIN TAYLOR
WALLACE S. HARTSFIELD, SR.

Whose preaching, teaching, and very lives established
the highest of bars (homiletical and existential)
for which I and a host of others
are still striving.

Contents

FROM ASHES TO EASTER

ADVENT AND CHRISTMAS

FOREWORD

A few years ago, a series of television ads sponsored by Nike featured the then well-known athlete Bo Jackson who had stellar professional success in both football and baseball, and almost certainly would have been in a professional Hall of Fame except that his career was cut short by injury. The ads included the tag line, "Bo knows . . . ." "Bo knows football." "Bo knows baseball." I begin the Foreword to this book by saying "Bob Hill knows preaching." If there were a Hall of Fame for Preachers, Robert Lee Hill would certainly be included. These fifty-two sermons exhibit the best of contemporary preaching with respect to spirit, theological acuity, timeliness, concern for justice, human insight, homiletical variety, evocative language, and poetry.

Bob knows joy. The spirit of joy comes across in the title of the book, *Life Is to Be Celebrated*, which is also the title of the forty-seventh sermon in the book. These sermons have an overflowing sense of the goodness of life that comes from a good, loving, blessing-bestowing God and that are mediated through a preacher who has an overflowing sense of the goodness, the wonder, and the delight of life. To be sure, this preacher has known his share of struggle. As we note below, the sermons never flinch in the face of injustice, suffering, sin, and death. But Robert Lee Hill is animated by awareness of something More, a loving Power who will never be content with those things, and who offers possibility to every moment. Because this presence permeates the world—and especially this preacher, as the title of the first section of the book says so well—ordinary days can become the occasions of extraordinary times.

Bob knows theology. I have to say my greatest general disappointment with contemporary preaching is its theological vapidity, or in too many cases, theological confusion or even amnesia. Preachers transfer the religious platitudes from the local hair salon to the pulpit. Apparently unaware that they are preaching different theologies, lectionary preachers often commend the theologies of the wisdom literature one week, the end-time passages another week, the Deuteronomic blessings and curses still another week, and the Greek world view coming through still other texts. Every one of these sermons is theologically consistent with a God of unrelenting love who seeks to bless the community of humankind and nature in all its wondrous diversity. This God continually offers individuals and communities pathways out of the destructive effects of sin and towards the pathway for blessing. For this preacher, "everyone's a theologian," everyone in the ecclesial community is called to think theologically about all of life.

Bob knows the news. Some preacher's sermons sound as though they could have been preached in almost any time and place. But every sermon in this volume makes direct reference to the moment in which it is preached. The sermons herein are not just condensed versions of the stories on the news with a little commentary on the side. This preacher reveals the complicated dynamics of contemporary events and interprets them theologically. These sermons are not just bits and pieces of theological reflections but, taken together, put forward a theological vision that can empower a life.

Bob knows justice. Robert Lee Hill knows justice in its deepest and most expansive biblical and theological sense: as God's desire for all in the human and cosmic community to live together covenantally in love, peace, mutual support, security, dignity, freedom, and abundance for all. From the beginning of his ministry, Robert Lee Hill has had a prophetic voice in the pulpit and a body active in movements for justice. The reader's eye will immediately catch a section of sermons in the book entitled *"Justice, Justice, You Shall Pursue,"* but the preacher's concern for justice is not limited to these five sermons. Bob Hill's passion for justice permeates the entire volume. It is a passion, similar to that of God as portrayed by Whitehead, "whose nature is best conceived [as that of] a tender care that nothing be lost."[*]

Bob knows honesty and courage. Bob has the integrity and courage to name things that need to be changed — things in individual, personal lives; things in the religion *("When Religion is Sick")*; and things in the larger culture. Moreover, the sermons can point directly to the consequences of neglecting the changes that need to be made. Yet, this preacher from Kansas City speaks not out of anger or vengeance but out of the painful love, and he always shines a light towards the possibility for all lives to manifest qualities that turn towards celebration. Bob Hill has been ahead of the Eurocentric game when it comes to racial justice, and that theme surfaces again and again.

Bob knows variety in preaching. So many preachers find a "style" and stick with it week after week as listeners become more and more anesthetized. These sermons put forward a steady theological vision. The congregation knows what it can rely on from God and what it needs to do in response. But the sermons vary in style and approach. Some sermons begin with the Bible and come to life. Some messages begin with life and make their way to the Bible. Some sermons go back and forth between the Bible and life. Some messages have the quality of precise, linear theological reasoning, whereas others are more lyrical and exploratory. Some of the sermons have the spirit of poetry even when expressed in prose. Some sermons leave the listener needing to make a decision while others have opened a door for meditation. And Bob's styles and approaches embrace a good many other things in between.

Bob knows language. I do not know of a contemporary preacher who has a better eye and ear for just the right word, for the expressive phrase that opens up a fresh perspective on the world, for the sentence that makes me think, "Oh, why did I not think to say it that way?" He imagines how things could be in ways that prompt the listener to think, "Why not?" Moreover, Bob tells real-life stories — including some autobiographical stories — that have the complexities, tensions, and resolutions of real life. Bob has an eye for just-right details. He has just the right words for feelings.

---

[*] Alfred North Whitehead, *Process and Reality*. Corrected Edition, edited by David Ray Griffin and Donald W. Sherburn (New York: The Free Press, 1978), 346.

Bob knows poetry. I have already mentioned that parts of some sermons have the feel of poetry expressed in prose. Robert Lee Hill is also a formal poet who has published volumes of poetry. Poetry appears in some of these sermons, always to excellent effect. Poets must walk a delicate line between using language with enough color and nuance to be truly expressive, but not using the language in such a way as to call attention to itself. The best poems create linguistic worlds in which listeners enter for a time, only to emerge with eyes and ears better attuned to their everyday worlds. Bob's poetry is of the latter genre.

Bob knows Introductions. The *"Introduction"* to **Life Is to Be Celebrated** is a bonus for preachers and for people who want to learn more about what goes into preaching. Introductions to books are often designed to catch the reader's attention, to tell the reader a little bit about the book, and to give the reader a little background on the author. The introduction to **Life Is to Be Celebrated** goes beyond those things to provide the reader with a most-engaging introduction to preaching—why we preach, what goes into sermons, when and where does preaching take place, and even how to do it. For preachers, this Introduction is a review of a basic course in preaching. Lay listeners will benefit from looking into the study window to see what goes on in sermon preparation. Surprisingly, this discussion of the theory and practice of preaching is written in a way that is more engaging than most sermons.

I do not know of a book on preaching that better brings a life-giving theology to our time. I hope it receives the wide readership that it deserves. And I hope that wherever it is read, it sparks celebrations of life.

Ronald J. Allen
Professor of Preaching, and Gospels and Letters, Emeritus
Christian Theological Seminary, Indianapolis

ACKNOWLEDGEMENTS

For support all through the process and utterly thoughtful steerage to the welcoming embrace at Caroline Street Press, my deepest thanks to Alex Greenwood, wonderful friend and extraordinary writer indeed. Thanks, too, to Sonja Shaffer, for visual excellence, and great thanks, as well, to Jason McIntyre, for artistry and deft finesse with his overall design.

For the keenest proof-reading skill I've ever been privileged to witness, I offer David Buchmann heartfelt gratitude and admiration.

For the Foreword by Ronald Allen – first-rate colleague, generous friend, and homiletician of the highest rank – abundant blessings and fervent thanks. Your encouragement and affirmation across the miles and the years have meant and have made a world of difference in the preaching task.

For the listening hearts, minds, and souls who constituted Community Christian Church, as well as the other congregations who received these sermons, I abide in profound thanksgiving. Your patience, enthusiasm, good humor, integrity, graciousness, joyfulness and persistent inclination toward celebration have shown me what the "Beloved Community" is all about.

And for perduring love in life and constant support in preaching and all else, I am first and foremost grateful to Priscilla, premier critic, keenest appreciator, and ever and again the best … always.

INTRODUCTION

Preaching is both craft and art, both direct statement and refined rhetoric, both exhortation and supplication, both proclamation and persuasion. Some sermons seek to soar toward the heights of holy ecstasy, while other sermons dive into the depths of human struggle. Some sermons effect life-changing transformations, while other sermons provide life-reinforcing assurance. Every one of these sorts of sermons (and so many more, too numerous to mention) become part of the homiletical experience for those preachers fortunate enough to preach over enough years.

The sermons within these pages are offered with a few caveats.

- Preaching always happens in a community of faith, tempered by relationships, tried and tested by shared commitments. Over the course of my 30-plus years of service at Community Christian Church in Kansas City, Missouri, and especially during the latter half of that span, a theme predominated: *Life is meant to be celebrated and not merely tolerated.* Aspects of that theme are detectable in nearly every sermon in these pages.
- Preaching is nearly always an amalgamated approximation of what we humans think we know about God and our traditions and maybe even some speculative insights about ourselves.
- Sermons are situated in definite times and places, with specific hearers and worshipers, engaging issues that hearers and worshipers contend with during their undeniably, unavoidably particular lives. There really aren't any "timeless sermons," however much we may applaud great pulpit masters of the past as having achieved such gems. (About the final form of these sermons here, please note that some of the sermons are from original manuscripts, others are transcriptions of recordings, and still others are combinations of those two sources. For clarity and readability, editing has also been applied.)
- Sermons also always aspire toward universal truths and ideals to which people across time and space cling with fervent hope. Preaching that hopes to connect with anyone must connect with the hopes of us all.

There are always *what, where, when, how, why,* and *who* questions on the way to the task of preaching.

The *what* dimension of homiletics is sometimes deemed to be the most challenging task of the preaching life. Figuring out a message, squeezing out an interpretation from the thick and time-worn texts of Holy Writ, seeking to find some trustworthy, non-profaning cadences for sharing something of God that has been found in one's daily walk of faith — all these are the *what* of preaching and the regular (usually weekly) task of a preacher in a regular pulpit. Nearly all the time, the preacher knows that one's reach will absolutely exceed one's grasp in the task. The enunciation of a vision, the reporting of what has been heard from the surprising whisperings of God, the searing truths too hot and too fervently felt to be kept inside oneself, the articulation of what it means to be a human being, what it means to be a child of God, what it means to be a soul reaching toward the saving light in the midst of uncertainty, the announcement of love and joy in the face of the gracing ways of God –all these are the *what* of preaching.

"*Where* can sermons be preached?" preachers ask when we set out as novices. "Anywhere and everywhere imaginable" is the eventual and only honest answer. Most sermons are preached from a pulpit. But the substance and structure of those launching pads of meaning are as varied as the people who preach and the congregations who listen. Most of the sermons in these pages have been preached in Kansas City, Missouri, at Community Christian Church, a 131-year-old congregation within the Disciples of Christ communion, a progressive community of faith that afforded this preacher more grace and tolerance than he ever deserved and more welcoming affirmation than any preacher could ever have considered possible. Over the course of my service at Community, I preached sermons in the sanctuary of the main building (designed by Frank Lloyd Wright), in the intimacy of its Bonfils Chapel, on the church's rooftop deck, in its Centennial Hall, in the Narthex welcoming area, in nearby Southmoreland Park, and in the Theiss Park amphitheater along nearby Brush Creek. Some sermons were offered in United Church of Christ, United Methodist, Baptist, Unitarian, and sister Disciples congregations. One sermon was proffered in a Reform Jewish congregation. After heeding the advice and encouragement of Fred Craddock, some of these sermons became "traveling" sermons and were offered in Arkansas, California, Indiana, Kansas, Kentucky, New Mexico, Ohio, Texas, Tennessee, and Washington, D.C., beyond the originating dates and places listed herein.

When are sermons preached? When were these sermons preached? Mostly on Sunday mornings. But, also, on other days of the week, as it turns out, when I look back over my preaching schedule and annual calendars. One could easily expect that Wednesday and Friday would be marked by preaching, given the liturgical scheduling of Ash Wednesday and Good Friday preaching occasions, as well as Maundy Thursday. But it's been surprising to recall a Shrove Tuesday preaching assignment. And then, taking into account that Christmas and Christmas Eve, unlike Easter which is anchored to Sunday, are moveable feasts and thus rotate to different days of the week, it's natural that the sermons contained in this volume have been preached on every single day of a normal week.

"*How* are sermons to be preached?" may seem to be a thoughtless kind of query. But in addition to the tectonic shifting of homiletical strategies that infused the last quarter of the twentieth century, the startling revolutions within media and technology and their compounding impact on how people receive any and all sorts of discourse have made the "*how*" of homiletics one of the most pressing questions for preaching in the twenty-first century. Words, of course, are the stuff of sermons. But they are no longer the only "texts" employed by preachers in proclamation. The use of images, film, and video have increasingly become important tools in the preacher's toolbox. Just as poetry may impressively sum up the essence of human experience or an encounter with the divine, so may a scene from a movie powerfully illuminate a foundational truth of scripture. Some of the sermons herein (particularly those from 2009 onward) were accompanied by slides or film clips. For the sake of continuity with the rest of the sermons, however, I've chosen not to include the slide and film cues. In the end, words remain the primary vessels bearing the message for this preacher.

"*Why* preach?" every generation asks in its own way and with its own attendant, vexing challenges. The answers to that question are multitudinous and multi-valent. Because one may and one must preach. Because of duty and need. Because one has been prompted by an arresting vision in a moment of crisis. Because one has been startled by a sliver of a glimpse of a truth out of the corner of one's eye. Because a text like Matthew 14:16 (paralleled in identical fashion in the other two synoptic accounts, Mark 6:37 and Luke 9:13) continues to haunt a preacher with Jesus' mandate about something more than food: "You give them something to eat." Because of the dearth of coherence which so many folks feel in their lives, and because of the steadfast hope of countless souls for more substance and less fear.

And then there is the *who* dimension of preaching. Who is a sermon for? The simple response to such a question is "the people," usually in a congregation, a specific group of people who display the textures of a shared history, gathered for worship and praise, sharing their sorrows and celebrations and most everything in between. And is the sermon for the preacher as well? Of course, "Yes" has to be the answer to that question, since all preachers are stumbling, stammering, and stuttering toward a holy moment when we can hear a pronouncement of grace and justice, of mercy and compassion, for our own souls as well as for those in our charge. But perhaps there is more. Might it be sometimes that God Almighty shows up to hear a sermon, to receive a confirmation of some truth that has been proffered down through the ages, to see if the people are catching on to a new angle on an eternal verity that has been granted to the community, to see if a preacher and a people will behold the new thing that God means to do in a new time in order to bring forth a new realm of grace and goodness, light and love?

All these are among the questions I attempted to ask along the way in the preparation and presentation of the sermons in this volume. For the privilege, honor and ground-shaking blessedness afforded me in the preaching of these sermons, I remain abidingly, utterly grateful.

– Bob Hill

ORDINARY DAYS,
EXTRAORDINARY TIMES

1

ON SEEING THE ELEPHANT
& HEARING THE OWL

Texts: Romans 14:7−8 and Psalm 118:24

I'd like to think the title of this sermon has quickened your curiosity and whetted your interest. Sermon titles are meant to do that, you know –that and more. Ultimately the title and the sermon itself should keep your interest long enough and seriously enough so that something important can happen between us, between preacher and congregation, so that something significant can occur in a worshipful moment.

The title of this word intends no trickery to keep your interest nor funky surprises to arrest your attention. Instead, I mean to focus on one of the fundaments of faith: facing death with grace.

This sermon borrows its title from an old phrase connected with the harrowing encounters experienced by Western pioneers and soldiers engaged in combat.[1] In old Zane Gray novels and in some Louis L'Amour novels, "seeing the elephant and hearing the owl" means to face something that stops you "dead in your tracks," either literally or metaphorically.

That's a good phrase, I think, for dealing with this very touchy subject. If we're bluntly honest, questions about death arise in each of us along the faith journey: How do we pass the "test" of facing our mortality with grace and peace? What will it be like when I have to "meet my day"?

Of all the "First Things" of faith – along with trusting God enough to let go of our anxieties and holding on to love for dear life, knowing that love is the greatest power accessible to human beings– facing death with grace is surely among the most important tasks for us as people of faith. Try as we might, we can never finally evade the truth of death's inevitability. As John Irving put it so tellingly in his brilliant novel *The World According to Garp*, "we are all terminal cases."[2]

And yet, we do try, don't we? It used to be, say, in the Victorian age, that folks reveled – sometimes gloried –in death-talk, while, at the same time, evading like the plague any reference to sexuality. These days, the opposite is the case, isn't it? We revel at every turn and all times in all things sexual, while, simultaneously, avoiding any references whatsoever to death. As a friend once said to me in all seriousness, "Death's a real downer, man."

But death, and dealing with it, need not be such a downer for any of us. In fact, if our faith is truly empowering, we can see the elephant and be ready to hear the owl with renewed purpose and surety.

The apostle Paul gives us our direction for facing death with grace. In his grand correspondence with the Christians situated in Rome, he speaks to them about what it means to live at peace.

Paul delivers an urgent call to unity among their supposed factions. There were apparent squabbles going on among the Roman Christians about matters that were proving to be divisive. Dietary differences and observances of certain holy days were apparently prompting expressions of judgment and condemnation between the brothers and sisters in the Church. In the midst of calming their passions, he describes one of the most memorable and profound theological truths in the New Testament: "If we live, we live to the Lord, and if we die, we die to the Lord; so then, whether we live or whether we die, we are the Lord's."[3] His claim, on the surface of his declaration, is about their unity as Christians. But the implications and the depth of his insights are about so much more.

Death, Paul is asserting in our morning scripture, need not be feared nor rejected nor evaded. Why did Paul believe this? Why did he have such confidence in the face of that common denominator which divides its way in the lives of all human beings? How did Paul have such audacity to resolve a dispute about kosher laws and worship observances with such deep theology?

Somehow, Paul knew that everyone of us will eventually see the elephant and hear the owl call our name. And he knew that we can have supreme confidence in meeting those moments with the powerful presence of a loving God. His phrase tells it all: "We are the Lord's."

In proclaiming "We are the Lord's" Paul was emphasizing the communal nature of faith. The Christian journey is at its basic level a "we" proposition." Yes, there are always dimension of individuality among those who follow after the master carpenter from Nazareth, most noticeably responsibility and accountability. But, ultimately the dimension of community is the trump card in this path we call "Christianity." "We are the Lord's," Paul affirms. Not just some, not just a few, but *we*.

Secondly, Paul asserts that "We are the *Lord's*." Meaning? We do not live or move or have being apart from our Creator. We belong to God. We are with God, from the moment we take in our first breath beyond the womb. And we continue with God all of our days. We are with God even in the midst of our dying. "We are the Lord's." God is always in communion with us.

No doubt, some of you hear in the sermon title an echo of Margaret Craven's novel *I Heard the Owl Call My Name*. In that beautiful story, Mark Brian, a young Anglican vicar, is sent by his bishop to the Tsawataineuk tribe at Kingcome Village in British Columbia. The bishop has sent Rev. Brian there in order that he might "know enough of the meaning of life to die."[4] Rev. Brian takes on his new responsibilities with vigor, love, courage, and a deep, abiding respect for the life and ways of the Indian folk who become his family.

While the lives of the people of the village are Rev. Brian's focus and his principal concern, death also dominates his presence in the village: the death of village members, the death of the culture of the Tsawatainek and his own impending death. This latter death is kept from him, until late into his stay at the village when he "hears the owl call," the traditional Indian sign that one's death is approaching. But though the terminal nature of his disease had been hidden from him for so long, and though he is young, what the bishop intended by sending him to Kingcome Village has been accomplished: he knows enough of the meaning of life and he is ready to die with a sense of nobility, with peace, and with a rare resoluteness.

This is the focus for the apostle Paul too. If we know deep down that life is communal ("We are the Lord's") and that life is communion ("We are the Lord's"), we have enough of the meaning of life to be ready to live and die with grace.

Some of us may also hear in the sermon an echo of our own experience.

Last August, slightly more than five months ago, I experienced an event which makes this morning's sermon a very personal one indeed for me. I've recently dubbed this my "intimate brush with extreme mortality." Its technical name is Acute Myocardial Infarction (AMI). And as you know, I was blessed by a quick response from the EMTs (two and a half minutes!) and equally quick treatment by Dr. Ken Huber and his team at St. Luke's Hospital. Because of their rapid response, the damage to my heart was minimized and my recuperation quotient was maximized. Now, after good food, wonderful medicine, and excellent guidance by the cardio rehab team, your unceasing prayers, and mega doses of Priscilla's love, I'm in the best shape I've been in for more than twenty years.

In the middle of the heart crisis, and then over the course of the immediate recovery period that followed, I had ample time to reflect on the AMI experience. It was then that I remembered something startling. I recalled Dietrich Bonhoeffer's words just before the end of his life: "This is the end—for me the beginning of life."[5] I didn't exactly have Bonhoeffer's sanguine attitude when the AMI was upon me, but, I remember, in the midst of the crisis of my heart, there was no panic. Priscilla and I both met the event unagitated and with equanimity. I recall that when the EMTs showed up, I went limp and relaxed. And even though they had a bit of trouble getting my blood pressure to rise enough so they could administer some pain medication, I was calm. "This could be my time," I supposed, as the ambulance raced to the emergency room.

After the trauma came the time for reflection. There, in the peace and tranquility of our West Wing (our name for our den), it startled me to recall the calmness which colored the entire experience. I wondered if I had passed what my friend Forrest Church used to call "the death test."[6] We ministers so often assist others in meeting death and preparing for life's final earthly transition. But how and what do we when it comes time for us to meet death?

I also pondered the countless Community members and numberless other Christians who have faced death with peace and surety.

Then I resolved I'd tell you one day what I had discovered.

#1—We can follow in the footsteps (and in the heartbeats) of those who have gone before us and trust that their ways are good ways for meeting the moment when we see the elephant and hear the owl. We can face death with grace by learning

from the graceful ways of that communal resource of faith. The Christian faith tradition has immense blessings in it that are truly magnificent, if we will but allow it to soak into our souls. On the faces of those we love—those who love us so much—is written, at the time of extreme crisis, the very grace of God. I believe the reason for such calm in our household on the fateful day of August 14, 2010, was the calm and resoluteness and peace in the hundreds of people I have accompanied on their final journey. Equanimity prevailed that day because there has been equanimity in the hearts and heads and hands of numberless folks who have taught us the true meaning of life. How does one learn peace in the face of the *extremis* of death? By going to church, and worshiping regularly, and saying our prayers, and practicing daily our faith. Such routine matters are the stuff of which greatness and great grace are made.

#2—*A heart attack, literally and metaphorically, is a demand that a person slow down.* If we know clear down into the sinews of our deepest selves that "whether we live or whether we die, we are the Lord's," then we need not live life in haste nor waste time being frenetic and frantic. Life is meant to be savored, appreciated, luxuriated in. Not gulped or gobbled or swallowed whole. In fact, when we do gulp, gobble, and swallow whole, we may just be hastening our deaths and shortening our lives.

#3—*It's time for all of us to give up the delusion that we are not going to die.* Our denial that gravity will not get us all is a self-imposed fantasy and has no basis in reality. By accepting that our earthly lives are finite, we can, in fact, increase our engagement with them and our enjoyment of each other, making every minute of our time together count. Death can be approached not as a terminus but as a transformational moment. In the grand grammar of grace, we realize that, as one folk preacher once said, death is not a period but a comma.

#4—*You really can't take it with you.* So, you'd better give it away. And better than giving away our material possessions and our money is the opportunity to give away something else. Not money or possessions. Not treasured heirloom antiques or property. Not things at all. The only "substance" that makes life valuable in any ultimate sense is the love we share with others.

Our greatest asset is the love we give away. It is the only aspect of our lives that truly increases in value over time. Better than the finest wine, more precious than the rarest gemstone. And it is the only aspect of our lives that is magnified when we transfer it to others. No one is ever lessened by giving love away. In fact, our love's shelf-life multiplies when it is given to others. So, a clear-eyed sighting of the elephant and open-eared hearing of the owl empowers us to love one another with fierce clarity and refined tenderness. When we know that death is a comma and not a period, we are freed to live a life of love, love, and more love.

#5—*Get busy rejoicing!* Our temporal earthly lives, when measured against the backdrop of all that has gone before us—billions of years of chronological time—and all that will come after we've departed from this zip code—also billions and billions of years, at the very least!—are fleeting and preciously brief. So, without haste or frenzy, we are called to get busy rejoicing. The Psalmist put this insight into absolute clarity when the happy declaration was made: "This is the day that the Lord has made, let us rejoice and be glad in it."

Yes, there have been yesterdays, and they are good to recall and learn from and treasure. But we live in this day.

Yes, there's always tomorrow, and it beckons us to be hopeful and to prepare as best we can so we won't be caught off guard. (To fly on a plane tomorrow I need to buy a ticket beforehand.)

But the greatest gift we have been given, the best occasion for living our lives, is today. This is the day that the Lord has made!

And what else can or would we want to do with such a gift than rejoice?! We have been made as rejoicing creatures. We are so constituted that we are not fulfilled until we rejoice. Life has been given to all of us for celebrating and not merely tolerating. So, get busy rejoicing!

If you are at your home, choose something to celebrate. On your job or in the classroom, there's always time for a quiet celebration, perhaps even a silent celebration. At the end of a day, when you are wrapping up the leftovers of your work and putting to bed the demands of your on-going tasks, there's always time for a little celebration. There's always time for rejoicing and being glad! The God of the universe who got you up this morning waits to rejoice with you throughout the day and then to meet you in gladness before your weariness carries you away into sleep. The God who brought you into this world, hopes for you to rejoice each and every day of your earthly journey. And, if we are out-and-out plainly, bluntly honest with ourselves, this same Lord will rejoice with us even in the moment of our deaths, when what appears to us to be a period is revealed to be the cosmic comma that it is.

So, remember: #1 – Life is always communal. Life, when it's at its best, is always communion with God. Other footsteps (and heartbeats) can show us the way. #2 – Slow down. #3 – It's time for all of us to give up the delusion that we are not going to die. #4 – You really can't take it with you, but the love you give way will last for an eternity. #5 – Get busy rejoicing!

And, as you will continue to hear me say, most nearly every Sunday, God bless us all, I love you. Amen.

NOTES

1. An early literary reference to *"seeing the elephant and hearing the owl"* can be found in O'Henry's short story "The Higher Abdication" in *Heart of the West* (New York: Doubleday, Page & Company, 1913), p. 137.
2. John Irving, *The World According to Garp* (New York: E. P. Dutton, 1978), p. 609.
3. Romans 14:8
4. Margaret Craven, *I Heard the Owl Call My Name* (New York: Dell Publishing, 1973), p. 144.
5. Eberhard Bethge, *Dietrich Bonhoeffer: A Biography*, revised edition (Minneapolis, Fortress Press, 2000), p. 927.
6. From personal conversations with Forrest, over several years. Please also see his excellent book *Love and Death: My Journey through the Valley of the Shadow* (Boston: Beacon Press, 2008).

2

TAKING LOVE SERIOUSLY

Text: I John 3:14–18, 4:7–12

Say the word *love* and an endless array of images blossom in the human mind. Hear it and imagine: "Love."

Are you thinking of a certain person? Are you experiencing a specific feeling? Are beautiful colors associated with the word *love* for you? Do you have in mind a particularly lovely place when you hear the word *love*?

Or, are you, instead, encrusted in an indifference to the word *love* and anything or any person or any place it may relate to? Some have been wounded in love in the past, and they'd just rather not hear about it or talk about it or even think about it. Others have been fooled into thinking they had experienced love when, really, they had only known a reality far different from love.

It may be hard for anyone in our culture initially to plumb the depths of love's reality because of the misuse and abuse to which the word *love* has been subjected.

On the other hand, when we take the time to assess honestly who we are as human beings, who we want to become as Christians, and how we want to make a contribution to life and to shape our world for the better, we know that love must be at the center of all those concerns.

This morning, I'd like to offer a prescription for love. What we all need is not an algebraic or a calculus understanding of love. What we all need, what we all can be blessed by, is a prescription for love.

In the early days of the church, what was the premier currency among the pioneer Christians? Words. Simply words. They received and shared words whenever they came together. Words like *hope* and *grace* and *shepherd* and *Our Father*. Barbara Brown Taylor uses a fetching phrase to describe what they shared, and what we share, too, whenever Christians gather: "gospel medicine."[1] This morning I'd like to provide you a prescription for a particular gospel medicine called *love*.

In the first epistle of John, we discover a veritable pharmacy of love. The faithful souls to whom John addressed his correspondence were themselves in need of a prescription of love. From what we can tell about their situation, there may have been some struggles going on within the church to whom John wrote. There was very likely some misunderstanding. Because the dynamics of the church— at the time of John's letter—were different than when it began, there may have been some growing pains.

In the midst of their struggles, in the midst of their growing pains, John reminds them of their origins and foundations: "For this is the message that you have heard from the beginning, that we should love one another."[2]

John first reminds the Christians then and there, and all of us here and now, that love is to be equated with life itself.

"We know that we have passed from death to life because we love one another."[3] Love is what keeps us alive and well. Love is what compels us to move beyond hatred and enmity. Love—forgiving love, grace-filled love—is what pulls us out of the "stuckness" of grief and regret and hopelessness and despair. Dr. John's prescription to love means this: Love can literally resurrect a life, can resurrect your life, can resurrect the lives of others.

One of the best ways– and by that, I mean one of the most effective and useful ways—we can participate in love's resurrecting power is by offering encouragement to one another. No extreme situation is required. No hill at Calvary is needed. We don't need to find someone in the throes of physical death. All we need to do is offer words of encouragement. Words like *You can do it!* Or *Great job!* Or *Thank You.* Or *I really appreciate you.*

This past week I was dutifully going through the paces of my cardio rehab at St. Luke's Center for Health Enhancement (deemed once by a newspaper writer as "Club Med").

I had added upper body strengthening to my workout, and it was a real treat. After finishing the upper body exercises, I set out on one of the favorite parts of my workout routine, simply walking. I was reeling around the track when Bobbie Testa, the head manager of cardio rehab of Club Med, began clapping and saying "Way to go!" I was puzzled by her applause and asked her why she said that. She motioned toward an area in the gym where I had done what is, for me, one of the hardest exercises, simple chair squats. "I saw you doing your squats. Great job. Perfect form. Way to go!"

I suddenly smiled and had an extra zip in my stride after that. A simple expression of encouragement— "Way to go!"— became a resurrecting dynamic in my life. The rest of the day I wondered how many spirits Bobbie has lifted and inspired because of the simple words of encouragement she shares.

Think right now of someone in this congregation to whom you could offer words of encouragement. Think also of someone outside our family of faith to whom you could say "Way to go!" If and when you offer encouragement, when you say "Way to go!" you will be participating in the dynamic of love's resurrecting power. You will be helping another person move from death to life. Taking love seriously means knowing that love gives life to others and that encouragement is one of the best ways to love others.

For Dr. John, as well as for all of us, love consists in genuine caring and sharing. And genuine caring consists of action. I once had a friend in Nashville, a former CPA who ended up homeless and alcoholic. Eventually, with help and prayer and humility, he became a raging quasi-social worker who helped out with people reentering society after spending time in prison or jail. His name was Bill Frith. If I heard Bill say it once, I heard him say it a thousand times: "People will never care how much you know, until they know how much you care."

Now that may seem like so much "Dear Abby" advice, like a trite bromide, but there's great wisdom in Bill's adage. Because it's true! He was talking about the difference between words and deeds. He was warning about the perils of hypocrisy.

Hypocrisy may be second only to self-righteousness as the premier danger for religious people. Every week I run into someone, somewhere in the greater Kansas City area, who will critique the entirety of the church of Jesus Christ because of its hypocrisy. Too often they're accurate in their critique. Way too many Christians crow about how they love their neighbors and then refuse to actually love a neighbor when one shows up. Or they narrowly define who a neighbor is. Or the neighbor somehow disqualifies herself or himself because of the way they look or the way they dress or by the color of their skin or their sexual orientation or their political preferences.

Dr. John's prescription to love is an eternal elixir which can fix any and all hypocrisies: "Let us love, not in word or speech, but in truth and action."[4] When we do acts of genuine caring and sharing, love is truly manifested and no one can claim any hypocrisy.

Clarence Jordan, who founded Koinonia Farms in Americus, Georgia, and inspired the creation of Habitat for Humanity, was also a Greek scholar and translated significant parts of the New Testament into colloquial English. You may have read his inspiring *Cotton Patch* versions of the gospels and certain of the New Testament epistles. Jordan translates a portion of our text for the morning like this: "Let's not [merely] talk about love. Let's not [merely] sing about love. Let's put love into action and make it real."[5]

Whenever you offer your tithes and offerings in weekly worship, whenever you volunteer to tutor a youth in reading, whenever you provide transportation for a senior citizen, whenever you help out at the hospital or work in a food ministry, whenever you ring bells for the Salvation Army or participate in the justice work of MORE2, you're putting love into action and making it real.

The real gist of what Dr. John prescribes for us, however, doesn't begin with what we say or do or enact. The first step, the foundational move, the fundamental posture, the primal attitude to be initiated isn't even ours. God is the originator of all gospel medicine, including love. Why are we to love one another? "Because love is from God; everyone who loves is born of God and knows God. Whoever does not love does not know God for God is love."[6]

This past summer I became acutely aware of a force, a cultural reality which has become a riving, destructive power. It was clearly present among so-called Christians as they were hawking their schemes and scams on television and radio. The image and personality of God that I saw being portrayed, more often than not, was an all-demanding, constantly judging, eternally dividing, incessantly criticizing, infinitely damning deity.

There never was a bigger lie! The God of both the Hebrew Bible and New Testament, the God who is Father to his son the Christ, the God of Psalm 23 and John 3:16, is a God of love.

Love is the ground of God's being, the heart of God's nature, the essence of God's presence. If you paint a picture of God without the tones and tints of love's colors, you have a false portrait of the Creator of Life and the Keeper of Eternity.

Why is this so central? Dr. John knew, and we know, too. If we have to rely on our own power, however magnificently well-intentioned and positively orchestrated, we're sunk. Our capacities are limited, our resources are not self-generating. We need Another. We need God's love which is outside of ourselves but ever possible within us by God's generous provision and prodding. "In this is love, not that we loved God, but that he loved us." [7]

The first instruction on Dr. John's prescription of love for us, then, is to receive love freely. Know that you are loved. God made this day– in all of its autumnal brilliance (or in all of its subtle and muted glory)– just for you. And for you and for me. For us all! God has given us powerful and peculiar talents and gifts and graces. God has quickened within us the ability to breathe and to have blood pulsing through our veins and the bedazzling capacities of our five senses. God has loved us into the living of this very day.

I hope and pray you will receive God's love freely and deeply and intimately. If you will do this, you will be empowered to offer encouragement to others on an amazing, perduring basis. Just by being alive and following the loving example of Christ causes God to echo in time and eternity a cosmic word of encouragement: "Way to go!" By receiving freely the abounding love God has for us, we put love into action and make it real for others and indeed the whole world. If we don't love, we don't know God. If we do love, God will surprise us with what can happen and what can be accomplished for a world much in need.

I urge you this morning to take the gospel medicine of love and follow the instructions of Dr. John's prescription. It will save your life. And by it you will help to save the lives of countless others.

And one more thing. This love won't cost you a thing. Like a candle that loses nothing by kindling another candle, this love is for you, and it's free. No cost to you. The price has already been paid. On a hill far away, by One who loved us all from the beginning until now, who loves us still, and who will keep on loving us until we get it right. Now that's a bargain and a prescription, I would suggest, that is impossible to refuse! Amen.

NOTES

1. See Barbara Brown Taylor's *Gospel Medicine* (Lanham, Maryland: Cowley Publications, 1995).
2. I John 3:11.
3. I John 3:14.
4. I John 3:18.
5. Clarence Jordan, *The Cotton Patch Version of Hebrews and the General Epistles* (El Monte, California: New Win Publishing, 1997).
6. I John 4:7-8.
7. I John 4:10.

3

LETTING GO OF ANXIETY
Text: Matthew 6:25–34

Happy New Year! On the surface of things, the passing of a day on a calendar is a rather lackluster event. But human beings, time-keepers that we are, love to mark particular days—birthdays, anniversaries, etc. —with such attention. The arrival of a New Year is a special marking-time occasion. Parties, confetti, fireworks, parades, football games, resolution-making, and general festivities mark New Year's Eve and New Year's Day as one of the most cranked-up occasions of revelry in our culture.

It's helpful to have a purpose-shaped focus for the acknowledgment of the passing of time. In religious terms, the marking of time as special and holy, as part of the overall discovery of the holy, is called "hagiology".

On the second day after the dawning of a new year, rather than urging you to craft some fresh New Year's resolutions, I offer a sermon series, "First Things First." focusing on key essentials of faith. These can surely provide us purpose and focus to shape our faith. And if we will attend and enact these essentials, I believe we all will have a Happy New Year and much, much more.

Our exploration of "first things" begins in the middle of Jesus' most famous oration, the Sermon on the Mount. Whether you're familiar with the Bible or you don't know where to begin in the Bible, you are likely very familiar with Jesus' words: "Do not worry about your life, what you will eat or what you will drink, or your body, what you will wear."[1] This is a charge to let go of anxiety.

That we are concerned and fearful from time to time is obvious to most of us, if we are honest about ourselves and our place in the world. Being concerned about the health of our families, the predicaments of our friends, the stability of our jobs, the growth of our faith, or the fulfillment of our dreams is natural and impossible to avoid. Our choices are not fearlessness as opposed to fretting. Our concerns about encountering threat or avoiding danger are real and help us live meaningful lives with purpose.

But when concern becomes agitated stress and grows into worry, we become counter-productive and less effective in handling our concerns. And then our worries can transmogrify into acute anxiety, panic, obsessions, and even phobias.

It's been proven scientifically that worry can debilitate our health, physically and mentally. My friend Forrest Church put it nicely: "Worry eats away at the body while gnawing at the mind."[2] Robert Soploski's research at Stanford University has revealed that chronic stress related to fear causes our adrenal glands to produce steroid hormones called glucocortocoids.

"Over a lifetime these hormones collect near the hippocampus the region of the brain that stores memories and collaborates with the amygdala in outwitting danger. If after many years the hormones reach a certain level, they create a toxic atmosphere, impairing our capacity to recall memories and to perform certain tasks."[3] Add to this the ill effects of worry raising our blood pressure, and the bald truth reveals itself: Worry kills or, at the very least, reduces our years and the quality of our lives.

Jesus knew the profound reality of worry's potential to harm us and thus addressed its threat in his most famous sermon. His focus is curious, isn't it? Among the thousands of sermon possibilities Jesus had to choose from—a call for world peace, a challenge to fashion a global ministry of mercy, the need for world-wide human understanding—he chose to center in on worry and overcoming anxiety. Somehow Jesus knew—instinctively, intuitively, profoundly—that lower-level worries and seemingly small anxieties, if left untended and unremedied, can lead to larger problems. It is poetically appropriate that the origins of our English word *worry* means "to choke" and "to strangle." Jesus knew that base level concerns which mutate into worrisome fears and chronic anxiety can choke and strangle the life out of us.

Jesus first addresses our anxieties about the basics: food and drink. Obviously, these base-line necessities need and deserve proper consideration. But a culture that has spiking incidents of eating disorders and a world with one third of its inhabitants, many of them children, suffering from malnutrition and too little potable water are just the sort of thing Jesus had in mind when he spoke about worrying.

And his remedy for such worry? An urging for us to look at the birds. Now that would be a comical suggestion if it weren't so patently and powerfully revealing.

This week I had an occasion of doing just this sort of looking. Right in front of Brookside Market, before I got out of my trusty Jeep in order to enter the store in search of food and drink, three little sparrows appeared in the evergreen hedge in front of me. This was right at the time that the big chill was racing into Kansas City like a runaway train and causing fearsome chills in us all. And what were the birds doing? Nothing at all. Not chirping. Not singing. Not whining. Not flitting about. And certainly not worrying. Simply nesting in the evergreen, as if everything would be all right.

So, I asked, "Aren't you cold?"

One of the birds, Simon, spoke up and said, "Of course we are! Do we look like dumb birds?"

And then I responded, "But aren't you going to freeze to death being out in dastardly, harmful nature? Would you like to come home with me and stay in our garage?"

"Don't be silly," Simon replied, "nature is our friend. That's why we're here in this evergreen bush. It will keep us warm just right. And there's no way we'd ever dream of using your garage. We'd starve to death in there. We have plenty of food to forage from if we stay out here in what you call 'dastardly, harmful nature.' Man, haven't you read any Wendell Berry? Nature is our friend."

"But," I asked, "doesn't nature ever let you down?

"Oh, wow, you really don't know anything, do you? God, who made all of nature, has always, always, taken care of us. And you call yourself a minister of the gospel of God!"

The gospel birds came all the way from the 6th chapter of Matthew to provide me, and indirectly you, with a basic truism about our basic being provided in the New Year 2011: We need not worry about what we will eat or what we will drink. God will provide all that and more for sure. If we but look at the birds and have as much fundamental faith as they do.

Jesus also mentions what seems to be a basic concern but can serve as a metaphor for our worrisome cultural obsession with outward appearance.

Now, I'm not a person opposed to fashion. A good-looking tie always catches my eye, and I have a closet full of them. And I always admire how all of you look so fetching each and every Sunday. Color and style and texture and material are part of the human equation. They are part of what makes us distinctly and peculiarly human. We are called to celebrate our individual preferences and choices. But they don't determine destiny.

When I think on the people who have made a difference in my life and an impact on the world, I discover something strange and liberating: I can't remember one iota of distinctive flair, spangle, or bling about what they wore. Martin Luther King, Emily Dickinson, Ralph Waldo Emerson, Mahatma Gandhi, and my grandmother were surely some of the most boring dressers ever. How about you? Did anyone who profoundly affected your life ever do so by the clothes they wore?

Jesus said to the crowd who heard his Sermon on the Mount– and he says to us on this first Sunday of the New Year– anxiety about the surface concerns of our life will not add a single hour to the span of your life and it won't enhance the substantive quality of it either.

The challenge to us regarding our penchant to let concerns become worrisome fears and chronic anxieties? Let go! Let go!

This morning, I want to offer you two simple methods by which I am confident we can let our anxieties go and thus be free for more purposeful and enjoyable lives in 2011.

- Resist the temptation to allow the menace of your worries to become monsters. Succumbing to such temptation gives us the excuse of victim-hood.
- Resist the option of trying to do something about the things you can't do anything about. Our overblown imaginations can sometimes lead us to fantasize about heroic actions that are absolutely impossible for us to perform

The Serenity Prayer– which was prayed countless times over a 24-hour period in the New Year's "Alco-thon" gathering in our Centennial Hall this past weekend– has it just right: "God grant me the serenity to accept the things I cannot change, the courage to change the things I can, and the wisdom to know the difference." In other words, let go of your anxieties about things you cannot control. Rather than worry yourself sick– physically, mentally and spiritually– over those things beyond your control, let go and then think and act on the things you can control.

Jesus' solution for our human penchant for mutating concerns into worries is another curious turn in his sermon. In order to conquer our fretting about the little things in life, we are to – are you ready for this? – consider the bigger picture from God's perspective. Jesus calls it the Kingdom of God: "strive first for the kingdom of God and God's righteousness and all these things will be added to you."[4] I like the older translations of this verse a bit better than the new more literal, wooden translations: "seek ye first the kingdom of God."[5] Seeking after the bigger picture, with our own, very human efforts, is what makes for a good life, keeping us free from the death-like effects of anxiety and panic and our prolific phobias.

This week I urge you to make a commitment and try a little experiment for the next four weeks.

Mark one day a week on your new calendars for "seeking after the kingdom of God." Mark it clearly, place it where you can see it when that day of the week arrives. And then "seek." By that I mean search for, look for, hunt for.

Seeking may mean doing something good for another human being, a neighbor, a member of the congregation, or a stranger.

It may mean seeking after a new faith insight, or reading a new novel, or checking out a new movie or a play in one of Kansas City's many theaters.

It may mean sharing a meal with someone you've been meaning to break bread with for a long time, but you simply haven't taken time to do so. Do so.

It may mean a new involvement in a non-profit organization, getting involved in making life better for someone else.

Remember that Albert Schweitzer was exactly 100% right when he said: "I don't know what your destiny will be, but one thing I do know: the only ones among you who will be really happy are those who have sought and found a way to serve."

And this we can surely do with eyes and ears and hearts of faith, seeking after the things that God will use, through us, to make the world right.

On this first Sunday of the New Year, I offer you my whole-hearted belief that there is nothing we cannot accomplish, nothing we cannot fulfill, if we follow the directions Jesus gives about overcoming worry. Jesus proffered to his hearers then– and to all of us here and now– a sure-fire remedy for conquering our anxieties: Trust God. Trust what God provides for you for your daily living. Trust what God knows about your capacities to provide for yourself and others. Trust what God believes about you.

Last Sunday, Rev. Michelle Harris-Gloyer told a wonderful story about her encounter with the legendary Cornel West. The measure of a story's power is its capacity to compel re-telling. Michelle's recounting of her encounter with Dr. West is just such a story.

During the question-and-answer session that followed a lecture by Dr. West, he recalled the great affirmations which he experienced growing up. His recollection, in essence, was "My community told me all sorts of good things about me. And I believed them!"[6]

Jesus the Christ, a poor peasant in a backwater province of the Roman Empire, a lowly carpenter from Nazareth who ended up penniless and crucified, wearing only a loin cloth in public ignominy in Jerusalem, would conquer death and shame and lovelessness and all personal and social debilitation by hearing God's affirmations about his life and its trustworthiness.

Could it be that the power of his Sermon on the Mount emanated from the memory of the day of his baptism when the skies parted and a voice from beyond proclaimed, "This is my beloved Son, with whom I am well pleased."?[7]

Could he also have been remembering what Mary and Joseph said of his abilities and the trustworthiness of his life being in God's hands?

Jesus' life is evidence enough that such trusting works. Let us hear God's affirmations about our lives and how God can be trusted to take care of us. Then, let us believe them! As we do so, watch out world! We and the world will never be the same again!

Again, Happy New Year! I love you. God bless us everyone.

One final reminder. Remember to look at the birds. If you see Simon, convey my thanks for the lesson he taught me. Amen.

NOTES
1. Matthew 6:25.
2. Forrest Church, *Freedom from Fear: Finding the Courage to Act, Love, and Be* (New York: St. Martin's Press, 2004), pp. 25-26.
3. Ibid., p. 26.
4. Matthew 6:34.
5. King James Version, Matthew 6:34.
6. Rev. Michelle Harris-Gloyer, sermon, "Simeon and Anna: Satisfied Lives," December 26, 2010, Community Christian Church, Kansas City, Missouri.
7. Matthew 3:17.

4

OVERCOMING THE HELL OF HATRED
Text: II Corinthians 5:16 – 21

In the history of Christian belief, no issue has been more problematic (or more divisive) than the teasing out, the discerning of what it takes to abide with God. The shorthand for this dilemma some would call, "Heaven or Hell."

In the Church's oldest creeds the issue is right smack-dab in the middle of the description of Jesus' life, ministry, death and resurrection:

"I believe in God, the Father almighty,
maker of heaven and earth;
and in Jesus Christ his only Son our Lord;
who was conceived by the Holy Ghost,
born of the Virgin Mary,
suffered under Pontius Pilate,
was crucified, dead and buried.
He descended into hell.
The third day he rose again from the dead."

If you are a cradle, non-creedal Christian like me, that phrase may sound passingly odd, and it should. Main line Protestants, for the most part, have eschewed creeds, including that portion of the Apostles' Creed, and thus don't recite it every Sunday.

Scholars have waged fervent debates, sometimes verging on fanatical fights, over the meaning of that phrase, "descended into hell," since there's nothing to confirm such a notion in any of the gospel accounts of Jesus' life. (Yes, there are a few references in Acts, Hebrews, and the book of Ephesians, which allude to Jesus doing battle on behalf of those who have descended into a netherworld. But there's no clear emphasis in the gospels on Jesus *descending into hell*. It's simply not there.)

Other scholars have maintained that the Apostles' creed describes Jesus *descending into hell* so as to magnify Christ's supremacy over the whole world, including the region and realm beyond earthly life, including any portion of it that isn't heavenly.

I suppose we have artists like William Blake and Dante to thank for the images that insinuate themselves into our hearts and minds about the threat of hell and the hellish consequences that await us after this life, if we don't shape up.

And even if you think that hell as a subject isn't a problem for you, in contemporary times, as a new generation of Christian leadership has sought to convey the blessings of the gospel to a brand-new, largely unchurched, generation, the past emphasis on the promise of heaven and the threat of hell has proven to be fairly offensive and "radioactive" to some folks. The judgmentalism— so very often smugly expressed and condescendingly delivered— that comes with dividing people into those who get to go to heaven and those who are cast into a lake of fire in hell is usually the last straw that sends some tenderhearted people running for the nearest exit out of a church building or religious gathering that spouts such theology. "If this is the way you're going to be, condemning people who aren't part of your club, I don't want to be a member of it!" they respond to the stereotypical challenge of "Turn or Burn!"

The saddest aspect about all these hellish matters is the simple fact that the emphasis on hell need not have happened at all.

This morning, I'm encouraging us to focus on the subject of Hell, but in a manner and a way that may be different for some, quirky to others, and altogether radically out of the main to still others. Instead of talking about the eternal destinies of our souls– which, by the way, will make a great theme for another sermon at another time– I urge us to focus on overcoming the hells that we ourselves make on this earthly side of the human journey. This is an appropriate emphasis since Jesus focused more energy on transforming the world through his way of life– that is, he was as concerned about bringing a lot more heavenly aspects into earthly life– than he was about anything else.

Too often, hell is made to be a burdensome topic by Christians themselves. Howard Thurman remembered to his last dying day that when he was eight years old, at his funeral, his family was treated with extreme insensitivity, and his father's character was besmirched and degraded. Because Thurman's father was not a member of the church, the funeral was not permitted within its walls. A traveling evangelist was engaged to lead the service and made everything worse, preaching Thurman's father into hell during the course of his oration, because he had "died out of Christ." All through the evangelist's hate-filled preachment, Thurman kept whispering to his mother, "He didn't know Papa, did he? Did he?"[1]

These days, hell can be seen in the hatred that is spewed with voluminous savagery in nearly every nook and cranny of contemporary culture. And it can be seen in great relief in the expression of two particular kinds of phobias.

While the purveyors of these kinds of hellish hatreds may intend, in their best moments, to alarm and caution us, the effects of their attitudes and actions simply create hell on earth.

If someone were to ask me bald-faced if I believe in hell, I would quickly respond, "Believe in it? Oh, I've seen it!"

In relation to two particular issues, the hell of hatred has been expressed and played out with great drama in the U.S. I refer to what has come to be called Islamophobia and homophobia.

I believe some of you, maybe a majority of you have known where I stand with regard to these dastardly fears. But for a long while, I haven't offered a clear sermonic word about these issues and how our faith intersects with them. Let today be the occasion for a clarification.

The phobia about Muslims and their apparent threat to the United States is a sad and regrettable mistake. Theologically speaking it is a grievous sin.

Jesus spoke of "other sheep" which he had to tend.[2]

The Jewish rabbi Gamaliel cautioned against Christian-phobia in the first-century church saying, "let [the apostles] alone; because if this plan or this undertaking is of human origin, it will fail; but if it is of God, you will not be able to overthrow them– in that case you may even be found fighting against God!"[3]

The book of Hebrews guides us "to show hospitality to strangers, for thereby some have entertained angels unawares."[4]

And in his *magnus opus* epistle, the book of Romans, the apostle Paul charged the Roman Christians "Do not repay anyone evil for evil, but take thought for what is noble in the sight of all.... Never avenge yourselves.... Do not be overcome by evil, but overcome evil with good."[5]

The Muslims are not only not be feared but, more importantly, they are not be regarded as evil simply because they're Muslims. To do so is to commit "thingification," that is, to consign them to the status of a thing and strip them of their humanity. We do not make ourselves righteous by making others unholy and despicable and evil. Yes, people do evil things, but people are not evil simply because they adhere to a faith that is different from ours. And besides, where do we draw the line? Shall we be like a church I know of in Nashville, Tennessee, that has on its cornerstone the inscription "Founded A.D. 33"? Shall we practice their kind of condemning exclusivism that relegates to perdition all people outside the membership of their so-called fellowship?

Islamophobia is rampant in our time and culture, and we have an obligation to resist it with Christian love. Terrorists who seek to do harm to the U.S. – either here or abroad– are equal opportunity thugs and are the poorest, most regrettable representatives of their faith. Just as we would not want Fred Phelps to be held up as a premier example of American Christianity, so we are bound to refrain from crowning Osama bin Laden as an exemplary practitioner of the religion of Islam.

Speaking of Fred Phelps, the second kind of phobia that is rampant in these times and sadly present in too many corners of American culture is homophobia.

I know that you know that I know that you know that Fred Phelps and his Westboro cult of hate-mongers twist and distort select pieces of the Bible to suit their needs, to foment division and hatred among all people. Their ceaseless drive for attention and their prideful penchant for publicity are exhibit A and exhibit B of the worst possibilities of which human beings are capable.

But I must admit that I sometimes have a secret hope that they would visit every congregation in America, of whatever stripe or kind, and cast their aspersions on every congregation for being sympathetic to homosexuals. I can't think of a better way to galvanize compassion and grace toward our homosexual brothers and sisters. It did so here at Community when Fred protested a funeral of one of our members 15 years ago. And we had some of the best-ever heart-to-heart conversations and discoveries among us about the issue of homosexuality. A lot of us have grown and shifted from previous positions, and many of us are still growing and shifting, but thank God we have evolved as a congregation.

I'm thankful and humbled when I notice how my mind has changed with regard to the issue of homosexuality. From a high-school framework of laughing at jokes about gays, through a rough-and-tough struggle with what scripture really does and doesn't say about homosexuality, and on through times of accompanying many families who have experienced their children's coming-out about their homosexual orientation, I've come to a rather peaceable yet firm position regarding homosexuality: We are to respect and appreciate however God made each and every one of us. I propose that you and I, as Christian brothers and sisters, exclude from fellowship and all the graces of life, in Jesus' way, those whom Jesus would exclude. I think that's as fair a proposal as I can muster. And since Jesus excluded no one from fellowship with him– and in fact incurred the wrath of the stodgy religious establishment because he wouldn't participate in such exclusion– we shouldn't either.

As a way of overcoming the hellish effects of these two great hatreds– Islamophobia and homophobia– allow me to cast a spotlight on the practical wisdom and heavenly principle of reconciliation that Paul proclaims in II Corinthians. Allow me to do so by highlighting the three R's of Reconciliation:

REGARD others as Christ regards them: as precious creations of God. Look on others in a Christlike way– whether they are different from you religiously or sexually. Regard every person as a precious creation from God's own gracious and holy hand.

REMEMBER that God's main working paper is to reconcile the world! The word in Greek is *katallagete*, meaning be reconciled, be made whole, be part of the whole family of God's household, no longer counting their trespasses against them. God has done it. God has made us right in Christ Jesus and now we have been given the responsibility to be made right with all other human beings.

REPEAT the good news message of reconciliation. What do you do with a message you've been given? Simple. You repeat it. So, we are to repeat the message of reconciliation to any and all as long as we have breath.

You know, I'm not sure I would have done such a gracious act as God did in Christ. I think it's really much simpler to set up the world with an us-against-them dichotomy and then simply blast to smithereens whoever is the other, the opponent, the different one, the so-called enemy. Oh, my adversaries might not be Muslims or homosexuals, but I'd be just as sinfully slimy if left to my own designs. I'd love to blast oil companies or investment bankers or the snake-oil salesmen known as television evangelists and send them all to perdition for their incessant malfeasances. But God didn't do that. No, God simply reconciled the world to God's Self. And since God did so, I can't afford to blast anyone.[6]

Which leads me to this conclusion: Those who commit Islamophobia and the likes of Fred Phelps and others who express such sickening homophobia are not outside God's grace either. They too are among those whom God reconciled whether they humbly acknowledge that fact or not. It's enough if we do, with or without their consent, on their behalf.

Amen.

NOTES

1. Howard Thurman, *With Head and Heart: The Autobiography of Howard Thurman* (New York: Harcourt Brace Jovanovich, 1979), pp. 5-6.
2. Other sheep.
3. Acts 5:38-39.
4. Hebrews 13:2.
5. Romans 12:17, 19, 21.
6. I'm grateful to Will Campbell for illuminating this understanding of reconciliation in Paul's theology.

5

THREE STAGES OF FORGIVENESS

Texts: Genesis 33:1 – 11

Last Sunday we began our *Finding Forgiveness* series with an exploration of the dialogue between Jesus and Peter, the premier apostle among Jesus' first followers, about the manner and the method for measuring forgiveness. Next Sunday we'll look at one of the most beloved stories about Jesus and his posture of forgiveness toward others: John's account of Jesus' encounter with a woman caught in adultery.

Today we're learning about forgiveness from the story of Jacob and Esau's reconciliation in Genesis 33. As we interpret this story, we'll be reminded to take a cue from Lewis Smedes's wise words about the dynamic process of forgiveness.

Jacob and Esau were the twin sons of Isaac and Rebekah. If we were to make a list of the great and famous twins in human history, according to all categories, including literature and mythology, I'm fairly certain most of us would include the following:

- Apollo and Artemis
- Romulus and Remus
- Helen and Clytemnestra
- Elvis Presley and his twin brother Jesse Gordon, who died at birth (now he would have been the ultimate Elvis impersonator).
- Ann Landers and Abigail Van Buren
- Chang and Eng Bunker (a.k.a. "The Siamese Twins"), who were conjoined at the side.
- Mary-Kate and Ashley Olsen.
- Tia and Tamera Mowry.
- The Minnesota Twins – for all you for Minnesotans!
- Markieff and Marcus Morris – for all you KU fans!

We would be remiss, however, if we omitted Jacob and Esau. For they are surely two of the most famous twins of all time. (Now, please note that even though Esau was the older of the two, because of who Jacob is, because of what he does, and because what he becomes, these twins are remembered as "Jacob and Esau" and not "Esau and Jacob.")

From the beginning of their lives, Jacob and Esau knew tension and rivalry. Jacob's name means trickster, supplanter, heel-stealer, referring to the account of how Jacob came out of his mother's womb, clutching with a near death-grip onto Esau's heel, wanting himself to occupy the place of honor as the first-born.

The dysfunctional family that we behold in the nine sordid chapters between the 25th and the 33rd chapters of the book of Genesis puts to shame any other family we see on television or in the movies!

Esau, the first-born, presumably heir to the leadership mantle and position of privilege within the tribe of Isaac, is born red and hairy. Isaac is a "smooth man."

Esau becomes a hunter, acquainted with roughness of the out-of-doors and all that goes with it, and he's his father Isaac's favorite of the twins. Jacob is quiet and keeps to the tents, inside, and he becomes his mother Rebekah's favorite.

In time, Jacob tricks Esau out of his birthright, which pertains to the property that would have been rightfully his. He does so by the enticement of some red lentil stew. Older translations of the text refer to a bowl of "pottage," but it should read "red lentil stew," something that obviously stimulated Esau's olfactory nerves and exacerbated his hunger to the point that he sold his birthright for a bowl full of Jacob's concoction.

But the linchpin story about the rivalry between Jacob and Esau– and the biggest betrayal, perhaps the most pronounced scam in the entire Bible– is found in the 27th chapter of Genesis. The time has come for Isaac's verbal blessing– a moment of mysterious power and the conveyance of unique privilege. Isaac is old, decrepit, and blind. He requests Esau to fetch some of his favorite game and prepare a meal. Then he intends to bless Esau as the inheritor of the legacy of Isaac's father (Esau's grandfather), Abraham.

As soon as Esau departs the stage to fetch the game and prepare the meal, Rebekah commands Jacob to kill two kid goats and prepare a delicious meal for his father, then to don some of Esau's clothes and the skins of the slaughtered animals so he will smell like Esau. Jacob dutifully does as his mother tells him, cooking the food, and donning the clothes and the hairy skins of the animals. Although old, blind Isaac suspects that something isn't quite kosher, he can't put his finger on it and proceeds with his blessing: "You sound like Jacob but you smell and feel like Esau. You have my blessing. And God will be with you. 'Cursed be everyone who curses you, and blessed be everyone who blesses you.'"[1] And from that time on, Jacob has the prime position of importance and leadership to carry on the legacy and mission given first to his grandfather Abraham.

When Esau discovers that he has been supplanted once more, he swears that, after their father Isaac dies, he will kill Jacob.

Of course, Jacob flees from Esau's planned wrath and the two do not see each other for twenty years.

But after a while two events combine to change Jacob. First, in a life-altering dream, he is visited by a vision of a glorious ladder going up into heaven and by a voice from the beyond promising to bring him back to the land he has fled. And second, after marrying Leah and Rachel and laboring long for his father-in-law Laban, he determines he will go to his brother Esau and attempt to leverage his favor. Along the way he beds down near the river Jabbok and there ensues an exhausting night of wrestling with a powerful angelic presence. The presumed angel gives him a blessing and a new name,

Israel. Jacob, the one whose name could be interpreted to mean crooked has now been deemed by the divine as Isra-el, made straight by God.[2]

Then Jacob and Esau meet, a story which we heard read earlier in worship this morning.

Now, the last words Jacob had heard from Esau's lips were the pledge of an avenger. Understandably then, even though he had been blessed by a beautiful dream and had wrestled successfully with an angelic force at Jabbok, Jacob still seems to fret fitfully about Esau and what he is capable of. Sometimes– more often than not, in fact– we "project... into the imagined feelings of others the condemnation [we] inwardly visit upon [ourselves]."[3] Worried about the avenging Esau and attempting to avert a gruesome meeting, Jacob puts out a veritable host of his family and livestock as tribute to Esau. In this way he hopes to "find favor" with his estranged brother.

But something has happened to Esau, too. Something (or Someone!) has somehow visited Esau during the two decades of his living and roaming apart from Jacob. And though he has 400 armed men at the ready, when he sees Jacob from afar, he runs toward Jacob with forgiveness in his gaze and welcoming reconciliation in his arms.

Here we see two things about the relationship between these two twins:

(1) "[I]n and through it all, God uses Jacob for God's ultimately good purposes. . . . If God can use Jacob, then there is hope for all of us."[4]

(2) Like the loving father in the parable of the prodigal son in Luke's gospel, Esau's running toward Jacob in reconciling love shows us something essential about God's very nature. "Esau, not Jacob, represents the radical notion at the heart of Judaism and Christianity that the justice God requires is not revenge but forgiveness."[5]

Jacob is so overcome with Esau's greeting of unexpected grace that, at first, he doesn't seem to know what to do with his intended tribute. What he had intended as leverage to gain favor now becomes a gift for the favor that Esau has initiated out of his own heart. Jacob insists that Esau receive his gift, "for truly to see your face is like seeing the face of God."[6]

"To see your face is like seeing the face of God." Of course, Jacob would say this. The one who is overwhelmed by Esau's gracious greeting and generous welcome is the one who had earlier wrestled with an angelic force and had "seen God face to face."[7] Jacob now knows what the visitation of the holy looks like.

To see your face is like seeing the face of God. This is the statement of one who knows what forgiveness is all about, who has received loving largesse, Godly grace, holy healing from on high.

To arrive at such a personal posture in relation to others, Jacob and Esau have participated in what Lewis Smedes has called the basic stages of forgiveness.[8]

First, there is hurt and disgust. The pain is so deep and unfair you can't forget it. You wish the person who caused your suffering to suffer as well. These are natural and unavoidable emotional states of being.

Second, there is the growing, sometimes incrementally increasing movement toward healing. Somehow, we are given what Smedes calls "magic eyes" by which we see the other person in a new light and rediscover the humanity of the wrongdoer. Jacob was given such vision in a dream and in the wrestling with an angel. He was a changed person after those encounters and knew that his life would not be fulfilled unless he attempted a healing reconciliation with the brother he had wronged. Esau, in his own right, changed over time as well. How and just exactly when we can only make conjectures. Perhaps he grew bored by the bitter taste of revenge in his mouth. Perhaps he felt burdened by the weight of hate he carried around in his heart. Perhaps he grew weary and worn out by the fantasy of carrying out his anger against Jacob. Frederick Buechner says, "Of the Seven Deadly Sins anger is the most fun. To lick your wounds, to smack your lips over grievances long past, to roll your tongue over the prospect of bitter confrontations yet to come, to savor the last toothsome morsel of the pain you are given and the pain you are giving back– in many ways it is a feast fit for a king. The chief drawback is that what you are wolfing down is yourself. The skeleton at the feast is you."[9] Perhaps Esau discovered that his own fruition as a human being was bound up in a reconciliation with his estranged brother. Perhaps he walked and roamed and wondered long and hard and finally– by the impact of a force outside of himself and by virtue of his own internal discomfort– came to the same conclusion that Jacob had come to: reconciliation must be attempted. However, he came to that notion, both Esau and Jacob moved toward healing.

Then, Smedes says, coming together occurs, as you invite the person who hurt you back into your life. This is what I call "reconciling hospitality." In this stage of forgiveness, we finally release from our lives the power of the wrong we have suffered and the hurt and pain the wrongdoer has done to us. We engage in wishing the wrongdoer well. This is Esau's posture. No longer feasting on his own anger but instead releasing himself from his pledge of revenge, he wishes Jacob well.

This is not the progression of logic but of love. This is not the product of cunning calculation but of compassionate generosity.

Alexander Pope declared "To err is human, to forgive, divine." But Esau and Jacob know better. To err is certainly human, but to forgive is not simply God's prerogative. To forgive is to engage in those attitudes and actions that will restore us to the image in which we were created. W. H. Auden, in his poem "For the Time Being: A Christmas Oratorio," has Herod say, "I like committing [sins], God likes forgiving them. Really the world is admirably arranged."[10] And for many people who live their lives in the cynically shallow end of the existential pool, that fits fine. But for Esau and Jacob, and for the rest of us who follow in their path, that just won't do.

Between humanity and God, the greatest justice of God is finally to forgive. And so also for the circumstances between brother and brother (twin or not), between friend and friend, between neighbor and neighbor, between parent and child, between nation and nation: Ultimate justice occurs when we forgive, when we act from the best within us, from the very image in which we were created by God.

Two thoughts and a story, before we go.

First, when you read the follow-up story about Jacob and Esau, you'll notice that they part ways. Theirs is a reconciliation, ultimately, by separation.

As Walter Brueggemann notes so rightly, "Reconciliations are seldom as unambiguous as we anticipate."[11]

And as Smedes reminds us, "The act of forgiving is a wonderfully simple act; but it always happens inside a storm of emotions. It is the hardest trick in the whole bag of personal relationships."[12]

The second thought is this: one gets the feeling that Jacob and Esau are not quite finished with their forgiveness. And this, too, seems appropriate. Which brings us to this proverbial wisdom: "Only God can forgive in a single breath."[13] But that doesn't mean we are kept from forgiving others to some measurable significance with the breaths we have.

Now for the story. A tale out of the Cherokee tradition recalls how an elder was once teaching a child of the tribe.

"There is," said the wise elder, "a great struggle going on inside of me. It is a battle between two wolves. One wolf is ugly and gruesome, full of hatred, anger, envy, arrogance, vengeance, resentment, regret, and greed. The other wolf is beautiful and altogether lovely, full of grace, forgiveness, generosity, joy, peace, and love. This battle is going on inside of you, too, and inside every human being."

The young child pondered long and hard about what the elder had said and then asked, "Which wolf will win?" To which the elder replied, "The one you feed the most."

Moving through the stages of forgiveness, Jacob and Esau each came eventually to feed the beautiful and lovely wolf inside of them the most.

And so can it be for each one of us.

When we do, forgiveness and reconciliation reign, and the world moves ever closer toward the beloved community in which God desires us all to dwell.

Let it be so. Amen.

NOTES
1. Genesis 27:29.
2. My heartfelt thanks to Rabbi Michael Zedek for this nuanced, poetic insight.
3. *The Interpreter's Bible,* (New York: Abingdon Press), vol. 1, p. 730.
4. John Buchanan, "The reach of grace," *The Christian Century,* August 12, 2008.
5. Ibid.
6. Genesis 33:10.
7. See *The Interpreter's Bible,* vol. 1, p. 730.
8. Lewis B. Smedes, *Forgive & Forget: Healing the Hurts We Don't Deserve* (New York: Harper & Row, 1984).
9. Frederick Buechner, *Wishful Thinking: A Theological ABC* (New York: Harper & Row, 1973), p. 2.
10. W.H. Auden, "For the Time Being: A Christmas Oratorio," in *Collected Poems,* Edward Mendelson, ed. (New York: Random House, 1976), p. 303.
11. Walter Brueggemann, *Genesis* (Atlanta: John Knox Press, 1982), p. 273.
12. Smedes, p. 2.
13. Lewis Smedes's phrase, quoted in Celestin Musekura, *An Assessment of Contemporary Models of Forgiveness* (New York: Peter Lang Publishing, 2010), p. 75.

6

GOD WANTS YOU TO LAUGH
Text: Genesis 18:9—15

Everybody ought to have Judy Joyce as a friend, or at least someone like her.

During my recent recovery, Judy presented a prescription bottle that had a different kind of medicine broadcast on its label: "LAUGHTER. Take one tablet at least three times daily as needed. Unlimited Refills. No Expiration Date." Inside the stereotypical medicine bottle were four dozen of the absolutely corniest jokes I had seen in a long, long time! Still, they were also, at once, some of the funniest. Judy knew that humor and laughter are part of any healing process. Judy knows intimately what God hopes for us all: God wants us to laugh.

God wants you to laugh, in season and out of season. On high, bright sunny days, and on gloomy ones as well. God wants you to laugh, in the midst of *in extremis* situations and when everything is smooth sailing. God wants you to laugh, as a Christian, in order to have fun and express your joy. God wants all of humanity to laugh. God wants you to laugh.

The mandate to laugh is so very clear from Scripture. It is almost as if it were a duty! Some of the most famous and memorable lines of Holy Writ focus on the necessity of laughter and all the emotions and activities that attend the experience of laughing- elation, exhilaration, joy.

In two of the most somber passages of Scripture in the Old Testament, the note of joy is sounded:

"Strength and dignity are her clothing," the book of Proverbs says about a good woman, "and she laughs at the time to come" (Proverbs 31:25).

"Weeping may tarry for the night, but joy cometh in the morning" (Psalm 30:5).

The preacher Qoheleth offers one of our favorite quotes about laughing: "For everything there is a season and time for every matter under heaven: . . . a time to weep, and a time to laugh" (Ecclesiastes 3:1, 4).

And Jesus, too, is all about joy and its gifts, which include laughter. In the Sermon on the Plain in Luke's gospel, Jesus says, "Blessed are you who weep now, for you will laugh" (Luke 6:21).

And twice in John's gospel, Jesus proclaims the centrality of joy and its gracing benefits through laughter:

"In the world you have tribulation; but be of good cheer, I have overcome the world" (John 16:33).

"These things I have spoken to you, that my joy may be in you, and that your joy may be full" (John 15:11).

27

The Church caught on to the Scripture's insistence on the necessity of laughter when it created Easter Mondays and Bright Sunday experiences. A thousand years ago, the Monday after Easter and the Sunday following Easter were times of great hijinks and laughter. Clergy played jokes on one another. Members pulled pranks. Jokes were told in church. And all of it was done in service of celebrating the fact that God got the last laugh, that death's grasp could not keep Christ from his divinely granted resurrection, and that death could not and will not be able to keep any of his followers down, either. In the twenty-first century some congregations have in fact adopted a Holy Humor Sunday, when the sermon amounts to a series of jokes, and not all of them of great comedic value, I might add. It sounds risky, but maybe we should even try it around here!

One of the most forwarded and copied sources of humor on the internet is the collection of so-called *"Letters from Children to God."*[1] And I'm 100 percent half-way convinced that they must have been composed by children, because no adult could be that inventive to create such gems. Gems like:

- Dear God: Who draws the lines around the countries? Nan.
- Dear God: What does it mean when the Bible says that You are "a Jealous God?" I thought You had everything. Jane.
- Dear God: Thank you for the baby brother, but what I prayed for was a puppy. Joyce.
- Dear God: I bet it is very hard for You to love all of everybody in the whole world. There are only four people in our family and I can never do it. Nan.
- Dear God: If You watch me in church Sunday, I'll show You my new shoes. Mickey D.
- Dear God: I didn't think orange went with purple until I saw the sunset you made on Tuesday. That was cool! Eugene.

And just think of the power of humor to humble the haughty and embolden the used and abused.

Think of Forrest Gump and the wisdom he imparted to our culture, and you can't help but at least smile, even if you're the edgiest, meanest grump in the room. Think of the memorable adages that Forrest Gump's laughter-inspiring character has given to us. Like Forrest's Mama said, *"Stupid is as stupid does."* Or *"Life is like a box of chocolates: you never know what you're going to get."*

Or consider the legacy of Seinfeld and the shenanigans of Jerry, George, Kramer, and Elaine. Remember the gems such as: *"A show about nothing."* *"Low talkers."* *"Close talkers."* *"The man-zier."* *"Serenity now!"* And of course, how will we ever forget, *"Yada, yada, yada."*

And besides what media does, remember your own glee when you tell someone else about a funny thing that happened to you or that you saw or heard or read.

Humor is a natural elixir that we simply must have more of. Laughter may not be able to cure cancer– yet!– but it can surely ameliorate the sadness, confusion, hurt, and uncertainty that comes with cancer.

Humor may not be able to secure a job for you in a down economy. But it sure can lighten the load and keep you from self-pity and make your joblessness endurable so that you can detect your many other blessings.

Humor may not be able to stop all the craziness and brutality in the world. But it can certainly serve as a reminder of the best and the most humane possibilities that abide in us as human beings.

It all started with Sarah and Abraham. In the 16th and 17th chapters of Genesis we hear laughter for the first time in the Bible. In the account that was read this morning we encounter Abraham and Sarah after they have been given new names as well as new identities as the establishers of a new, free, and blessed people. They are told by God that Sarah will bear a son to Abraham. Furthermore, they are told that through them, and the lineage of their progeny, there will come great nations and kings. When they hear this news Abraham and Sarah laugh. In fact, Abraham falls on his face when he laughs (Genesis 17:17). Sarah laughs to herself (Genesis 18:12).

Now most male commentators have been kinder to Abraham than they have been to Sarah about their respective laughter, "judging her severely."[2] But they needn't have been.

At first glance it seems that God is rebuking Sarah for her laughter. Is Sarah's laughter incredulity? Is it scoffing laughter? Is hers the kind of laughter that is unnatural in a situation like hers? Sensitive receivers of this story must say "No" to all such questions.

Who wouldn't have laughed in Abraham and Sarah's situation? They are decades beyond picking up their first Social Security checks. They've been on Medicare so long they can't remember not being on it. And now their Medicare benefits are going to cover the cost of a brand-new baby? God has got be kidding!

They're laughing instead of crying; they're laughing instead of going crazy.

But God questions Sarah. Why God doesn't question Abraham, we don't know.

Maybe Abraham, as he has been on many other occasions, is too dense. Maybe only Sarah can ascertain what God truly wants, which is a relationship based on an on-going conversation. And notice that as God and Sarah engage in conversation, "God makes no judgment on Sarah, even when Sarah denies that she laughed."[3]

I believe that God, in essence, wants Sarah to laugh. God wants a dialogue to be maintained between Himself and his highest creatures. It is as if God were saying "Do you see how comical, how wonderfully funny you and all the rest of my creation are to me? And besides, I'd much rather laugh than weep over your behavior. So please, go ahead and laugh. I want you to laugh! That is part of the on-going conversation I desire with you."

Now, before I close, it would be well for us to count the benefits– the holy gifts– of laughter as well. I believe God knows them intimately, but we know them far less well:

- *Laughter can keep us honest about ourselves.* Laughing truly can help us not to take ourselves too seriously. Gary Simpson, pastor at Concord Baptist

Church of Christ in Brooklyn, New York, tells the story of his father, who was also a pastor in Ohio, as he dealt with a rather unwelcome pie that a church member once made for him. Now, the member who had made the pie was not a good pie-maker. In fact, they had missed their calling and everybody knew it. When Gary's father got home, he threw the pie away. The next Sunday, the pie-maker, greeting Dr. Simpson at the door, inquired, "Well how did you like that pie I baked for you?" "Well," responded Dr. Simpson, "such a pie as you created doesn't stay around our house very long!"

- *Laughter helps us heal physically, psychologically and spiritually.* Norman Cousins has documented how he participated in his own healing by laughing himself into health. When he discovered he had a heart ailment he began taking massive amounts of vitamin C and making himself laugh. Later, he would be burdened by "reactive arthritis," and he applied the same remedy. He wrote about it all in *Anatomy of an Illness*, which is still in print today. Cousins said that he made "the joyous discovery that ten minutes of genuine belly laughter had an anesthetic effect and would give me at least two hours of pain-free sleep."[4]

- *Laughter helps us maintain balance in a world that is overly earnest, overly brutal, overly vindictive.* In her memoir, *Growing Up Laughing: My Story and the Story of Funny*, Marlo Thomas tells how, when she was growing up, her father, Danny Thomas, would ask her, "'Anything funny happen at school today?' He was always looking for the fun."[5] And so, Marlo included laughter and fun into the very fabric of her life. And she went on to become a celebrated television actress in her own right and the inheritor and wonderfully generous steward of her father's philanthropic legacy, St. Jude's Children's Research Hospital. Could you use Marlo as an exemplar for your own life? Could you make fun and laughter a plan for your own life? In a world as harsh as razor blades, as brutal as a sledgehammer, and as humorlessly vindictive as a cobra, should we not try massive doses of laughing for the living of our days?

- *Laughter helps us, as individuals and communities, stay sane.* Maya Angelou recalls that in the antebellum American south, slaves had a practice of going to the "laughing barrel" to express themselves.[6] Laughing was disallowed on many plantations, so when they couldn't help themselves, they'd go to a barrel and lean way over, as if they were trying to retrieve something, and laugh themselves silly. Again, laughing instead of crying.

- *Laughter empowers us to live more and more into the Imago Dei (the image of God) in which we were created.* Could it be that laughter is part of the divine image, the Imago Dei, in which all of humanity has been created? Could it be that it is in laughing that we behold an angle of God's personality? With all due respect to those who yearn to grasp the depths of God in their very souls, let us allow—no let us embrace and proclaim— the notion that God wants us all to laugh, that it is a holy mandate to express ourselves with gales of laughter and chortling and jesting and cackling!

This past week, our pastoral staff was inspired, touched, and divinely disturbed by "The Maafa Suite" presented at the St. Paul Community Baptist Church in Brooklyn, New York. *Maafa* is a Kiswahili word that roughly translates to "catastrophe." Just as *holocaust* conveys the horrors of what was done to Jews by Hitler's demonic minions, so *maafa* is meant to convey something of the ravages of the transatlantic slave trade. The motto of the presentation, established by the MAAFA founder and St. Paul's former senior pastor for 34 years, is "The Way Out Is Back Through."

In the middle of "The Maafa Suite" presentation there is a long prayer, entitled "The Preacher's Prayer," in which a singular figure rages in a soliloquy of anguish: "Why don't you help us, why don't you come and relieve us of this oppression? I want an answer! I want You to answer me now! Now! Now!" And then there's a dramatic pause, and the preacher says, "And if not now, then as soon as possible." At which point the entire audience breaks out in laughter. Not only because there is a theatrical need for some relief from the dramatic anguish, but because it is a real human need. We all need to laugh, even in the most devastating of circumstances.

These are but a few reasons God wants us to laugh — today, tomorrow and every day of our lives. Laugh long and hard and loud. Or softly, politely, demurely. Whatever you do, laugh. At yourself and the pretentious foolishness we too often get ourselves into. Laugh at the foibles of everyone, and then know that we all have a common bond in our brokenness. Laugh at the outrageous possibilities God wants to implant and then see them come to fruition in us.

So, laugh! Tell jokes, even bad jokes, do skits, practice jesting, hold on to the comical. Laugh! Laugh, instead of complaining. Laugh, instead of whining. Laugh, instead of remaining silently indignant. Laugh, instead of living in regret. Laugh, instead of abiding in resentment. Always remember that it is your holy duty as a person of faith to laugh. God wants you to laugh! Amen.

NOTES
1. http://tgulcm.tripod.com/ohc/humor.html#Hunter
2. *The New Interpreter's Bible*, (Nashville: Abingdon, 1994), vol. 1, p. 463.
3. Terence E. Fretheim, *Abraham: Trials of Family and Faith* (Columbia, S.C.: University of South Carolina Press, 2007), p. 113.
4. Norman Cousins, *Anatomy of an Illness as Perceived by the Patient: Reflections on Healing and Regeneration* (New York: W.W. Norton & Company, 1979), p. 43.
5. Marlo Thomas, *Growing Up Laughing: My Story and the Story of Funny* (New York: Hyperion, 2011).
6. I first heard Maya Angelou's recollection of *"the laughing barrel"* at the Trinity Institute's "God with Us Conference," at Grace Cathedral, San Francisco, Calif., January 25-27, 1990.

7

WHAT DO YOU DO WITH PSALM 137 (AND OTHER TROUBLING BIBLE PASSAGES)?

Texts: Luke 6:27–30, Ephesians 6:5–9, Psalm 137:9

Jacob Bronowski, famed host of the long-ago PBS series *Ascent of Man,* as well as being a scientist and poet, discovered an interesting phenomenon among the Sherpas who serve as the guides for expeditions up the Himalayan mountains. The Sherpas who do this extraordinary work only know the face of Mount Everest from their perspective, from the valley below where they live. When they have been shown pictures of Mount Everest from other vantage points, they can hardly believe their eyes. "Their disbelief changes to . . . amazement when they realize that something with which they are so familiar can have other sides to it."[1]

That's the way it is with us, I believe, and the Bible. Over the course of the three sermons in this *Festival of the Bible* series, I have been hoping and praying that we Community Sherpas will experience the transformation of disbelief into utter amazement as we, too, realize that something with which we are so familiar can have other sides to it, can, in fact, have many other sides to it.

During the past two weeks, you have heard me emphasize how the Bible is holy to us and how it is our Bible now and that it always needs to be connected to the real lives we live as Christians in the twenty-first century. By the way, I hope you've taken your Bible out for a ride this past week and made those connections I suggested in last week's sermon!

I hope and trust you've heard me say that the Bible has untold and immeasurable ways to move us and deepen our faith. If you missed receiving that emphasis, let me say it again clearly this morning: The Bible has an immense capacity to thrill and to inspire, to challenge and to change, to embolden and to encourage.

For me one of the most profound examples of the Bible's powerful and nearly limitless capacity to inspire occurred in relation to a man named Otis Moss.

It's almost as if it happened yesterday. There we were, almost three years ago now, in the middle of the sanctuary of the St. Paul Community Baptist Church in the East New York neighborhood of Brooklyn, New York. On a Wednesday night, the Rev. Dr. Otis Moss II, Pastor Emeritus of the Olivet Institutional Baptist Church in Cleveland, Ohio, was preaching. I can't imagine ever forgetting the powerful word he uttered to all of us there that evening.

Dr. Moss spoke about the "Three Dimensions of Spiritual Maturity." He garnered the three dimensions from the first verses in three consecutive psalms.

- Anguish. "My God, my God, why hast thou forsaken me?" (Ps. 22:1)
- Adoration. "The Lord is my Shepherd." (Ps. 23:1)
- Affirmation. "The earth is the Lord's & the fulness thereof."(Ps. 24:1)

The first verses from three consecutive Psalms. Wow! What a powerful preachment it was. What a masterful use of scripture. And what a powerful capacity was revealed in scripture's ability to illuminate what we experience along the journey of faith.

Now, the Bible possesses numerous passages which trouble people of faith. This morning let us ask if there is a possibility of discerning new ways of interpreting old passages of scripture so that we can embrace the overall thrust of the Bible without succumbing to the hackneyed, outmoded presuppositions and destructive injunctions posed by certain scriptural passages.

I'm assuming that all of us have been troubled by one passage or another in Holy Writ. It is natural to be so bothered. In fact, it's really a sign of faithfulness to wrestle with scripture, sometimes, Jacob-like, even into the wee hours of the morning, so as to seize a meaningful blessing from a Bible passage. This morning I promise not to keep you too long. But I do invite you to put on your wrestling gear and come along with me as we explore how troubling and how motivating and moving the Bible can be.

I.

A first example pertaining to the bothersome-ness of scripture can be found in the sixth chapter of Ephesians. The verses you heard earlier in the service have been used endlessly to diminish one group of people by the domination of another group of people. From the time immediately after the birth of the church and well into the 1700's, slavery was justified by slave owners and slavery defenders by use of this passage and its parallels in other epistles by Paul. "Slaves be subject to your masters...." It would be well into the eighteenth, nineteenth, and twentieth centuries before Biblical critics would drive home the point that certain portions of the Bible were culturally conditioned — that is, certain parts of Holy Writ, including Ephesians 6:5-9, were products of their times.

The Apostle Paul was, in significant ways, a product of the Hellenistic culture of his day. And while he gave emancipation advocates some of their favorite watchwords– "In Christ there is neither slave nor free."– he did nothing during his itinerant ministrations, neither in Asia Minor nor along the European frontier he evangelized, to dismantle the structures of racism, most especially slavery.

Later on, this passage in Ephesians was used to justify the Confederacy's position regarding slavery in the U.S. Civil War. Families were torn asunder and brothers shed each other's blood over the issue of slavery and the Bible's seeming support for it.

In our day and time, we can say that a critical evaluation of this passage in particular (and others like it) pertaining to slavery leads us to the following conclusion: Not all of the Bible is applicable to our lives today. Our best response to such scriptures can be to note the best principle, the premier symbolism, the most powerful metaphor, the finest ethic for living in the passage and then to see how it resonates with the teachings and way of life of Jesus.

II.

Another example of a troublesome passage can be found in the sixth chapter of Luke's gospel. In these verses we find not so much words that are culturally conditioned and out-of-date for our time, but words that are hard to live out, ideals that are supremely difficult to embody in our day-to-day existence.

"Love your enemies, do good to those who hate you." In all three synoptic gospels these words fall from Jesus' lips. Has there ever been a more difficult section of holy scripture to live up to? "Turn the other cheek"? Yeah, right.

But even though we find these sayings hard, even though we might say on certain days that these words are impossible to live out and up to, we still would say these words surely qualify the Good Book as holy. Yes, these words are hard to hear and hard to live out! And in that hardness we are certainly troubled.

Which leads us to note that the Bible often reveals just how hard faith can be. And it shows us what our best selves can be like. What do we do with these sorts of troubling passages? Simple.

Firstly, give thanks for them, because they show us what is possible within the human experience. Give thanks that we are not left to our own devices but have been shown "a still more excellent way," the way of love and sacrifice and sharing and mercy.[2]

Secondly, we can marvel at those who have embodied this passage of scripture and thereby transformed the society in which they lived.

Think of Jane Addams in Chicago and her work with children.

Remember Mahatma Gandhi, who, even though he wasn't a Christian by birth or by conversion, lived out the love ethic of Luke 6 more vividly than nearly anyone else in the world during his lifetime.

Think also of Martin Luther King and how he and millions of his followers helped our nation live up to its best ideals by using the ethic of love as counseled by St. Luke.

Yes, it is an irksome passage of scripture, but please give thanks for it, because, perhaps in a way supreme in all of the New Testament, it inspires us to live up to "the better angels of our n nature."

III.

As a final example, consider Psalm 137, which is front and center in the sermon title today. In this passage we encounter something which is not simply out of date or hard to live up to. In the ninth and final verse of Psalm 137 in particular, we encounter a passage that is utterly disgusting: "Happy shall they be who take your little ones and dash them against the rocks." Harry Emerson Fosdick could not stomach this passage at all: "Even Guonod's glorious music cannot redeem [the closing words of Psalm 137] from brutality."[3] Walter Bruggemann was likewise stymied by Psalm 137: "I cannot see how such a psalm fits with Christian faith."[4]

While the opening lines of Psalm 137 are rightly famous as words of anguishing lamentation, the closing words in verse nine are repulsive. Yes, we want to affirm that the experience of exile and the mocking of one's religion are some of the foulest humiliations we can ever know. But we are insulted by the gross brutality that is countenanced in verse nine.

There are at least four main insulting experiences we can have in relation to Psalm 137.

- We are insulted that such a piece of literature was ever found to be acceptable and included in the Bible in the first place. "How in the world did such a piece of vindictiveness ever make it into the Bible in the first place?" we are likely to ask.

- Psalm 137 is insulting to our understanding of God. It sullies our image of God. Surely God wouldn't approve of such a wish, such a prayer.

- And Psalm 137 is insulting because there isn't a divine answer given to this psalm as there seems to be in other psalms? Why didn't God just blast the Psalmist for uttering such violence?

- Psalm 137 is insulting in its resonance with our emotions of vengeance and our own embodiment of vengeful action. How dare the Psalmist remind us of our shadow sides! This may be one of the "undertow" dynamics of this psalm (and others) that likewise curse enemies instead of loving and forgiving them.

IV.

In the case of these sorts of troubling passages of Holy Scripture, let us ask an all-important question: What shall we do with them?

- Know that the way out of a passage, even one as troubling as Psalm 137, is through. It never helps when we evade a piece of scripture simply because we don't like it or don't understand it. Admitting that certain portions of scripture make us uncomfortable can be the first step into an incredibly fruitful season of spiritual growth. It's all right—in fact, it's A-OK— to have ultimate problems with certain portions of the Bible. Our faith is too important not to have an occasional lover's quarrel with the Bible. It may be that we're not reading it deeply enough or closely enough if we aren't at least a little bit troubled by scripture. Criticism isn't condemnation.

- Remember that the Bible isn't a recipe book but rather a collection of stories and sagas and poetry and, most importantly, a gathering of testimonies about the vitality and blessings that arise and evolve from knowing God ever more closely day by day by day. And as such, it behooves us to admire it but not make an idol out of it. And it's consistently a mistake to "look to the Bible to close a discussion; the Bible seeks to open one."[5]

- Trust that the God of the Psalmist is the same God whom we worship this morning and note that there is not one recorded account in any other psalm or any other portion of Holy Writ that God answered and responded to the vengeful plea by fulfilling the brutal ending in verse nine. This is no small comfort and a humbling challenge to us all when our own prayers go seemingly unanswered. The answer of God at the end of Psalm 137 is silence and non activity. Psalm 137 says curse my enemies, but God will not. Psalm 137 says beat the babies against the rocks. But God sends a baby instead that will heal the world of all its bruising and cause all manner of stones to drop from the hands of those who have known only vengeance and hatred. In the seeming silence of God in response to the unredeemable brutality at the end of Psalm 137, we hear a holy hush and quivering quietude, a sacred silence in which God speaks volumes to us. Far from being the basis for a justification of vengefulness, Psalm 137 reminds us that as real as our own sense of vengeance may be from time to time, God will not give up on us. God will keep on being full of mercy and grace until we can come home to his heart of grace.

Are you bothered sometimes by what you read in the Bible? If so, you have company— so am I. But if we listen into and through and beyond the troubling passage, we just might hear an invitation from God's heart of grace: "Come home. Come home to my love and forgiveness and a peace that defies understanding and that only I can give. This is the ultimate message of the Bible. This is why I sent my Son Jesus, your Christ. This is how and why I love you so much and will keep on loving you until you get it right."
    Amen.

NOTES
1. In "Century Marks," *The Christian Century*, May 17, 2011, vol. 128, no. 10, p. 8.
2. See I Corinthians 12:31-13:13.
3. Harry Emerson Fosdick, *The Modern Use of the Bible* (New York: The Macmillan Company, 1925), p. 26.
4. Walter Brueggemann, *The Message of the Psalms: A Theological Commentary* (Minneapolis: Augsburg, 1984), p. 77.
5. William Sloane Coffin, *The Heart is a Little to the Left: Essays on Public Morality* (Hanover, New Hampshire: University Press of New England, 1999), p. 48.

8

THE BETTER ANGELS OF OUR NATURE: ABRAHAM LINCOLN

Texts: Mark 3:25 and Colossians 3:8 – 11

This morning we're shining the light of appreciation and gratitude on another "Great Soul" as we continue our new *Great Souls, Great Faith* series of Sunday morning messages. The focus of our considerations is the faith of a gaunt, Kentucky-born, sad-eyed man from Illinois . . .

- whose losses in life (politically and otherwise) were four times as numerous as his victories;
- whose religious sensibilities were patently obvious but would elude definitive description;
- whose ultimate stature was heightened by his adamant refusal to engage in any brand of self-aggrandizement; and
- who began in rustic, humble circumstances and yet became esteemed as perhaps the greatest President in U.S. history.

According to the rankings by eminent historians—including folks like Arthur Schlesinger and presidential scholars like my friend Forrest Church—and according to countless polls among folks all across the country and over many decades, Lincoln ranks consistently, along with George Washington and Franklin D. Roosevelt, in the top three of the greatest presidents in U.S. history. Just below them, are usually ranked two other luminary American heroes, Thomas Jefferson and Theodore Roosevelt. And for all of us in the Midwest, don't worry—Harry comes in shortly thereafter.

This morning, let us allow a clear, backward gaze toward U.S. history and then, employing our imaginations—sanctified by the lens of grace and the purposes of our faith—let us consider the lasting meanings of Abraham Lincoln's witness and faithfulness to the God of his life and ours.

Frederick Douglass esteemed Lincoln to the highest degree:

> In all his education and feeling he was an American of the Americans. He came into the presidential chair upon one principle alone, namely, opposition to the extension of slavery. [I]n the light of the stern logic of great events, and in view of that divinity which shapes our ends, rough hew them how we will, we came to the conclusion that the hour and the man of our redemption had somehow met in the person of Abraham Lincoln.[1]

William Sloane Coffin said, in a manner completely "Coffinesque": "There was something monumentally untrivial about Abraham Lincoln."[2]

Arthur Schlesinger offered one of the most sensible and striking assessments when he averred that Lincoln "was no saint buy rather a human being who grappled with what could be accomplished in an imperfect world."[3]

Carl Sandburg, who was so enamored of Abraham Lincoln that he wrote a six-volume chronicle of Lincoln's life, said it well when he described Lincoln as "a mystery in smoke and flags/ Saying . . . /Yes to the paradoxes of democracy,/ Yes to the hopes of governmen."[4]

And Walt Whitman, perhaps the most eloquent and surely the most florid of eulogists for Lincoln wrote in "When Lilacs Last in the Door-yard Bloomed" how he "mourned, and yet shall mourn with ever-returning spring."[5]

Lincoln does not lack for enthusiastic champions of his superlative character in U.S. history.

Our focus this morning, however, is not merely to praise Lincoln but to see what about his soul is worthy of emulating by all of us here in this day and in this time.

Abraham Lincoln was born in Hardin County, Kentucky, on February 12, 1809. He would lose his mother when he was nine years old. After his father, a fairly successful though uneducated farmer, remarried, the Lincoln family would move to the frontier of Indiana, where he would come to maturity and find himself a commercial, legal, and political career, and grow steeped in faith. Professionally he was a lawyer, and his ambitious heart would inspire him to seek public office. He was first a member of the Whig Party and later became the banner holder for the fledgling Republican Party which came into existence in 1854. His electoral pursuits were many, first in the Illinois legislature, then the U.S. House of Representatives, then the U.S. Senate, and ultimately the presidency of our nation. In our country's most trying time, the Civil War, he would lead the citizens of the nation with perseverance, persuasion, and a holy patience. Tragically, though the war was finally over, President Lincoln would fall to the bullet of an assassin, being shot in Ford's Theater on Good Friday and then dying on Holy Saturday, April 15, 1865.

I.

Now, let us consider the substance of Lincoln's faith by assessing what I call his "Four-Chambered Soul." As hearts have four biological chambers which impact a human being's physical functions and activities, so, I would suggest this morning, Lincoln's soul had four chambers which described his spirituality.

One chamber of Lincoln's soul simply must be described as the Chamber of Loss and Sorrow.

Starting out as an adult, Lincoln tried many an occupation– riverboat pilot, postmaster, surveyor. The earth of his performance didn't quite meet the sky of his intentions. And after that, despite his ascendency to the highest office in the land as our 16th president, behold the litany of his losses:

1832– Defeated in run for Illinois State Legislature

1833– Declared bankruptcy as his general store went under

1835– Anne Rutledge, his sweetheart, died

1836– Had nervous breakdown

1838– Defeated in run for Illinois House Speaker

1843– Defeated in run for nomination for U.S. Congress
1849– Rejected for land officer position
1854– Defeated in run for U.S. Senate
1858– Failed to attain U.S. Senate seat

Yet, despite these losses and perceived "failures," Lincoln lasted and persevered. Perhaps this is one of the reasons he could have such compassion toward others. In the middle of the Civil War, he would pardon Union deserters; at the end, he would grant a general amnesty to all Confederate soldiers as well. While he was firm in his position of saving the Union (and eventually became completely opposed to slavery), he mightily resisted any expression of self-righteousness.

Out of those losses and that resistance against self-righteousness, there continued to arise a throbbing, abiding compassion.

In the face of unthinking cruelty and (even worse) willful, snaky mendacity, Lincoln had compassion. Of all the virtues the prophets embody in the Hebrew scriptures — including especially Isaiah, Jeremiah, Amos, Hosea, and Micah — compassion is the premier, signal characteristic. Richard Lischer has identified this key characteristic of the prophets in his book *The End of Words*. He says we too often stereotype the prophets' dominant tone as that of anger. But no, Lischer says, the dominant tone of the prophets is not anger but sorrow.[6]

We could do with a lot more compassion — Lincoln's sort of compassion — to the point of sorrow.

Compassion for the ones blinded by ambition and blindered by provincial perspectives.

Compassion for the most vulnerable. (We all know "the seventh law of thermo-spiritual dynamics," even at six o'clock in the morning: Parents always play favorites among children; a mother or father always loves most the child that needs them the most at a given moment.)

And compassion to the point of sorrow even for those who succumb to stupidity like xenophobia, or to cynicism that leads to despair, or to grievous hurt that leads to hate and even greater hate.

II.

A second chamber of Lincoln's soul was devotion.

At first, Lincoln was what used to be called a Hard-Shell Baptist. Among his favorite hymns was "Rock of Ages."

Despite his origins, he never joined a church in Kentucky, Indiana, Illinois, or in Washington, D.C. When he was in the nation's capital, he would attend the New York Avenue Presbyterian Church, where he is memorialized by a pew on the right side, facing the chancel, toward the front, known as the "Lincoln pew" to this day.

He was also a student of the Bible, knowing it well and deeply. Pastor Phineas Gurley, the pastor at New York Avenue Presbyterian Church when Lincoln was attending, spoke glowingly about conversations in which the President would articulate his beliefs and his take on Bible passages. And Lincoln's eloquence in one memorable speech after another echoes the cadences and inflections of the King James version of the Bible.[7]

Through his reading of Holy Writ and his evolving faithfulness, Lincoln got it right about invoking God's power for one's side in a conflict. His is an attitude and a perspective we would do rightly to emulate. In the middle of the Civil War, Lincoln was asked if he knew for sure if God was on the side of the Union. "Sir," Lincoln replied, "my concern is not whether God is on our side; my greatest concern is to be on God's side."

It was from his own life of Bible reading, devotion, and prayer that he would come to grips with our nation's initial fall from grace— slavery— and forge a vision of what he called a "new birth of freedom," knowing the truths that our texts for this morning proclaim: (1) that a house divided cannot stand; and (2) that ultimately, "As I would not be a slave, so I would not be a [slave] master." Or, as the Apostle Paul put it to the people of Colossae: "there is no longer Greek and Jew, circumcised and uncircumcised, barbarian, Scythian, slave and free."

III.

Which brings up another chamber of Lincoln's soul, and that is the power of words. Not only could he carve out memorable phrases and quotable quotes, but he was also a master shaper, crafter, and codifier of our national self-understanding.

In his first Inaugural Address, he would remind us of "the better angels of our nature."

At the dedication of the national cemetery at Gettysburg in November 1963, after the former president of Harvard orated for more than two hours, Lincoln gave one of his most memorable addresses, citing in only 265 words the bravery and courage of those who had hallowed the battle field at Gettysburg with their blood, and thus had provided all succeeding generations hope "that this nation, under God shall have a new birth of freedom; and that the government of the people, by the people, for the people shall not perish from the earth."

And then in 1865, in what most consider his greatest speech, his Second Inaugural Address, Lincoln intoned the ravages of war and how from both the divine and the human perspectives the Civil War needed to be drawn to a close as soon as possible. This, at his soaring conclusion, would become a holy etching on our collective national memory:

> With malice toward none; with charity for all; with firmness in the right, as God gives us to see the right, let us strive on to finish the work we are in; to bind up the nation's wounds; to care for him who shall have borne the battle, and for his widow, and his orphan— to do all which may achieve and cherish a just and lasting peace among ourselves, and with all nations.

IV.

And let us never forget what is likely the most important chamber of Lincoln's soul, namely that he was almost always in over his head. Either by the historical situations that put him in positions of extreme stress or by his own ambition, Lincoln rose from one rung of leadership and activity to another, always stretching toward a new level of mastery and influence.

How could he do it? How could he not merely endure but prevail and grow when he found himself in over his head? By being saturated, completely infused, with a hopefulness that welled up within him and from beyond him. Could it be that the origin of this impulse for hope was in the American oversoul? Perhaps. Did Lincoln's hopefulness arise from his appropriation of the prophets and Jesus' saving, loving character, which rested on the foundational thesis that there was always more mercy in God than there is sin in us? Partly. I think it was a combination of his sensitive soul, which could overcome loss with compassion, his devotion to the highest in God and the best in humanity, and his trust in the best words of his mouth and the meditations of his heart—those things which were the most valuable to him and ultimately to the nation—that propelled him to abide in hope.

In the end, Lincoln knew that hope is the dynamo at the center of peacemaking which drives the engine of activism.

He knew that hope is the kernel of every faith worthy of the name.

He knew that hope is what moves us forward and raises babies above the flood-waters of a hurricane and shines a piercing light into the reckless rubble rendered by the lightning-quick earthquake.

He knew that hope is the motivation for every person who wants children to read, and cultures to prosper, and music to be magnified, and truth to triumph.

Lincoln knew that hope—that innate given, that incessant impetus for the throbbing of all souls, your soul, my soul, every soul—is what moves us to pray and work and live for peace until the cows of Bashan come home, and the ways of war are ground down into silent uselessness and every person inherits the possibility of experiencing tremendous capacities for beauty and attainment and grace and love.

Amen. I love you. And may God bless us all.

NOTES
1. Frederick Douglass, "Oration in Memory of Abraham Lincoln - Delivered at the Unveiling of The Freedmen's Monument in Lincoln Park, Washington, D.C., April 14, 1876," in Mayo O. Hazeltine, editor, *Orations from Homer to William McKinley*, (New York: P.F. Collier and Son, 1911), vol. 18, pp. 7681-7683.
2. William Sloane Coffin, *The Collected Sermons of William Sloane Coffin: The Riverside Years*, (Louisville: Westminster John Knox Press, 2008), Volume I, p. 45.
3. Quoted in Kevin Mattson, *When America Was Great: The Fighting Faith of Postwar Liberalism* (New York: Routledge, 2004), p.111.
4. Carl Sandburg, *The People, Yes* (New York: Harcourt, Inc., 1936).
5. What Whitman, "When Lilacs Last in the Dooryard Bloom'ed," *Leaves of Grass and Selected Prose*, Sculley Bradley, ed., (New York: Holt, Rinehart and Winston, Inc., 1962), p. 273.
6. Richard Lischer, *The End of Words: The Language of Reconciliation in a Culture of Violence* (Grand Rapids, Michigan: Wm. B Eerdmans Publishing Co., 2005).
7. Edgar DeWitt Jones, *Lincoln and The Preachers* (New York: Harper and Brothers, 1948), p. 37. (Cited in http://www.mrlincolnandfriends.org/the-preachers/phineas-gurley/)

9

THE STRENGTH OF MEEKNESS
Text: Matthew 5:5

Meekness does not get a lot of positive play in culture these days.

Meekness is hardly what we want to teach our children in facing the tough issues of life, is it? While we would never have them become callous, we do desire for them some wizened toughness, don't we?

And no one in the leadership structures of the military wants soldiers to be meek and mild. You won't find any class or workshop, regular or remedial, called "Shock and Awe: The Meekness Way."

Meekness is not a venerated virtue in our culture. Not now. Maybe it never has been. As Erik Kolbell wisely observes, "our culture consecrates the strong by castigating the weak."[1]

We've seen this inferiority of meekness highlighted in drastic relief in the media lately. In the debates, or should we say the mud-slinging contests, over the financial situation of our nation. In the saber-rattling by nations small and large, from Iran to North Korea to the United States. We'll see the inferiority of meekness and the superiority of strength flung at us in every replay and every commercial we behold this afternoon.

The wielders of worldly power would have us know this about how power really works: strength is the opposite of meekness. In fact, meekness is really weakness, plain and simple.

That's right, isn't it? We have it right, don't we?

Well, actually, we don't. Meekness, right after recognizing our sacred tears, is highest on Jesus' list of the values he most esteems. That which appears to be lowest and least among the dynamics that are effective for successful living, turns out, according to Jesus' perspective, to be one of the most powerful and productive.

Emmet Fox, whose writings were passed along to me by at least five friends who are involved in Alcoholics Anonymous, wrote a powerful book about Jesus' Sermon on the Mount. When he was purveying his religious thought at the New York Hippodrome through the time of the Great Depression, his secretary was the mother of one of the two men who founded A.A. In his powerful book, Fox says our text for the morning is "one of the half dozen most important verses in the Bible." It is "the secret of overcoming every difficulty. It is literally the Key of Life. It is the Jesus Christ Message reduced to a single sentence. . . . that [which] turns the base metal of limitation and trouble into the gold of 'comfort' or true harmony."[2]

So, let's understand meekness anew this morning, and see why Jesus promised that the meek would inherit the earth.

I.

As people of faith, when we speak of meekness, let us be clear: we're not talking about weakness. Meekness is not to be equated with weakness in either character, or physicality, or devotion. In fact, one who is meek has more lasting power available for one's life and for the benefit of others than those who are "strong" by the world's standards.

Nor does meekness mean passivity — waiting for the world to happen to you rather than making it happen. Meekness is not a haven for those who wish to avoid involvement in the world. Some interpreters have said that this meekness beatitude has to do with passively enduring subservience and subjugation and waiting for the blessedness of a heavenly reward in the future. Nothing could be further from Jesus' purposes.

Meekness doesn't mean being a spineless milquetoast, allowing the world, either by impersonal force or by personal affront, to treat you like a doormat.

Meekness is none of these sorts of synonyms.

II.

Rather, meekness is, at its foundation, gentleness. The Greek word for meekness which Jesus uses in the fifth verse of the fifth chapter of Matthew's gospel is *praus*, meaning "under control."[3]

A certain ancient papyrus from Africa recorded a description by a wealthy patron of the horse trade. The description went into detail about the stellar character of a particular horse, how high it stood, how broad in the shoulders it was, the veritable power it displayed in all of its physical splendor. And best of all, said the description, "It is a meek horse."[4] Meaning? Meaning that the horse had taken to the bit and could be ridden with ease and surety. Meaning, the horse had allowed itself to be used and guided and controlled by one who would care for it and tend it and see to its every need. Meaning, the horse had been "gentled" out of its wildness and had been put into good service of its owner's purposes.

This is the gist of our beatitude this morning: We are called to allow our lives not to be controlled by the things and substances and status symbols of the world. Money is not finally, or ever, ultimate power. Amassing massive amounts of money — and of what money can buy, such as property, financial instruments, cars, and impressive houses — isn't even a way out of poverty. Too often, amassing money and what it can buy is only a fancier form of poverty.

Politics will not save us, either, although good politics and good politicians are always to be preferred.

Nor will popularity save us or ever prove to be ultimately powerful.

No, real power lies in the gentleness offered by meekness, Jesus says. If we have been "gentled" into a posture and an attitude and a lifestyle of meekness, then we can trust there is One who will care for us and tend us and see to our every need.

III.

Which leads us to humility. If meekness means gentleness — being controlled and guided by One who will take care of us like nobody's business (literally!) — then meekness also connotes humility.

Another way of putting this came to me straight away this week: Meekness doesn't flinch in the face of the too-much-ness of the world. Those who are meek know that God's enough-ness can counter any and every sort of too-much-ness the world ever casts upon us. How do we overcome the world's too-much-ness and rely upon God's enough-ness? By humility.

Now, remember that humility doesn't mean self-abasement. Humility is sensing and knowing deep within our souls how God has graced us and continues to grace us with gifts. Or, as one pastor's class member once put it to my pleased astonishment, "Being humble means being proud of God."

IV.

And if we have been gentled and humbled, what else can we do but love our lives and the God who gives life to us? In love, with gales of loving laughter, we can receive God's forgiveness for our foolishness and live in astonishment at the daily blessings we enjoy, no longer taking them in flippantly but accepting them with true, deep, strong reverence.

Just recently I came across a new poet, or, to put it more accurately, a poet new to me. Her name is Jo McDougall, and she is a grand talent. She's also a cancer survivor, or, better put, a cancer endurer. In one of her signature poems, *"Mammogram,"* she writes about reviewing the X-rays taken of her and the possibility of cancer in her breast:

> "They're benign," the radiologist says . . . .
> I suddenly love
> the radiologist, the nurse . . . .
> I step out into . . . the Taj Mahal . . . .
> . . . . of the parking lot.[5]

Jo McDougall knows what meekness is as Jesus recommends it in his Sermon on the Mount. Jo McDougall has been gentled and humbled into a posture of love toward the whole world. In the face of the world's too-much-ness, she has laid claim to the holy enough-ness that is hers. And suddenly the parking lot to which she returns after her talk with the radiologist has become magical, mystical, gloriously impressive, and altogether lovely. Perhaps this is what it means, finally, to "inherit the earth."

V.

When we become gentled and humbled and abide with a loving posture toward the world, Jesus promises that we will "inherit the earth." Jesus is quoting Psalm 37:11, which was itself a promise to the exiled Israelites in the midst of their exclusion from their homeland, a time when they were oppressed and, seemingly, had no power.

This is truly where the beatitudes become radically transforming. There's no mere otherworldly fruition as the only blessing to be anticipated. There's no forestalled fulfilment to be solely relied upon. No, the promise of this beatitude is an inheritance of *this* earth. Meaning? That the powers of brutality and principalities of harshness, though they seem to be in charge, always fall. Meaning? That the positive ways of gentleness and humility and love are the premier forces that move the world forward. (Sibelius was right on target: "Pay no attention to the critics. No statue was ever erected in honor of a critic.") Meaning? If we will but put our hearts and souls and minds under the positive control of God — in gentleness, humility and love — we will have everything we need and more! We'll have life, and abundantly so.

How else can I put this point? Let me remind you of the words of one commentator, who wrote, "In a world where our knowledge and control of the forces of nature may well at any time . . . threaten the very extinction of human life, genuine meekness becomes [humanity's] only hope."[6] Or, as William Sloane Coffin once put it more succinctly in our Centennial Hall, "Unless we do become meek, there will be no one left to inherit the earth."[7]

What else can I say to reveal the extraordinary gift of this beatitude and its trustworthiness? Let me tell you a story. Nobel Peace Laureate Archbishop Desmond Tutu knew all about the power of meekness to transform the world. He stands today — and he did throughout his stellar ministry as a leader of the Anglican Church and a champion for freedom with few compeers — less than five-and-a-half feet tall. You wonder why his smile is almost as wide as his shoulders, given what hellish conditions he endured under the oppression of South African apartheid. But then, when you understand his faith, his persistent enduring, and his unflagging endorsement of meekness, the smile makes sense, and his stature rises to what seems to be ten feet tall. Before the liberation of South Africa, indeed during some of the most painful days of apartheid, Tutu would lead followers up to the top of Table Mountain, the plateau that hovers over the beautiful city of Capetown. Once atop the promontory, Tutu and his band of followers could see Robben Island, where Nelson Mandela and a host of other resistance leaders were imprisoned. With the police and army personnel analyzing and scrutinizing his each and every word, Tutu would remind his hearers that their persistence in Christian love would one day conquer the hatred and the shameful oppression of apartheid and that the freedom they had been working for so diligently and with such dedication and humility and humor would one day in fact be theirs. One commentator has said Tutu's words were "an act of worship, of renewal, and of defiance; a gesture of faith, ultimately vindicated by the power of persistence."[8]

I know of no record of the exact words which Tutu uttered on any of those occasions when he and his followers were atop Table Mountain looking out to the Atlantic Ocean and the sight of Robben Island where Nelson Mandela would reside for 18 of the 27 years he spent in prison under the hated apartheid system. But I have to think that on more than one occasion, Archbishop Tutu reminded his hearers, and himself, of the words of Jesus and said, "Blessed are the meek, for they shall inherit the earth." Amen.

And, again, allow me to offer the meekest and, at once, the most powerful statement I know: I love you, and God bless us all.

NOTES

1. Erik Kolbell, *What Jesus Meant: The Beatitudes and a Meaningful Life* (Louisville: Westminister John Knox Press, 2003), p. 57.
2. Emmet Fox, *The Sermon on the Mount* (New York: Harper & Row, 1938), p.28.
3. See *The Interpreter's Bible* (Nashville: Abingdon, 1951), vol. 7, pp. 282-283; *The New Interpreter's Bible* (Nashville: Abingdon, 2000), p. vol. 8, 179; William Barclay, *The Gospel of Matthew* (Philadelphia: The Westminster Press, 1975), vol. 1, pp. 96-98.
4. As remembered from a story Carlyle Marney told a long time ago, on a recording that I have since lost after first hearing it, in a context and a place that, regrettably, are also forgotten.
5. Jo McDougall, "Mammogram," *Satisfied with Havoc* (Pittsburgh, Penn: Autumn House Press, 2001).
6. *The Interpreter's Bible*, vol. 7, pp. 282.
7. One of the many quotable quotes Dr. Coffin shared during a preaching workshop in Community's Centennial Hall, April 1995.
8. Erik Kolbell, p. 59.

10

A WORD ABOUT WATER

Text: Psalm 104:1–13, 24–26

In this culminating Sunday in our *ECO: For the Beauty of the Earth* series, we're now finishing a complete orb around and through our major concerns connected with our island home.

You'll recall we began this series with a look at "Loving the Earth" and how necessary and holy such love is for any of us to have a positive future on the planet.

Next, we were held within the embrace of some of the most spectacular organisms in the world: trees. And we discovered a slew of significant trees throughout scripture, and how, as "A Timbered Choir" (using Wendell Berry's fetching phrase), they speak volumes to us about God's powerful provision and abiding, caring love for the world— if we will but pay attention to them.

Last week, we heard impressive words from Tom Haley and Ryan Thrasher about how, according to St. Francis, we are to become "Instruments of God's Peace" as responsible caretakers of the earth and all of its treasures: earth, wind, and sky.

This morning, we are here to share a word about water. Water is one of the central symbols of the Christian faith. In ritual, music, architecture, art, and general symbology, water occupies a premier place in the traditions of the church and our experiences of the gospel. With the water imagery of Psalm 104 as a base, I want to explore with you the powerful images of water, what they can mean for our mutual care for the earth, and what they can mean for our faith.

Now we all know how right Psalm 104 is to declare, "O Lord, my God, you are very great. You are clothed with honor and majesty, wrapped in light with a garment. You stretch out the heavens like a tent, you set the beams of your chambers upon the waters."

But not only that: "[Y]ou make the clouds your chariot, you ride on the wings of the wind, you make the winds your messengers, fire and flame your ministers." The Psalmist knows the core necessity of water for our world: It's absolutely essential—for our survival and for the earth's thriving.

Without it, trees would not grow, and the sky would not be clear enough for us to see the Milky Way in Namibia or anywhere else. Without water, neither we nor the rest of creation would be sufficiently hydrated to behold the rest of the wonders of the world, including the aurora borealis in Alaska. Or an Easter sunrise in San Francisco. Or the wide-open plains of Montana. Or the sky above my friend Maggie Finefrock on her 500-mile pilgrimage along El Camino de Santiago in Spain. And we wouldn't be able to enjoy the surprising and gracious miracles of one season turning into another from a Brookside wintry street, to a Missouri spring country creek, to a European vista in summer, to an autumn display out at Tall Oaks Camp.

Now, in the play and movie *The Rainmaker*, the title character Starbuck preaches a mini-sermon when he says: "Rain is rain, brother. It comes from the sky. It's a wetness known as water — *aqua pura*. Mammals drink it. Fish swim in it. Little boys wade in it. And the birds flap their wings and sing like sunrise. Water! I recommend it."[1]

That poetic proclamation by Starbuck to the scoffing and incredulous Noah Curry, and to Noah's brother Jim, sister Lizzie, and father H.C., about what can be done to alleviate the drought-ravaged dustbowl of their lives, is surely a soliloquy we all could affirm. Who wouldn't recommend water?

As Psalm 104 declares so directly about God's gifts of water: "You make springs gush forth in the valleys; they flow between the hills, giving drink to every wild animal. . . .From your lofty abode you water the mountains; the earth is satisfied with the fruit of your work." And as Psalm 42:7 says: "Deep calleth unto deep at the thunder of thy cataracts."

As Psalm 104 goes on to affirm, "[The waters] rose up to the mountains, ran down to the valleys, to the place that you appointed for them. You set a boundary that they may not pass, so that they might not again cover the earth."

And the Psalmist is right again when he declares that "You cover [the earth] with the deep as with a garment . . . . O Lord, how majestic are your works! In wisdom you have made them all . . . . Yonder is the sea, great and wide."

The composer of Psalm 104 has water as a core focus in his reverie and celebrations, and we are given clear and caring guidance about the motivation for the care of the earth:

• We are not the originators of the ocean. God is.

• We are not the wonder-working fashioners of waterfalls. God is.[2]

Our scripture for the morning does not say, "How manifold are humanity's works" in the care and stewardship of the earth, as good and necessary as that might be.

No. It says that God is the One to whom majesty is to be ascribed. God is to be given praise and glory. Such celebration is the first action of those who yearn to take care of the earth.

To put it very simply and straightforwardly, we raise our praise to God first, before we recycle. We worship God first, before we work on new legislation to protect the environment.

In a sense, Psalm 104 is the original environmentalist's manifesto.[3] But the motivation for caring for the earth in Psalm 104 is founded on the acknowledgment that God has created all that is, and, because of that fact, it is sacrilege to sully it or sacrifice it for anyone's greedy needs.

But a question remains: How do we come to a closer relationship to our Creator God revealed in and through the wonders of water and all that God has made, including water? I think there are three simple steps:

I.

Psalm 38:4 says: "Taste and see that the Lord is good: blessed are those who trust in Him!"

When was the last time you really tasted a glass of water? When was the last time you luxuriated in a drink of clear, cold, thirst-slaking water? When was the last time you remembered that medical professionals recommend that we all drink at least six to eight 12-ounce glasses of water per day? And that if you do so, you are likely to lose weight and breathe easier and generally feel more rejuvenated than those who don't do likewise?

I recall one summer in my high school years when water tasted so absolutely delicious at the end of a "Day's Work." Now I don't mean a day's worth of real work, which I did, working at a grain elevator underneath the oppressive August heat on the coastal plains there along the Houston ship channel. What I mean is how great water tasted after chewing an entire plug of "Day's Work" chewing tobacco, which any decent, self-respecting ship channel elevator worker enjoyed. Oh, how the water tasted when quitting time came and you went home and spit out the "Day's Work" chewing tobacco and took a long drink of water. (The contrast between the burning acidity of the tobacco and the utter sweetness of the water should have been a tipoff that the tobacco probably wasn't that good for me — or anyone else!)

"Taste and see that the Lord is good," says the Psalmist. This is a revelation connecting us to our Creator and the glories of water, through our earliest and most primitive sensory way of knowing the world and the God who made it and us.

So, your first piece of homework as a result of today's message is to taste — really taste! — a simple glass of water each and every day of your life. As you taste that water, know that you are not only doing something good for your overall health, you are partaking of a theological reality: the water is objective, sensory evidence that God wills good for you and your life and for all of God's creatures.

II.

Your second homework assignment is to listen to the water God has created.

Sometimes we can hardly hear anything because of the ceaseless chatter going on within our own hearts and minds. Frederick Buechner cautions us: "What deadens us most to God's presence within us . . . is the inner dialogue that we are continuously engaged in with ourselves, the endless chatter of human thought. . . .[T]here is nothing more crucial to true spiritual comfort. . .than being able from time to time to stop that chatter."[4]

So, stop the chatter and listen to the water. Whether it is the splashing splendor of the fountain across the street from the church or a stream caressing the slopes of a wooded hillside or a quietly flowing river, listen to the grace that such water offers to the world. In that sound is the sound of nourishment to a farmer's fields. In that sound is the delight of children amazed at the crystalline beauty of water pierced by beams of sunlight. In that sound is the reason for the rejuvenation of all forests and all trees and everyone in the human family.

And when you hear such a sound, when you really hear it deeply in your heart, mind, soul, and body, then you can't help but be grateful and give thanks!

So, the next time you hear a river, or listen to a fountain or even gather next to the gurgle of a water fountain, say it out loud: "Thanks, God, for the beautiful sound of water and everything that water makes possible!"

III.

Your third homework task is this: Touch and Know. When you wash your hands, when you take a shower, when you hold your hand underneath a running faucet or in the rush of a streaming creek, touch and know intimately the grace which God wants to give to you and to each and every member of the human family.

Touch the three-dimensional representation of the grace which God wants to pour over your life.

Touch the basic symbol of your forgiveness and know that God's love is made real in that watery renewal experience.

Touch the life-giving character of water and know the life-saving nature of God who yearns for none of us ever to go thirsty for the waters of the earth or the waters of eternal life.

So, remember: 1—Taste and See! 2—Hear and Give Thanks!! 3—Touch and Know!

And when you do this, you'll begin to get a glimpse of the meaning of one of the greatest movies ever made about water, *A River Runs Through It*. Montana is the setting for Norman Maclean's story of a Presbyterian pastor and his caring wife and their two sons. In a peculiar way, it is a kind of Prodigal Son parable in reverse, in which the young prodigal does not really, finally come home but finally falls away. And the older, dutiful brother is not embittered but embodies full grace and eventually, with his family's blessing, leaves home for graduate school.

There are memorable lines in Maclean's utterly memorable story about grace and art: "[A]ll good things—trout as well as eternal salvation—come by grace and grace comes by art and art does not come easy."[5]

And about the holy connection between religion and fly fishing: "[O]ur father was a Presbyterian minister [who] told us about Christ's disciples being fishermen, and we were left to assume . . . that all first-class fishermen on the Sea of Galilee were fly fishermen and that John, the favorite, was a dry-fly fisherman."[6]

And about love: "We can love completely what we cannot completely understand."[7]

And about perfectionism: "Many of us would probably be better fishermen if we did not spend so much time watching and waiting for the world to become perfect."[8]

The very best declaration about life and water and grace Maclean saves for the end, when the older brother, now an old man, ruminates about all that has transpired: "Eventually, all things merge into one, and a river runs through it. The river was cut by the world's great flood and runs over rocks from the basement of time. On some of the rocks are timeless raindrops. Under the rocks are the words, and some of the words are theirs. I am haunted by waters."[9]

Maclean could have just as easily said, "I am inspired, I am blessed, I am enthused, I am graced by waters!"

But even if Maclean doesn't say it that way, the task to affirm it falls to us, and we can say: *Eventually, all things merge into one, and a river runs through it.*

We are graced by waters. Amen.

NOTES

1.   N. Richard Nash, *The Rainmaker* (New York: Samuel French, 1954), p. 40.
2.   James L. Mays, *Psalms* (Louisville: Jon Knox Press, 1994), p. 334.
3.   J. Clinton McCann, Jr. "The Book of Psalms," *The New Interpreter's Bible* (Nashville: Abingdon Press, 1996), vol. 4, p. 1099.
4.   Frederick Buechner, *Telling Secrets* (San Francisco: HarperSanFrancisco, 1991), p. 104.
5.   Norman Maclean, *A River Runs Through It and Other Stories* (Chicago: University of Chicago Press, 1976), p. 4.
6.   Ibid., p. 1.
7.   Ibid., p. 103.
8.   Ibid., p. 37
9.   Ibid., p. 104.

11

HAVE MERCY!
Text: Matthew 5:7

It's interesting to note the connections and interrelatedness among the beatitudes we've been exploring in our current *"Bountiful Blessings"* series. We began, as you'll recall, noting how sacred our tears are in our lives. Next, we underscored the proper ways of being meek. And last week we took up what it means to hunger and thirst for righteousness. The video of Narayan Krishnan has visited me continually since we saw it together last Sunday.[1] And it's appropriate that one who hungers and thirsts for righteousness so generously should precede this week's emphasis on mercy. His hungering and thirsting for righteousness are indeed merciful, and it is out of great mercy that he seeks to embody righteousness for the people of the village of Madurai, Tamil Nadu, India.

In today's beatitude– "Blessed are the merciful, for they shall receive mercy"– we encounter one of the great truisms of the Christian gospel. There's nothing more pertinent, nothing more germane, nothing more central to following in the footsteps of Jesus than mercy.

To his first disciples Jesus embodied all mercy, as they continually mangled their discipleship. To those who gawked at his wonder-working healing power and were inspired by his teaching and preaching, he consistently proffered mercy. Toward the vast crowds that listened to his Sermon on the Mount he had a merciful posture. I get the feeling that he was manifesting gentle mercy even standing before old Pilate, when he responded to Pilate's question about being "King of the Jews" by saying, "You say that I am."[2] And we can never forget Jesus on the cross uttering those words that have become famous as the height of mercy, "Father, forgive them, for they know not what they do."[3]

If Christian faith is about anything, it's about mercy. If Jesus' ministry and life and death and resurrection to new life are about anything, they're essentially about mercy.

This morning, I want to ask something of you, and it may seem like a strange question. When did you first hear about mercy? And, there's another question that's closely related to it: When did you most recently witness mercy? As you ponder those questions, I want to offer several moments that have been soundings of mercy for me. Perhaps, in my recounting of these soundings, something will resonate, maybe even harmonize, within your own heart and soul.

The first time I clearly recall hearing about mercy was from my grandmother Mammy. Once, while she was visiting us in the Rio Grande Valley in Texas, she declared "Have mercy," as she read something in the newspaper. What it was in the paper that prompted her to say "Have mercy" I don't exactly know. But there was about her declaration a note of humble petition toward God to help someone in trouble. She was expressing some sort of sympathy about another person's plight.

This is what mercy is, to be sure: sympathy. To feel something for another's situation, to have a feeling of tenderness within us toward another. When the picture flashes across your computer screen or your television of the untold millions struggling to make it through the day– whether in Haiti or Peru or Indonesia– we have a feeling of sympathy.

That's partly what our Week of Compassion offerings this week and next Sunday are all about: sympathy with our brothers and sisters around the world. One of the greatest outpourings of sympathy which we've ever expressed here at Community occurred right after the tidal wave floods that decimated Indonesia in December 2004. With extraordinary sympathy, Community eventually collected more than $14,000 for that crisis alone. Great, generous sympathy. Some may call this pity, but the better word for this kind of sympathy is mercy.

The next time I recall hearing the phrase "Have mercy" was in California, on an election day, in the living room of Mary Reynolds' home, on E. 22nd Place in south central Los Angeles. We were feasting on the best pinto beans and homemade cornbread I'd ever put in my mouth. But even more delicious was the taste of democracy in the air that day, as vibrant older folks working the polls told of the battles fought and the victories won to ensure that all people could vote. Then in came Mr. Soto. "Hey, Mr. Soto!" the ladies shouted. "It's Mr. Soto, y'all!"

Mr. Soto was an immigrant. He had become a naturalized citizen and a favorite in the neighborhood. That day he was more than a little worried because he couldn't find his voter registration card, and he wanted to vote. When the ladies holding forth at the registration table heard his tale, one of them said "Have mercy, y'all! Mr. Soto's in a fix, and we've got to help him." Then they reassured him that they would walk him through the process for confirmation of his registration and that he would indeed be able to vote that day. And he did.

There it was again: "Have mercy, y'all!" This was an invitation to empathy.

Beyond feelings of sympathy, it was a word urging others to conjoin their lives with Mr. Soto's so that he wouldn't have to bear his burden alone. "Have mercy, y'all!"

Empathy. Yes, in addition to sympathy, empathy is surely what mercy means.

More recently, I heard the phrase "Have mercy" while on a spiritual retreat in Tucson with the other members of the leadership circle of the Bethany Fellowships.

On a calm and balmy Thursday afternoon, we found ourselves away from the retreat site and in the parking lot of a Safeway shopping center. We were there to pray.

We read two brief pieces of scripture– "A voice was heard in Ramah, wailing and loud lamentation, Rachel weeping for her children; she refused to be consoled, because they are no more"; and "Comfort, O comfort my people, says your God. Speak tenderly to Jerusalem."[4]

Then we read the names of the six people who died on the day of horrors, January 8, 2011, and offered our prayers of anguish and love. It was a somber moment to repeat the names of Phyllis Schneck (79, a homemaker from Tucson), Dorothy "Dot' Morris (76, a retired secretary), John Roll (63, chief judge of the U.S. District Court for Arizona, named to the federal bench by President George H. W. Bush in 1991), Dorwan Stoddard (76, a retired construction worker), and Gabriel "Gabe" Zimmerman (30, a community outreach director for Rep. Gabrielle Giffords), and Christina-Taylor Green (age 9).

We also prayed for the thirteen wounded and maimed. We prayed that their memories of that day would be transformed into dreams of different and new days, when family members and friends and their communities of faith would gather round them with comfort and tenderness.

And we prayed for Jared Lee Loughner, the broken young man, who expressed tragically less than the image of God in which he was created and committed horrendous crimes of murder and mayhem. We prayed for clarity in his soul and "a recognition and acknowledgment and somehow, someway a healing" in God's time and by God's heart of grace. When we concluded that part of the prayer, someone was inspired to say, "And we pray for his parents, too."

We prayed as well for the people who minister in Tucson, that they might possess "grace and grit enough to continue to provide the light of hope even when the darkness seems daunting," and to remind Tucson of the meaning of its name: "that it may abide as the place where the water 'at the foot of Black Mountain'– the waters of care and consolation, the waters of the river of life– are offered to one and all." What we were doing had a haunting harmony with those other occasions I had heard "Have mercy." Only this time, it was a simple request for healing and forgiveness: "Have mercy on Tucson, O God." It was a petition for a healing of the people who had suffered loss and for a merciful forgiveness for the one who had caused such senseless loss.

Our simple time of prayer in that parking lot on that plain Thursday afternoon reminded me of the ancient refrains of the church's earliest liturgies: *Kyrie eleison, Christe eleison, Kyrie eleison.* (Lord have mercy. Christ have mercy. Lord have mercy.)

Those would have been words enough, even if we had not had a litany to read. *Kyrie Eleison, Christe eleison, Kyrie eleison.* Lord have mercy. Christ have mercy. Lord have mercy. Have mercy. Heal and forgive.

George Buttrick once offered wise and poetic guidance: "If no deed is possible, words have power. . . . If no words are possible, tears have saving grace."[5]

That afternoon our words were all we had. But they easily could have been summed up with the simple phrase "Have mercy." And if words had failed us that day, our tears would have sufficed. They too would have been expressing "Have mercy."

Have mercy– as sympathy, as empathy, as a plea for healing and forgiveness. Yes, each one is what mercy is about.

One of the most memorable occasions of hearing "Have mercy" was during a span when I lived across the street from All Peoples Christian Church in Los Angeles.

Not only were the people and the place memorable nearly beyond belief. So were the DJ's who prevailed on the radio at that time. With great voices and distinctive styles, they guided us in the procurement of the music our souls needed. One DJ had a signature way of greeting his listening audience and turning our attention to the next tune he was about to play. "Have mercy, Los Angeles!" he'd shout with commanding volume and compelling flair.

"Have mercy, Los Angeles!" With that signature announcement the DJ was not only alerting us to pay attention to the next tune he was playing. He was also beseeching us to assume a shared moral duty of taking care of one another. To use Shane Stanford's phrase, he was urging us to take note and see that "Mercy is spiritual glue."[6] He was also stating what Eugene Peterson has noted about mercy: "You're blessed when you care. At the moment of being 'care-full,' you find yourselves cared for."[7]

Have mercy, as a moral imperative, for all people to seek out the best possible outcomes for one another.

Have mercy, as an existential urging, for one and all to abide by the exercise of mercy, to know that we are called to be "a community of practical and active mercy,"[8] that we are to regard mercy as "something to be done."[9]

As Barbara Brown Taylor put it so eloquently in her very first literary offering, *Mixed Blessings*: "You are loved, act like it. You are redeemed, act like it."[10]

This is what the Jamaica Partners Medical Mission folks have done. Just four weeks ago we bade the 25 mission-trip partners farewell with a blessing in worship.

They returned ten days later to tell us that at one station they saw 89 patients the very first day they were there. Then, the next day, 114 more! Gayle Woods reported there was greater need by the Jamaicans this year than on any previous visit by the partners. The partners offered mercy just as they have received it. And in turn, they received even more mercy. They were, even if only for a short time, part of "a community of practical and active mercy."

"Have mercy." Two little words that pack a wallop. Have sympathy. Have empathy. Have a posture and an attitude of forgiveness and healing. Be sure always to share the mercy that you have received. "Have mercy!"

What if we were to hear that phrase with fresh ears and then begin to practice what we hear? "Have mercy!"

What if we were to say that phrase with new appreciation for its many nuances? "Have mercy!"

What if– just what if– we were to go around and say "Have mercy!" to everyone everywhere? "Have mercy, Lenexa!" and "Have mercy, Liberty!" and "Have mercy, Leawood!" And "Have mercy, Kansas City!"

What if we were the new DJs providing the stimulus to listeners throughout the metropolitan area with just the right emphasis about mercy? It just might be the start of a revolution of caring and sharing and love unlike nearly anything we've ever seen! "Have mercy!" "Have mercy!" "Have mercy!" Amen.

NOTES

1. http://www.youtube.com/watch?v=ZiC_9RHTvsA
2. John 18:37.
3. Luke 23:34.
4. Matthew 2:18; Isaiah 40:1-2.
5. *The Interpreter's Bible* (Nashville: Abingdon Press, 1951), vol. 7, p. 284.
6. Shane Stanford, *The Eight Blessings: Rediscovering the Beatitudes* (Nashville: Abingdon Press, 2007), p. 80.
7. Eugene Peterson, *The Message* (Colorado Springs, Co: NavPress), p. 1250.
8. Warren Carter, *Matthew and The Margins: A Sociopolitical and Religious Reading* (New York: Orbis Books), p. 134; Douglas H. Hare, *Matthew* (Louisville. John Knox Press, 1993), p. 40.
9. Barbara Brown Taylor, *Mixed Blessings* (Cambridge: Cowley Publications, 1986, 1998), p. 83.

12

EVERYONE'S A THEOLOGIAN

Text: Acts 17:16 – 28

Check any newspaper or magazine, electronic or hard copy versions, or check any television website, and you won't find "Religion" as a major header for their news items. But yet . . .

The bad news of the non-religious news seems always to trump the good news that's happening in the religious world. But yet . . .

And I have given up my campaign to rectify movies that portray religious figures as buffoons and idiots in popular movies. *"Four Weddings and a Funeral"* would be the premier example of how badly clergy suffer from negative stereotyping. But yet . . .

I say "But yet . . ." because, despite how badly faith and belief and spirituality and religion are treated (or neglected), there is still within us all a deep desire, an incessant yearning, to know the divine dimensions of life. Just think of it:

A little boy is awakened in the middle of the night. The immensity of God that he's learned about in Sunday school startles him awake into complete befuddlement.

An earthquake shatters Japan, and a tsunami rams into the coast of Sendai, leaving devastation and heartache in its wake. And the eternal question arises: Where was God?

A couple desires to get married. The court house and a judge would be nice, but this couple wants something different. Even though they're not members, they call up a church and schedule their wedding there.

A student prays hard. The exam's coming up. Yes, there's been a lot of late night and early morning studying. And the prayer isn't a petition for magical assistance. The student's prayer is for clear-headedness and mental acuity, so she'll do her best.

What do all these scenarios have in common? They all express– at one level or another– the desire to be connected to something greater than ourselves. We want, we yearn, to be more deeply related to the divine.

Today we launch a new sermon series– *CREDO: I Believe.* There is a deep hunger for God in everyone, and it's interesting to note how we express that hunger, sometimes even through idolatry, often through simple acts of grace and prayer, always with great yearning for completion and wholeness.

Credo is Latin for creed, which pertains to belief. The creeds we're going to dig into are not the traditional creeds. Neither the Nicene Creed nor the Apostles' Creed will take center stage here, though we may reference both of them in a forthcoming sermon.

Nor are we trying to be sneaky and dive into the Affirmation of Faith of the Christian Church (Disciples of Christ), as beautiful as it is. No, the creeds we're going to explore are the commonly held beliefs, those strongholds of faith that are commonly held and essentially practiced.

Today we're examining the thesis "Everyone's a Theologian." Which is another way of describing the 500-year-old tradition of "the priesthood of believers." Since the fertile beginning of the Reformation, Protestants have clung closely to the notion that every Christian has both rights and responsibilities for their own connection with God. There's no intermediary necessary for anyone to connect with God. We all have the right to relate to God personally and intimately. And we all have the responsibility to think through our faith carefully and thoroughly. Willful ignorance is not an option.

Which means that if we believe in the priesthood of all believers, then everyone's a theologian whether they recognize it or not.

And since everyone's a theologian, we have a lot of varied beliefs floating around, from the mundane to the sublime.

My mother had a strange theological notion. When I was anticipating something that would occur in the future, a project, the results of a test at school, a church event, she'd say, "Well, if you hold your mouth right, everything will come out well." Such a strange bit of theology. I never did figure out what that meant.

Just recently I received a mailer announcing that you and I had better get ready for the end of the world. Through certain "theological insights" and calculations about Biblical prophecy, the exact date for the end of the world had been determined: May 21, 2011. Strange theology.

Everyone's a theologian, and there's an astounding variety of theology going on everywhere.

Which is exactly what the Apostle Paul experienced when he was in Athens. Standing in the place where philosophers came to tease out their latest notions and where judicial disputes were adjudicated, the Apostle Paul delivers one of his most monumental missionary messages. At the Areopagus (as known as Mars Hill), Paul enters into the life and texture of the Athenian culture. He notices how replete with theologies they are and how idolatrous they have become with their theologies.

Paul's theological discourse sounds so strange, he gains a reputation as something of a babbler. The Greek word in verse eighteen– rendered as "babbler" in several translations– literally translates as a derogatory term, "seed picker." He's like a bird to the Athenians, bobbing his head up and down, picking at one seed after another, not making much sense– so it seems to the sophisticated onlookers, at least. Paul keeps mentioning something about Jesus and his resurrection. And in the end, he quotes Epimenides, a philosopher-poet presumably well-known among the Athenians, and talks about the one true God, "in [whom] we live and move and have our being."[1]

Now Paul does three things that are absolutely on target for registering his own theological claims:

- He connects with the local folks by using one of their own terms. He sees an altar at which a sign has been placed: "To an Unknown God."

And he uses that as his launching point for connecting their interest in the divine to the life and ministry of Jesus.

- He invites a simple investigation of his own faith. It's as if he's saying, "Check it out." No big hard sell. Just a description of what has been done, and how all the little gods the Athenians have fashioned for themselves are really pointing to the one true God whose gospel Paul has come to preach to them.

- He cites Aratus, another poet from secular literature, apparently very famous to the local folks, to make his point: "For we too are his offspring."[2] Paul is an adroit preacher. He knows not to antagonize his listeners. But at the same time, he doesn't compromise the gospel. He doesn't water down his message. He doesn't give the Athenians what Anne Lamott calls "grace lite."[3]

At this point, reasonable people ought to be asking one question: If everyone's a theologian, which theology deserves our most rapt attention and our most faithful devotion? Whew! I was worried that you were never going to ask that question!

Paul indicates the core of his beliefs and the most compelling piece of his preaching in two ways. One we know only from inference and not from direct quotation. The other we have in a quote by Paul that sums up beautifully what life along the path of Jesus is all about.

Early in the scripture that was read this morning, it is indicated that Paul is decried as a "seed picker" because he has told the Athenians about a "foreign" (that is, different) way of understanding God's presence. It all has to do with "the good news about Jesus and the resurrection."[4]

This is a theology that is straightforward and that all theologians in the Christian camp can wrap their hearts, minds, and souls around: "the good news about Jesus and the resurrection." It's not only simple and to the point. It's the truest distillation of the Christian message we can get, really: "the good news about Jesus and the resurrection."

Well, theologians, if you were wondering what basic tenet to which you could hook your wagon, here it is: "the good news about Jesus and the resurrection." If someone asks us about substitutionary atonement, we can respond "the good news about Jesus and the resurrection." If someone asks about the exact rules for obtaining God's favor, we can simply talk about Jesus' way of life and the possibility of new life for one and all who believe in the power of the resurrection.

Our theologies, I'm suggesting this morning— no I'm earnestly pleading for all of us to seize this morning!! — are all subsumed under the banner of life in the spirit and by the path of Jesus and the mysterious, wondrous, table-turning, life-altering renewal of resurrection, not only for Jesus but in our own lives, here and now and forever.

Everyone's a theologian, and we can have all kinds of potentially conflicting notions and ponderings and questions. And it will all be all right, if we we'll harmonize our thinking and living with Paul's seminal preaching on "the good news about Jesus and the resurrection."

The second thing Paul does is to quote a poetic soul who uttered or inscribed the memorable words *in him we live and move and have our being.*

Prior to this portion of his oration, Paul has described how the idolatrous altar with the inscription "to an Unknown God" is actually a reference to the God of Genesis who brought everything into being, the God who gives breath and life to every creature, the God who gives them the compulsion to seek after the divine connection in the first place, the God "in whom we live and move and have our being." I, like you, perhaps, and like countless Christians, love that phrase. It never fails to inspire me. I suppose that phrase is so powerful because of its simple powerful undeniability. In a beautiful triptych of simple words, the Apostle Paul gives voice to the most succinct truth we know: God is everything. With God, we have everything we need. Without God, we don't have anything worth having.

I like the way Clarence Jordan translates this phrase in the 28th verse: "in him we come to life, in him we are motivated, in him we find meaning."[5] Meaning? Alive, full of purpose and focus, and comforted into sanity and emboldened into generous love toward one another by God's holy presence.

I've finally come to the point in my life and in my journey as a pastor, that I cut to the chase as often as I can. If someone were to ask me what my main credo is, what my main theology is all about, I have a ready answer. I think it resonates with your answer to such a question, and I believe it harmonizes exactly with Paul's monumental message in the 17th chapter of Acts. If someone were to ask me to summarize my personal theology in less than 50 words, I'd say: "The way of Jesus and the key to understanding resurrection is knowing how powerful, cleansing, and healing love is. Love-real, genuine love, not some counterfeit substitute for it- is rather clear; love God, others, and yourself. As you do that, you will know God's grace forever." Or I could say, "In God 'we live and move and have our being.'" I believe that. More importantly, that's the core of the credo of the Christian life.

How about we go to Athens, wherever our Athens may be, and tell everyone the good news about Jesus and the resurrection?

What's the worst that could happen to us? That they'd call us "seed pickers"?

Amen.

NOTES
1.   Acts 17:28a; see *The New Interpreter's Study Bible: New Revised Standard Version with The Apocrypha* (Nashville: Abingdon Press, 2003), p. 1989.
2.   Acts 17:28c; see *The New Interpreter's Study Bible*, p. 1989.
3.   Anne Lamott, *Traveling Mercies: Some Thoughts on Faith* (New York: Pantheon Books, 1999), p. 163.
4.   Acts 17:18c.
5.   Clarence Jordan, *The Cotton Patch Version of Luke and Acts: Jesus' Doings and the Happenings* (New York: Association Press/New Century Publishers, 1969). p. 133.

13

WHEN RELIGION IS SICK

Text: Amos 5:14 – 15, 21 – 24

Who do you take your cues from? Whose wisdom guides your daily living?

Do you have a favorite hero figure who inspires you toward a better life? Do you remember a cherished family member whose wit and insight still resonate inside your heart and soul and spur you on in your job, at school, with your family, among your friends?

Over the course of the next four Sundays, I hope you will come away from your worship experiences here at Community with some new "hero" figures, some newly claimed sources of inspiration. Beginning today and continuing through October 10, we're going to be imbued with the beauty and sometimes blunt blessings of Biblical heroes. Your laughter will increase next Sunday because of Sarah. You'll be either touched or puzzled or both when we see how sacred dogs are to God. And then we'll examine what it means to choose life, day after day, step after step, breath after breath in our daily lives.

Today we begin with the unlikely hero and troubling figure of Amos. Amos' words are not foreign to us. Even if we may not know much about the Bible, we have heard the resounding rhetorical flourishes of the 24th verse in the fifth chapter of Amos: "let justice roll down like waters and righteousness like an ever-flowing stream."

Now that would be fine as a bumper-sticker or as a motto to imprint daintily on a wall-hanging or as a nice reminder of soaring eloquence. But you must also know the rest of Amos and his prophecy, especially what he has to say about sick religion.

Amos was a Hebrew prophet who proclaimed the coming judgment of God in the middle of the eighth century before Christ was born. From the southern Kingdom of Judah, in the little village of Tekoa, Amos, a humble sheep herder and dresser of sycamore trees, was tapped to speak a rough, harsh word of judgment to people luxuriating in the Northern Kingdom of Israel. This is certainly a recipe for unpopularity!

And, beyond the sterling examples of his beautiful ways with words, what does Amos proclaim? What does he foretell/forthtell to the people of Israel, and, by extension, to all who take heed of the prophet's witness, i.e., us? "The end is near."

No wonder the rulers and priests of his day considered Amos a rather stark, harsh, and all together unpleasant fellow. "The end is near," he, a southerner, says to the folks in the Northern Kingdom. "The end is near," he proclaims to Amaziah, the court priest in charge of the sanctuary at Bethel. "The end is near," he also preaches to any contemporary person whose waywardness today would match the waywardness of the ancient Israelites who first received his preachment.

This is not merely Eeyore-like downcast-ness. Amos is not a "sad sack" figure moping around with a hang-dog countenance. No, Amos is attempting to address real and abiding problems that the people of his day are suffering without even knowing they're suffering from them.

During my sabbatical the past summer, across the hot and humid stretch of the southern tier of the U.S., I had time and circumstance to do something I normally don't do: watch television programs that are purportedly religious. Most of these so-called religious programs were crammed with people of the Christian persuasion. And nearly all of the programs and nearly all of the featured hosts and guests of these programs were of a stripe that didn't represent the mainstream of the religion spectrum. One would rightly assess that the media battle had been won by fundamentalists.

To put it mildly, most of the programming was disturbing. In tone, content, and intention, the substance of what was broadcast in most of these shows was petty and pitifully pious, or, on the other hand, belligerent, mean, and self-righteously condemning. And rarely, if ever, was the ethic of love mentioned.

Then, while driving along the Nantahala River– a tributary that courses through Georgia, South Carolina, and North Carolina– Amos' words came rushing back into my mind: "For thus says the Lord to the house of Israel. . . . I hate, I despise your feasts, and I take no delight in your solemn assemblies."

There were three noteworthy aspects of this television reality:

- Many of the religious shows on television purvey a "prosperity gospel," which proclaims, to put it bluntly, God wants you to be rich.
- Many of the religious shows on television proclaim that life here and now, on this earth, is of decidedly secondary importance
- Almost all of the religious shows on television today lack any sort of a call to justice.

Amos' summary of all this would be: "Your religion is sick: Let justice roll down like waters and righteousness like an ever-flowing stream."

Amos prophesied to people who were experiencing the pinnacle of power. To Israel's dominating clutch of control, he offered a fiery rebuke: "The end is near! Your end is near!" Not only did it insult the rulers and leaders of Israel, it also didn't make much sense given their apparent prosperity, security, and vast possessions. Insulting, insane, and absolutely irritating– such was Amos' reputation.

I'm not sure what Amos would look like if he appeared among us or what he would actually sound like if he prophesied to our circumstance.

We have no way of really knowing what he in fact looked like 2800 years ago. We can infer with some degree of accuracy that he probably dressed like a shepherd of his day would dress, for he describes himself as a "herdsman and a tender of sycamore trees."

What we do know are Amos' words, and from his words, I believe, we have good guidance about the dangers of sick religion, not only in his time but in our own as well.

Guided by Amos, we need to be watchful for two old sicknesses and for two new ones.

First, *the disconnect between the worship that people rendered to God and their indifference to justice for hurting people* was the number-one infraction Amos was protesting. Not only in Amos' proclamations, but in the prophetic proclamations of Amos' contemporaries (Isaiah, Hosea, Jonah), the call to justice was of premier importance. Amos put it plainly: "establish justice in the gate." Ostentatious worship, saying all the right words and doing all the correct sacerdotal gestures, could not make up for Israel's indifference to justice.

Indifference toward the poor. Indifference toward orphans. Indifference to those without power. Amos would resonate with the wise counsel of Elie Wiesel: "The opposite of love is not hate, but indifference."

If Amos were here today, we would not be surprised to hear him decry the indifference to justice that too long prevailed in the Kansas City School District over the past two generations of students. I think he would be greatly appreciative of the efforts by Dr. Covington, spurred on by a rising tide of concerned citizen groups, including many Community members.

The second cultural, political and religious infraction Amos protested was Israel's basic *refusal of faith*. That is, Israel, the northern kingdom, and Judah, the southern kingdom, had both lapsed into a denial of God's power of provision. The most obvious representation of this denial was rapacious greed. Grasping after material possessions they sought to satisfy a ravenous hole in their lives that only God could fill.

I think Amos would be aghast and dismayed by the prevalence of the so-called prosperity gospel in our current culture. Surely, he would call us to resist such a perversion of Jesus' message of love and his redeeming witness of compassion.

But two new contemporary sicknesses also presently harm us. They are akin to what Amos witnessed in ancient Israel, but they are certainly modern in their impact and influence.

The first is *privatized self-righteous condemning of others*. From Pastor Terry Jones to equally bigoted fundamentalistic terrorists, from the bully on the playground to bullies on the radio, from television programs and print media, self-righteous condemning of others seems to be running rampant.

The second malady that seems to be plaguing religion more and more these days is *a lack of a vivid sense of God's presence*. There seems to be a withering of our claims of being touched by God. Now, I know, that many if not most of us are naturally reluctant to speak openly about how God "touched us here" or how God "visited us there." I know that reluctance myself. But it seems that there is something more going on, a more pervasive malaise regarding God's being really present in our lives. I've heard friends say "I don't sense God being real these days. God doesn't seem to be here." And this sickness of religion is part of all kinds of faith, fundamentalistic and liberal and every sort in between.

Now, we can be thankful for Amos's analysis and diagnosis. Now that we have the diagnosis, what about the remedies?

I have four simple suggestions that I earnestly believe can help us (and any anyone else) when religion is sick:

- *Do justice.* Amos was like unto Micah, another of Amos' contemporaries, who charged his hearers: "Do justice." (Micah 6:8) Remember Amos' clarion cry, "Seek good, and not evil"(Amos 5:14). Participate in some activity, some endeavor, some event that will provide care, comfort, and compassion for "the least of these" in our culture. Join a group, dig in and do a service project, sign a petition, become a member of an organization. Whatever your choices may be, remember that it is action and not merely attitude that fulfills the call to justice.

- *Don't count on money to save you.* Release your dreams of amassing piles of wealth to secure your future. The "prosperity gospel" promulgated by television preachers will sadly disappoint you. It is full of neither prosperity nor gospel. Let us never forget that Jesus pronounced a supreme blessing on those without prosperity: "Blessed are the poor."

- *Tell the truth,* and only tell it as well as you know it and never with self-righteous condemnation. I have a suggestion that I'd like to hatch this morning: Let us conspire to spread unadorned truthfulness wherever we go. How about it? What do you think? Want to try that?

  Last week my friend Dr. Jan Linn spoke a powerful word from Community's pulpit as part of a 9/11 service called "From Pain to Peace." Jan is working on a new book with the provisional title *Are Christians as Bad as Everyone Thinks?* I find his thinking provocative and winning as he tries to disentangle Christian belief and dominant public perceptions of it. One statement he made I will never forget: "We can tell all the truth we know without claiming to know all the truth there is." In other words, truthfulness is like a gemstone: we can only know the facets of it we can see. Jan is right in his statement, and this could serve as a motto for our truthfulness conspiracy: "Let us tell all the truth we know without claiming to know all the truth there is."

- *Practice the presence of God.* Shall we begin acting out our Christian commitments and our deepest beliefs with vitality? Shall we engage in regular worship and daily prayer with the foundational assumptions that God is present in our lives and in the lives of all people? Shall we wake up each morning with a positive refrain on our lips– with an "Aha!" instead of an "Alas and alack?" Instead of saying with a shudder "Good Lord, it's morning," shall we instead proclaim with joy "Good morning, Lord!"?

Can we begin to say that on a regular, disciplined basis, in honor of Amos and his challenging prophecy? If we will begin to repeat that greeting– along with doing justice, eschewing a reliance on wealth, telling the truth, and practicing the overarching presence of God with persistent vitality– we will begin to see a healing in our lives, a healing in our land, a healing in religions of all kinds and sorts, including our own. Amen.

14

VESSELS OF GRACE

Texts: I Corinthians 4:1 and II Corinthians 4:7

This morning we begin to focus on the heart of our current *Here We Grow* sermon series, as we seek to understand the unavoidably specific ways grace is made real and how spiritual growth happens.

The theological category we're diving into is one of those polysyllabic words that can cause some to yawn. But the word has a long and venerated history and is a treasured concept, really, especially at Christmas time. It sounds like a milk product, and it actually is the "mother's milk" of any relevant theology worth having. The word is *incarnation*.

Incarnation means "the word became flesh."[1] Meaning? Meaning: the notion became tangibly real. Meaning: the ephemeral idea became concretely manifested. Meaning: the flat abstraction became three-dimensional and touchable.

Incarnation is what Christianity is all about. My friend Chuck Blaisdell[2] has often reminded me that while the Easter message of resurrection is the distinguishing crux of the matter for us Christians, there is no resurrection without incarnation.

The "Incarnation" is reinforced by the name the angel quotes from Isaiah's prophecy when he announces to Joseph what he is to do: "and you shall name him Emmanuel."[3] And the meaning of Emmanuel? "God with us." In other words: "Incarnation."

This morning I'd like to offer you another word, an equally fine equivalent for incarnation. The word is plain and simple without any fancy ornamentation. Are you ready? Here it is: *Here. Here* is the word. God's love is here. Grace is here. Not over yonder where you cannot touch it. Not on another planet where you can never visit it. Not at an unattainable elsewhere, but here! Paul put it this way in his first piece of correspondence to the church at Corinth: We are "servants of Christ and stewards of the mysteries of God."[4]

We are responsible for bearing the great mysteries of God's grace and love and hope and peace to the world. Here, among us, is where the gospel gets translated into life.

Here is also where we grow. We grow in the unavoidably particular place called Community Christian Church. Those of you who are members, those of you who are visitors, and those of you who are trying to figure out whether you want to become members all know this: Life is lived best in the particular, specific here-and-now.

We grow not in a fantasized, nebulous nether-world but in specific places and with specific people. What was true about Jesus is true also about us: The words of faith– words like compassion, caring, hope, love, justice, mercy, generosity– become flesh (i.e., real) in actual people and places. Here we grow!

The Apostle Paul had another fetching way of putting it: "For we have this treasure in earthen vessels."[5] We live by faith, and we share the grace we have received in and through our fallible selves.

"Earthen vessels" is another way of saying "Here." What did Paul have in mind by this metaphor? I want to suggest three different kinds of "vessels" that bear in them the wondrous grace of God.

First, Paul had in mind the very mortal, imperfect ways he lived out his faith and the equally mortal, imperfect ways we live out our faith. The "earthen vessels" he had in mind were the clay jars in the first century after Christ's birth that were used to carry water. They were also used to hold wine, to protect valuables, to serve as repositories for items like treasured scrolls and important implements for worship.

Clay jars, Paul was saying, that's what we are. We're simple earthen vessels bearing incredibly valuable treasure within us.

Now clay pots can be fragile and are certainly breakable. Clay pots can crack, as any one of the gardeners among us can testify. What this means for our faith is clear: "So grand a treasure borne in such a menial, frail, seemingly inept container makes it understandable that the power enabling the whole enterprise is from God and not from us."[6]

It's important to know that we are "earthen vessels" in this way. Or, to put it like a friend of mine once averred, it's important to know that "we're all cracked pots." If we know we're fallible, if we know we're malleable, if we know we're fragile, we'll be more likely to be appreciative of and reliant upon God's grace as the source of our strength.

The apostle Paul knew intimately and thoroughly that his life was fragile, frail, often impinged upon by hurt and pain and the bruising of the world. Later on, in his second letter to the church at Corinth, Paul describes how he was given "a thorn in the flesh. . . . Three times I besought the Lord that it should leave me."[7]

But the answer Paul received about his very earthen thorn-troubled vessel was "my grace is sufficient for you, for my power is made perfect in weakness."[8] We are earthen vessels, clay jars, cracked pots. But we need not fear nor tremble with panic, for God's grace is within us, among us.

The second kind of vessel that bears the grace of God within it is a ship. The sailing vessel of a ship has long been an image and a symbol for the church.

It was natural and appropriate that such a symbol should find a prominent place in the development of the Church since many of the first disciples were fishermen. Some of Jesus' greatest miracles are associated with the Sea of Galilee and boats. And Jesus used the fishing endeavors of the disciples as a powerful metaphor of invitation when he said, "Follow me and I will make you fishers of people."

No wonder, then, that the World Council of Churches has as its symbol the figure of a boat, a sailing vessel, bearing the love and grace of God to a world desperately in need of being visited by both.

At Community we are something of a sailing vessel ourselves. A visitor once described our unique Frank Lloyd Wright building by saying, "You all remind me of *The Love Boat*." And while he meant it as derision, I think it's really a compliment.

For we *are* a "Love Boat" vessel that bears love to the world. The vessel of Community offers love in so many ways, through many programs, on so many occasions. This Love Boat, otherwise known as Community Christian Church, has a bow that points into the future, a hull crafted by all the saints of our membership over nearly 120 years of sailing, a map called the Bible for directing our journey on the seas of life, a captain named Jesus who stands on the bridge, and a Steeple of Light that serves as both a mast of mystery and a beacon of beauty and hope for all who behold our efforts.

And here in this Love Boat vessel at Community, we are inviting all of our members to respond affirmatively to a clarion call that goes like this: "All hands on deck!" Every one of us is valuable and prized as part of the vessel of Community's Love Boat. In our current Stewardship Campaign, this means all of our commitments and estimates of giving are absolutely essential for the best fulfillment of our family of faith.

I have wondered lately what would happen if every member, every household in our congregation, were to take the leap of faith and make a financial commitment to Community's crucial and important ministries. Just think of it. What if we, each and all, could stretch our stewardship to the extent of simply tithing on the 2010 U.S.poverty level for a household of one? If all of Community's housheolds could do that, it would mean the greatest financial support we've ever known for our congregation's overall programs. Surely, we must imagine such a possibility. Surely, we must consider growing by such a stretch, such a leap of faith!

The day is coming in the near future when we will need to expand our ministries for our children and youth. In the next few years, we will provide congratulatory scholarships for more of our high school seniors than we've ever done in the past. The good news is we now have an endowment for that purpose. The challenge will be to nurture and support our children and youth with expanded regular, weekly programs and sufficient staff to meet their needs. Can we do it?

Absolutely, if we make the commitment to grow in our stewardship support for the vessel here at Community Christian Church.

The third kind of vessel to which I want to draw your attention has nothing to do with clay jars or boats. Rather, these are the vessels that course through our bodies bearing life-giving sustenance to each and every organ, muscle, and tissue in us.

Blood vessels have become newly important and significant to me over the past two and a half months. I now know that there passes through each of us, throughout the 60,000 miles of blood vessels in the average child and the 100,000 miles of blood vessels in the average adult, over the course of our lifetimes nearly a billion barrels of blood. I know that on an average day our blood travels nearly 12,000 miles. I know, too, that all of that blood coursing through all of our vessels over all of those miles is a very, very good thing! In fact, it's a miraculous thing! And it sure beats the alternative. What I've begun to see, too, is that our blood vessels are profound metaphors for who we are as Christians and what we are to be as a congregation. We are to understand ourselves as vessels bearing grace and love to the world's body.

The organs and tissues and musculature of the world need us so!! We are to provide the oxygen of openness to the world. We are to give the hemoglobin of hope to the world. We are to offer the electrolytes of love to the world. Sometimes the world is in extra-special, extraordinarily desperate straits– such as in the case of natural disasters– and then we are to provide the Lipitor of love and the Plavix of empowerment to help people hang on and endure! We are called to be vessels bearing grace and love to the world's body.

What an "awesome trust God bestows upon each of us,"[10] what a privilege to be the vessels of God's good news of love. And what wondrous results there are — for the world and for us — when we fulfill our calling as such vessels.

Thanks be to God that we have been granted the opportunity to grow here at Community Christian Church, in our cherished family of faith, and to be vessels — clay jars, boats, arteries of affirmation and veins of victory — on behalf of Jesus Christ. Amen.

NOTES
1. John 1:14.
2. The Rev. Dr. Chuck Blaisdell is the retired senior minister of First Christian Church, Colorado Springs, Colorado, and a church consultant in Paxton, Massachusetts.
3. Isaiah 7:4; Matthew 1:23.
4. I Corinthians 4:1.
5. II Corinthians 4:7.
6. *The New Interpreter's Bible*, (Nashville: Abingdon, 2000), vol. 11, p. 81.
7. II Corinthians 12:7-8.
8. II Corinthians 12:9.
9. Matthew 4:19.
10. *The New Interpreter's Bible*, vol. 11, p. 83.

15

THE BLESSEDNESS OF THE BODY

Texts: Psalm 8:3-9, John 1:14, I Corinthians 6:19 — 20

Good morning! And again, Happy New Year! I don't know all the reasons for my enthusiasm behind saying "Happy New Year" this year, except one: it really is good to be fully into the new year 2012 and to see you this morning.

On the crest of what promises to be a very good year for all of us, we are commencing a new sermon series: *Health, Healing, and the Journey to Wholeness.*

For those who are wondering about the issue of *embodiment* itself; for those who are asking the question "Are human beings bodies who have souls or souls who have bodies?": this series is for you.

For those who are struggling with your bodies, to get them right physically, or medically, or biochemically, or any other way, this series is for you.

For those who have battled with body image and the attempt to measure up (or down) to what popular culture and advertiser tell us are so-called ideal bodies, this series is for you.

For those who are engaged in a colossal contest with bulimia or anorexia nervosa or obesity or hypoglycemia or diabetes or heart failure or hardening of the arteries, this series is for you.

For those who are seeking to escape pain and its ravaging effects on your entire system, this series is for you.

For those who have conquered the challenges of physical health (at least, for the time being) but are still fighting to maintain financial health, this series is for you.

For those who would love to have a sure sense of the Holy Spirit within the temple of your physical self, this series is for you.

For any one of us who simply has a body, this series is for you.

In short, our first sermon series of the new year focusing on *Health, Healing and the Journey to Wholeness* is intended for each and every one of us, for every body!

Over the course of the next several Sundays, this sermon series will find us all engaged in an exciting exploration of health and healing issues, including a consideration of the Biblical understanding of the body as the temple of the Holy Spirit, the significance of financial health in tough times, the central components for healthy relationships, the problem of pain, and the possibilities for healing in all aspects of our lives.

Today we take up the robust theme of "The Blessedness of the Body." Let us be straightforward about what our scriptures say about the human body. The Hebrew Bible— what we call the Old Testament— for example,

possesses an overtly positive regard for the human body. In the book of
Genesis, at the end of the story of creation, humanity is crafted by a loving
God, and what God had made is pronounced not simply "good" but "very
good."

Read the Song of Solomon and behold how male and female bodies are
extolled for their graceful grandeur and luxuriant beauty. I often will suggest
to couples that they read the Song of Solomon (also known as the Song of
Songs) to one another out loud, in order to get in touch with the wondrous
capacities our bodies have to stimulate intimacy and grace in relationships.

On the other end of the spectrum, behold how the Old Testament
doesn't evade pain and suffering but has the grand figure of Job suffering
horribly for apparently no reason.

For the most part, however, the view of the human body is positive and
affirming in the Old Testament.

The New Testament, over all, also has a positive view of the body. When
it speaks negatively about "the flesh," the New Testament is talking less
about your physical equipment and more about the existential condition of
humanity and our immoral actions. "Flesh," or sarx in the Greek, is the
weakest link in our human makeup. Soma, on the other hand, is the Greek
word for "body" and, more often than not, possesses a morally neutral
connotation. Some fundamentalists have taken the verses that deal with
"fleshly" concerns out of context and twisted them into a perverse distortion
of what embodiment and earthly life are all about.

This series will assume a positive view of the human body, and we will
specifically do so in this message this morning.

There are at least four sources, or reasons, for the blessedness of the
bodies with which we have been equipped.

First, our bodies are blessed because of their source: they are gifts from
God. Our texts for this morning tell us this searing truth.

- We have been made "little lower than the angels"; and
- The Word of God, which Jesus Christ was and is became not an idea,
  not a notion, not a phantom of someone's imagination, not a cipher,
  but "became flesh," that is, enfleshed in the skin and bone and tissue
  of humanity.

God made Christ's birth happen, and that birth is the structure of reality
through which God made it possible for each of us also to enjoy existence.
Mary Oliver puts it best:

The spirit. . . .
could float, of course,
but would rather

plumb rough matter.
. . . .
it needs the body's world . . . .
so it enters us [1]

Secondly, our bodies are blessed because of their wonders: they are full of miraculous capacities. All three of our selections from Holy Writ this morning affirm this reality. Paul's letter to the Corinthians especially emphasizes this grace. Our bodies are the bearers of the Holy Spirit, and that's why we need to monitor the unholy things we sometimes do to our bodies, on the one hand. And on the other hand, we need to affirm the sacredness of our bodies and the holy acts they can accomplish:

- The miracles of surgery
- The wonders of music
- The grace of architectural design
- The triumphs of athletic achievement
- The splendors of caring communities
- The amazements of communication
- The loveliness of compassion in times of crisis
- The awesomeness of art
- The sacredness of a forgiving embrace

Thirdly, our bodies are blessed because of their uses: we can be gifts to others. If we are— as Psalm 8 says we are— made "little lower than the angels," we can begin acting like angels toward each other. We can begin treating others with an assumption about "the better angels of their nature," rather than assuming they're devils.

This is what folks do when they become part of a blood drive and commit themselves to be tissue donors. This is what we do when we take the time to be tutors and volunteers and helpers for anyone in need.

In the most heroic circumstances, this is what happens when we help others at risk to our own lives. Parents will do this in a heartbeat for their children. Firefighters and police officers and soldiers do this for strangers every day.

How and why all these extraordinary efforts and angelic actions? Because, as Psalm 139 puts it, we have been "fearfully and wonderfully made."[2] God gave us enfleshed life so that we can be gifts to one another, in order that we can be of use.

Ultimately, our bodies are blessed because of their powers: we have been givens senses as luscious opportunities to engage and enjoy and revel in the world. By the five senses that are ours, we know we are alive. We can see and smell and taste and hear and feel the very textures of God's wide, wide world. We can encounter furry cats and sour lemons and savory cinnamon rolls and scratchy beards and smooth-as-silk babies' faces and inspiring sonnets and soaring arias and tough linebackers and rain and thunder and soothing sunlight and . . . .

Can you sense it? Of course, you can. You have been graced with the powers that come with the blessedness of being an embodied creature. Who needs superheroes with superpowers when we have the powers of our five senses right at the tips of our fingers and noses and tongues and ears and eyes?

Now, only one question remains: "What shall we do with these magnificent bodies that are ours?" Here are four guidelines for maximizing the blessedness of our bodies.

(1) *Honor your body as a holy temple for the next week.* I want to suggest that you do this, at first, for just one week. Business leaders tell us all the time that a task should be measurable and achievable, so lets do this for the next seven days. Not for forever, nor for a year nor for a month. Just for this next week. And here's how you honor your body as a temple: don't put anything in your body that you wouldn't put in a temple designated for God's holiest things.

(2) *Decrease the stress in your life.* Read a book. Listen to music. Take a hot shower. Talk with your dog or cat, or better yet, talk with the human beings with whom you live! One of the better ways to decrease the stress in your life is to do something of benefit to others. Remember the wisdom of Harry Emerson Fosdick: "At very best, a person completely wrapped up in himself makes a small package."[3] If you get involved in assisting or helping or aiding others, your world will naturally and immediately enlarge. And I guarantee that the stress in your body will begin to decrease.

(3) *Increase your exertion.* Go for a walk. Go for a run. Go bowling. Enroll in an exercise program. Do something with your body, knowing the wisdom of "use it or lose it." If you will increase the exertion in your body, the endorphin rush you experience will also increase, and you'll encounter a greater sense of calm and peaceableness.

(4) *Behold the wonders of the body each day.* See what your body can do and give thanks to God for it. Flex your hand, hold the hand of another person, look at yourself in the mirror. And count it as a true wonder. Behold how you navigate the world with your one precious body and know that you and everybody else in the world are wondrous creatures.

I ask you: What if we treated ourselves and every person we met, and what if others treated themselves and every person they met, as precious creatures from God's very gracious hand? Would we not see a decrease of strife, a lessening of conflict, possibly even the end of war? Can you imagine it? Can we behold it? Can we begin to live like we really appreciate the blessedness of our bodies?

I love you. God bless us all.

Amen.

NOTES
1.   Mary Oliver, "Poem," *Dream Work* (New York: Atlantic Monthly Press, 1986), p. 52.
2.   Psalm 139:14.
3.   Harry Emerson Fosdick, *On Being A Real Person* (New York: Harpers, 1943).

16

BUCK O'NEIL — LOVING YOU
Text: John 15:12—17

Good morning, friends! Good morning and welcome to the launching of a brand new sermon series, *"Great Souls, Great Faith,"* in which we'll explore the faithful lives of contemporary exemplars.

Today and over the course of the next two Sundays, we'll reflect on and learn from the witness of: (1) the greatest baseball man who hasn't been elected to the Hall of Fame in Cooperstown, (2) a Disciples preacher, whose genius revolutionized the practice and teaching of preaching and whose humility has much to teach us about prayer, and (3) a poet, memoirist, and civil rights activist who remains one of the greatest exemplars of authentic faith and grace.

Those looking for doctrinal purity or dogmatic hegemony here will surely be disappointed as we proceed through this series. But for those eager souls wanting to know how other souls have lived their faith, how they have prayed, how they have struggled spiritually, and for those wanting to garner insights from the paths others have walked and for those wanting to gain wisdom from the hard-earned maturity that others have won, this series can be enriching experience.

The Great Souls included in this series are neither the only ones nor the premier ones. But they are people who have distinguished themselves with passion, care and rare sensitivity along their faith journeys. They have kept close to God and to the reality of the blessings that can come when you maintain such closeness. By keeping close to such Great Souls, our faith can be enlarged.

What is plainly clear to all who are seeking to be faithful is the fact that we can use all the help we can get. This series is offered with the hopes that it will find a secure hold on the souls of everyone who wants to increase their encounters with God and their experiences of the gifts of faith as they open themselves to new light.

In this first sermon in the series we're focusing on Buck O'Neil and the sentiment he expressed in his signature song, "The Greatest Thing."

For those of you who have yet to become baseball fans, let me assure you today's message still has much to intrigue and inspire you. For we are talking about one of the greatest advocates of goodwill the earth has ever seen. To many people, both here in Kansas City and around the globe, Buck O'Neil was the embodiment of graciousness and caring love.

Buck began life humbly in Florida. He was born on November 13, 1911, in Carrabelle, Florida. At the age of 23, Buck left Florida and started playing semi-pro baseball with teams like the Miami Giants, the New York Tigers, the Shreveport Acme Giants, and the Zulu Cannibal Giants. During this time, he teamed up with the legendary Leroy "Satchel" Page. In 1937 he signed with the Memphis Red Sox of the Negro American League. Then, in 1938, the Red Sox traded him to the Kansas City Monarchs, where he would play and manage for 14 years.

In 1956, he became a scout for the Chicago Cubs, where he would discover talent like Billy Williams and Lou Brock, both of whom would become Hall of Famers.

In 1962, the Chicago Cubs named him as coach, making him the first Black coach in the Major Leagues.

In 1988, after his long service with the Cubs, Buck returned to Kansas City to become a scout for the Kansas City Royals. He also worked tirelessly to establish the Negro Leagues Baseball Museum in Kansas City and served on the museum's board of directors.

It was during this time that Buck came to national prominence through his association with and starring role in Ken Burns' award-winning *Baseball* television series on PBS.

Buck died peacefully on August 5, 2006, at Research Hospital. A public celebration of his life was held at Municipal Auditorium and a smaller home-going service was held at his home church, Bethel A.M.E., here in Kansas City, Missouri.

Four months later, on December 7, 2006, he was awarded the Presidential Medal of Freedom by President George W. Bush. Buck's brother, Warren, received the posthumous honor in Buck's stead.

Buck is remembered in Kansas City in some significant ways. At the entrance to Forest Hills Cemetery, on Troost here in Kansas City, there is a monument honoring him, close by his grave site where he is buried next to his wife, Ora Lee, who died in 1997.[1] And out at Kaufman Stadium, right behind home plate, four rows up, a special seat has been designated as the Buck O'Neil Legacy Seat and is awarded to 81 different individuals for each home game every year.

On July 25, 2008, a statue of Buck was placed at the entrance of the Hall of Fame in Cooperstown, New York, and the Buck O'Neil Lifetime Achievement Award was established.

Of course, you can read all about Buck in two superb books, one, his memoir, *I Was Right on Time*,[2] and the other, *The Soul of Baseball*,[3] by Joe Posnanski, who has probably scrutinized and studied Buck more carefully (and more lovingly) than anyone writing in sports journalism anywhere.

But more important than any of his baseball and civic accomplishments was the simple, profound fact that Buck lived a life of love. For all of the adult stretch of his 94 years, Buck lived a life of love. Beginning in Florida, and all through the baseball barnstorming days on the road and throughout his tenure with the Monarchs and then the Cubs and then the Royals and then with the Negro Leagues Museum, Buck lived a life of love. He embodied exquisitely and eloquently the love ethic as we have heard it in the gospel of John, in the 15th chapter: "This is my commandment that you love one another, as I have loved you. Greater love has no one than this, to lay down one's life for one's friends . . . . I am giving you this commandment that you might love one another." Now, Buck lived out that ethic in his own unique way. He lived it out first and foremost by dismissing the option of bitterness.

Buck lived a life of love by dismissing the option of bitterness. Buck had every right to be bitter, but he didn't find much reason to be so. He consistently dismissed the option to be bitter about anything or anyone. In the degradation of segregation of Florida, he didn't get bitter, he got better as a ballplayer, and he got out of his celery-field overalls and into a baseball uniform. When he didn't get to play in "The Show," having only ever played in the Negro Leagues, he didn't express bitterness. No, he dismissed the option of bitterness and instead worked to get others into the game and then later Negro League stars into the Hall of Fame.

At Cooperstown, on the glass behind his statue, just beyond the entrance to the National Baseball Hall of Fame and Museum, there's a statement of Buck's:

> Waste no tears for me.
> I didn't come along too early.
> I was right on time.

And when he missed being voted into the Hall of Fame by one meager vote, he was surely crestfallen inwardly. But he didn't show it outwardly. And he carefully and strongly dismissed the option of bitterness. "Ol' Buck's going to be all right," he said on the day he heard the news that he wouldn't enter into the Hall of Fame. "Ol' Buck's going to be all right. Buck's already in the Hall of Fame. I'm in the Friendship Hall of Fame." He said he never hated anyone. And the only thing he ever hated was cancer, because it took his wife Ora Lee from him.

Which leads us to the second way he lived a life of love. Buck lived a life of love by delighting in the daily. Every day was a beautiful day to Buck. And every person was beautiful to him. He would never regard anyone he met as beneath him or lower than himself. He would do as Jesus did, simply calling them— literally anyone who greeted him around the town— his friends.

His attention to the daily and his devotion to the loveliness in the ordinary was most clearly evident in his loving relationship with Ora Lee. Having met her on Easter Sunday in 1943 in Memphis, Tennessee, and after they got married in 1946, when he came back from serving in the Navy in World War II, Buck and Ora Lee loved and exulted in each other for 51 years.

Buck loved Ora Lee with devotion and dedication when she was discriminated against in downtown Kansas City stores, when she tried to shop for a hat.

And he loved her with fierce loyalty and a special grace, when Ora Lee was discovered to have cancer. As the *Kansas City Star* reported, "Buck would call her years of fighting the disease 'the greatest 15 years of my life.'"[4]

They were the greatest because of the sacred dailiness they shared together, such as the cherished meals in their home, especially when they had company and she treated everyone like royalty. What was special to

Buck was not the mounting acclaim that was accruing to his reputation and presence in Kansas City and across the nation. Ken Burns may have made Buck a household name after the *Baseball* television series. But the house and home and life he shared with Ora Lee— in all of its dailiness— were his greatest graces and best blessings.

Above and beyond dismissing the option of bitterness and delighting in the daily, Buck lived a life of love by daring to love others first.

We were privileged to host Buck at Community Christian Church on numerous occasions. At a steak cookout sponsored by the Men's Fellowship. During a COLOR's Juneteenth celebration, in a Martin Luther King Interfaith Service. And he always came dressed impeccably and ready to go, with a huge smile on his face. He always seemed interested in your welfare and what you were doing. He'd have a quick quip or two, and he would take as many pictures as you wanted. But he was genuinely interested in what was going on with you, what was going on in the world, and how he and you— how *we*— could make it better. He really did live a life of love by daring to love others first, before anything else.

This was even true at the end of Buck's life, when his strength was ebbing away, when he had lost much of his zip and most of his pizzazz. Even then, though, he expressed his love for others. Emanuel Cleaver recalled for me how when he went to see Buck at Research Hospital two days before he died, he could hardly get Buck to talk about his medical situation. Instead, Buck turned the tables on Emanuel and asked about his children. "How's Evan doing?" And "Is E3 preaching at St. James now? Is he really preaching there or is he half-stepping?"

In the midst of his *in extremis* situation, he dared to love others first, to call attention to their lives, to be concerned about the welfare of others over and above his own welfare. "He had the ability to reserve thinking about himself and express care for others first," Emanuel recalls. And when Emanuel told me that story, I couldn't help but think of the text for this morning's message: "No one has greater love than this, to lay down one's life for one's friends." And when I told Emanuel that John 15:12— 17 was my text for this sermon, he said, "Oh yeah, that's him, that's Buck, all right."

In Buck O'Neil we have beheld not a perfect person but one who sought to live as best he could a life of love that dismissed the option of bitterness, that delighted in the daily, and that dared to love others first before anything else.

It was natural, then, and perfectly in tune with the gist and grit of the gospel, that Buck's famed theme song was "The Greatest Thing":

The greatest thing in all the world is loving you.
The greatest thing in all the world is loving you.
The greatest thing in all the world is loving you.
The greatest thing in all the world is loving you.

May we learn to sing it in our own day, in our own way, and in our own key. And when we do, do not be surprised if there arises from the celestial realm beyond a heavenly and harmonious echo and a great and glorious laugh from Buck O'Neil. AMEN.

NOTES

1   The exact coordinates for the location of Buck and Ora Lee's graves are Section 103, Row 3, Grave 12.
2   Buck O'Neil with Steve Wulf and David Conrads, *I Was Right on Time: My Journey from the Negro Leagues to the Majors* (New York: Simon & Schuster, 1996).
3   Joe Posnanski, *The Soul of Baseball: A Road Trip Through Buck O'Neil's America* (New York: William Morrow, 2007).
4   J. Brady McCollough, "Buck and Ora were about love," *The Kansas City Star*, Oct. 8, 2006.

17

NEW YEAR'S RESOLUTIONS THAT MATTER

Text: Philippians 4:4 — 9

With the tick of the clock, we've entered into a new year, and a new time in our lives. We gather, it should be noted, at a time of an unusual coincidence: a New Year's Day Sunday worship service. Unlike Catholics, Episcopalians, and Lutherans, we Disciples normally have an "optional" attitude toward a service on New Year's Day: we normally opt out of going to church on that day. Except when it comes on Sunday.

But I'm so glad we're here and so very glad to see you and to share this rare moment with you.

Now with a quick spark of the imagination, as we ponder what the New Year may hold for each of us individually and for us as a congregation, the metaphors abound: At the starting line of a new race into a new year . . . as the earth commences another circumnavigation around the sun . . . as we raise the flag of another year's dawning . . . as we begin a new trek through another 365 days....

And there are even similes upon similes within those metaphors:

- We are like babies taking their first steps.
- We are like rookies taking the mound for the first game of the season, ready to launch the first pitch of their career.
- We are like farmers at the edge of the corner of a field on the first day of ploughing, ready to till the soil, plant the seed, and see what nature can make happen with a new crop.
- We are like writers before a blank page, about to inscribe the first word of the first phrase of the first sentence of the next great American novel.

Now there is a sense in which this day is like any other day. We are practical people, after all, and like to avoid the pie-in-the-sky approach to life and prefer to deal with things in a down-to-earth way. But let us be careful with our emphasis on the ordinary, lest we miss the mysterious and wondrous possibilities in the seemingly mundane. Let us not be like the two Kentucky farmers famously depicted once in a New Yorker cartoon. The two farmers are leaning over a fence and one turns to the other and says, "Anything exciting happen today?" "Nah, nothing exciting," says the other farmer. "Oh, there was a baby born over at Tom Lincoln's place, but nothing exciting ever really happens around here."

On this brand-new day of this brand-new year, resolutions are in order. Now, I'm normally loath to suggest New Year's resolutions for myself or anyone else. Most resolutions can be easily dismissed as overly idealistic or too saccharine to be taken seriously.

But this year is different. Even though I've never spoken about resolutions in sermonic form before, the apostle Paul's epistle to the Philippians has inspired a new approach. In a sense, Philippians has redeemed resolutions for me.

The entirety of the epistle can be viewed as a summing-up and a setting-forth for the church at Philippi, the first church Paul established on European soil. This is also the congregation to which he bequeaths his most fervent care and loving concern.

There is in Philippians what could be the most famous New Year's Day line of all: "Forgetting what lies behind and straining forward to what lies ahead, I press on toward the goal of the prize of the upward call of God in Christ Jesus."[1]

There is also in this letter some of Paul's greatest affection as he remembers how he and the Philippians have come such a mighty long way together: "I thank my God in all my remembrance of you, always in every prayer of mine, thankful for [our] partnership in the gospel from the first day until now."[2]

Then he comes to his resolutions, a series of resolutions, actually, which you heard earlier in the service. Now these resolutions are not your garden-variety intentions. They are not about losing weight or saving money or getting a new career or starting new hobby, as important as those endeavors might be. No, these resolutions are about ultimate concerns, things that matter.

The first set is all about rejoicing: "Rejoice in the Lord always; again I will say, Rejoice. Let your gentleness be known to everyone . . . . Do not worry about anything, but in everything by prayer and supplication with thanksgiving let your requests be made known to God."[3]

And then Paul offers a promise: "And the peace of God, which surpasses all understanding, will guard your hearts and your minds in Christ Jesus."[4]

Then comes the second set of resolutions focusing on principles and ideal qualities to be maintained in a good life: "whatever is true, whatever is honorable, whatever is just, whatever is pure, whatever is pleasing, whatever is commendable, if there is any excellence and if there is anything worth of praise, think about these things. Keep on doing the things you have learned and received and heard and seen in me."[5]

And then comes the refrain of the promise about God's peace: "and the God of peace will be with you."[6]

Now, those are as good a compilation of resolutions as the Bible can muster, for the New Year or any other.

Inspired by Paul, and yet knowing that the words of yesteryear need to become real in our own time, in new ways and with new applications, I've fashioned some new New Year's resolutions. With your forbearance, I offer them to you for your consideration as possibilities for our shared life together and for living the New Year in fresh and hopefully engaging ways.

1.   I will indulge myself and I will encourage others to indulge themselves in the gatherings and the graces and the lasting gifts of

life: meals shared with those we treasure, love expressed as often as we can, an abiding focus on what makes for justice and goodness for all, walking as humbly as we can, day by day, knowing that God wants us, all of us, all of God's children, to enjoy life to hilt.

2. I will give it all, and I will give it now. I will not hoard and save, for a later time or a better date, any compliment, poem, idea, notion, support for a worthy cause, any laugh, any hug when hugs are wanted and needed.[7] I will eagerly seek out and be open to the insights and gracings of others. I will rise to the challenging question: Why should any one of us be lost if someone else knows the way?[8]

3. I will spend what I don't have, that which I so much enjoy and treasure. I will share God's love that comes to us all freely and generously, a gift that is never to be possessed solely by any one person but is a universal spiritual currency.

4. I will let my heart be broken, broken open to a world in need of caring and hope. I am not an automaton but a human being and so I will maintain a bruisable heart, a vulnerable center of my personality, a capacity to be affected by the world and all of its inhabitants.

5. I will attend to the needs of children, never failing, so far as I can help it, to receive happily a greeting from any child and then return it with affection and enthusiastic appreciation. I will remember that all children — in this congregation, in this city, or in any other — are "our children."

6. I will forego violence in my language, in my actions, and, of equal importance, in my assumptions, my attitudes, and my responses toward what the world brings to my door, even if what it brings is chock-full of violence.

7. I will treasure three specific bodies – my own, for it is the only vehicle I have for negotiating life through this world; the body of the earth, which is the carrier vehicle for the entire human race; and the Body of Christ that gathers here at Community Christian Church, for it needs my efforts, my prayers, my support, if it is going to be hale, hearty, and healthy as a witness for good in the community and in the world.

8. I will smile at the world as often as I possibly can, sometimes through clenched teeth, to be sure, but knowing that negativity never has worked and only a glad heart can live a fulfilled life.

9. I will take in as many movies as I can and listen to as much music as I can and behold as much visual art as I can and read as many books as I can, for the splendors of human creativity are sheer gifts and glimpses of the divine.

10. I will be as truly human and humane and alive as I can muster and will live my days with attention and engagement and will not simply visit this world. As Mary Oliver puts it succinctly, about this year, or any other:

When it is over . . . .
I don't want to end up simply having visited this world.[9]

Now those are my New Year's Resolutions for 2012 and they are, I hope and trust, about things that matter.

Happy New Year! I love you. God bless us all.

Amen.

NOTES

1   Phil. 3:13b—14.
2   Phil. 1:3—5.
3   Phil. 4:4—6.
4   Phil. 4:7.
5   Phil. 4:8—9a.
6   Phil. 4:9b.
7   See Annie Dillard, *Give It All, Give It Now: One of the Few Things I Know About Writing* (New York: Welcome Books, 2009).
8   See Samuel Green,"Postcard: October 18/01 NYC," in *The Only Time We Have* (Waldron Island: Brooding Heron Press, 2002), p. 37, and *"Oct. 18 New York City," The Grace of Necessity* (Pittsburgh, Pennsylvania: Carnegie Mellon University Press, 2008).
9   Mary Oliver, "When Death Comes," *New and Selected Poems* (Boston: Beacon Press, 1992), pp. 10—11.

18

HOLY HIDING
Text: John 8:59

This morning, on Shrove Tuesday, on the eve of the commencement of the Lenten season, among this gathering of colleagues, I want to bring a word to you *as* a colleague. This is, I believe, a special word, specially shaped just for us, we purveyors of proclamation, we preachers of the gospel, we pastors of the flocks.

The word to which I would draw your attention is found in a brief half verse at the tail end of the ninth chapter of the gospel according to St. John. Hear now this powerful word: "So they picked up stones to throw at him, but Jesus hid himself and went out of the temple."

This morning I want to offer a brief word about "Holy Hiding."

Now by hiding I don't mean the kind of flight from conflict, when, with the assistance of Southwest Airlines, we just "want to get away."

Nor do I mean the kind of hiding that we do, or at least once did, when playing hide-and-seek.

Nor do I mean the kind of cowardice that causes us to shrink from the challenges of life.

No, the kind of hiding that I want to emphasize this morning, especially to us as ministers, is the kind of hiding that Jesus did in the days of his flesh prior to his crucifixion, death and resurrection. For by a brief focus on that kind of hiding, I believe we may discover a lifetime's worth of saving grace.

Now, you have to admit that the phrase at the end of the eighth chapter of John's gospel proclamation is a bit odd. This phrase has haunted me for quite some time. Why? It has haunted me because my Jesus is not a shrinking violet in the face of danger. My Jesus is not afraid of anyone, at any point, regarding any issue. My Jesus doesn't hide himself from any confounding consternation or damnable difficulty. My Jesus says, "Put 'em up, 'put 'em up, put 'em up." And then whoops everybody in sight.

Jesus wasn't ever afraid of the Pharisees— that "brood of vipers," he called them.

Wasn't afraid of Herod— the "old fox," as he described him.

Wasn't even afraid to offer a strong word to God Almighty. Who can ever forget that cry of despair and defiance: "My God, my God, why have you forsaken me?"

No, my Jesus doesn't hide at all.

Except that he does. He hides in John's gospel. And if we have careful eyes and caring hearts, we discover he hides elsewhere as well.

In John's powerful eighth chapter we see how Jesus is squaring off against the religious establishment. He has revealed his identity as being one with the Father. And the powers that be don't like it one bit. So incensing are his words about his identity, "I AM," that they are riled into near violence. They pick up stones as if to kill him.

The common contemporary interpretation just won't do. To say that Jesus leaves the scene of conflict so as not to contradict his previous comments that "his hour had not come" is way too weak. To that kind of interpretation I would say, "Nonsense." During his three-year circuit-ride through his territory, Jesus did plenty to incense the authorities, and it makes plenty of sense to aver that in John's eighth chapter, at the end, a near miracle occurs as Jesus avoids the seemingly certain wrath of the authorities who will not tolerate his apparent blasphemy.

What Jesus is doing is engaging in some "Holy Hiding."

Hiding the way he hid at the very beginning of his ministry.

"In the morning, while it was still very dark, he got up and went out to a deserted place and there he prayed." (Mark 1:35)

"The apostles gathered around Jesus and told him all that they had done and taught. He said to them, 'Come away to a deserted place all by yourselves and rest a while.'" (Mark 6:31)

At Capernum he sought to escape the madding crowd and retreated into a deserted place. (Luke 4:42)

The Greek word for "hid" in John's gospel is "εκρυβη." It's the word from which we derive the word *crypt* and *cryptic*: hidden, concealed, secreted, clandestined, under cover.

The way I would put it is that here in John's gospel and elsewhere, Jesus frequently found a path into his inward sea.

Howard Thurman, in his marvelous book *The Growing Edge*, puts it this way:

> There is in every one of us an inward sea. In that sea there is an island; and on that island there is a temple. In that temple there is an altar; and on that altar burns a flame. Each one of us, whether we bow our knee at an altar external to ourselves or not, is committed to the journey that will lead him to the exploration of his inward sea, to locate his inward island, to find the temple, and to meet, at the altar in that temple, the God of his life. Before that altar, impurities of life are burned away; before that altar, all the deepest intent of your spirit stands naked and revealed; before that altar, you hear the voice of God, giving lift to your spirit, forgiveness for your sins, renewal for your commitment. As you leave that altar within your temple, on your island, in your inward sea, all the world becomes different and you know that, whatever awaits you, nothing that life can do will destroy you.[1]

Now, that is a profound meeting with the Maker of us all. And if that's too much for you to handle, I can easily understand. So I've brought along some steps to take to arrive at a holy hiding place for your life:

(1) If you are tired, and beat up, and finally drawn and nearly quartered, maybe what you need is a nap. A siesta. Some sleep.

(2) Make an appointment with God.

(3) Create what Annie Lamott calls "God's inbox."

(4) Take off your shoes when you pray.

And remember that, all along his three-year ministry, Jesus hid himself in the heart of God.

In the face of wanton need . . . hiding.

In the face of greed and other destructive behavior . . . hiding.

Whenever he was beginning a new campaign . . . hiding.

Especially when he set his face toward Jerusalem and the certain death at Calvary . . . hiding.

Jesus constantly hid himself in the heart of God.

Holy hiding is what allowed Jesus to escape the certain wrath of the religious authorities.

Holy hiding is what gave Jesus the power to preach and heal and confront and challenge.

Holy hiding is what buoyed Jesus up when his closest associates failed him.

Holy hiding, I firmly believe, is what allowed Jesus to forgive others and to be kind to the ungrateful. Holy hiding is what gave Jesus his energy and his tenderness.

In his holy hiding Jesus heard repeated what he had heard at his baptism: "This is my beloved."

So, abundant blessings on your own holy hiding this Lenten season— and always! — and may you ever know that you are God's beloved!

Amen.

NOTES
1.   Howard Thurman, *The Growing Edge* (New York: Harper & Bros., 1956), pp. 43-44.

FROM ASHES TO EASTER

19

HUMBLE ASHES AND CRAZY HOPE

Texts: Genesis 18:26 – 27 and Romans 5:1 – 5

Ever since I came to Kansas City, Ash Wednesday has been a special moment for me. Chalk it up to a Protestant coming late to what Catholics have known for centuries about liturgy, drama, color, and ritual. (As I say to my Catholic friends, "Why should you guys have all the fun?") Or say that it's a fascination with this very obvious, public expression of one's faith. Or, perhaps, my engagement with Ash Wednesday is an attempt to express at least a portion of what Christians believe about their faith – namely, that it's OK to openly, straightforwardly announce that one is a Christian.

However it came to pass, this allure that Ash Wednesday poses for me has only intensified since I came to Community.

And, for some odd reason, Ash Wednesday has also been – consistently, insistently, persistently – a day of odd greetings. What I mean is that on Ash Wednesday, more often than not, I hear myself offering the greeting "Happy Ash Wednesday." And I do so with clear sincerity and unabashed ignorance regarding the incongruity between the statement "Happy Ash Wednesday!" and the solemnity with which Ash Wednesday is observed. At times I wonder if I come off like legendary gunfighter Kid Shelleen in the movie *Cat Ballou*. At one point in the story line Kid enters into a funeral scene so drunk that, when he sees a coffin and some candles, he mistakes the occasion for a birthday and begins singing, drunken slurs and all, "Happy Birthday to you, Happy Birthday to you . . ." And I say "Happy Ash Wednesday." Whew!

People didn't start out singing and greeting each other happily in the first observances of Ash Wednesday 1,700 years ago. For Christians, the use of ashes was practiced in association with the public display of penance. But then, by the fourth century after Christ's birth, the practice faded away. By the eleventh century, the use of ashes had come to be connected with the beginning of the Lenten season and its preparations for the celebrations coming at Easter.[1]

The use of ashes in Christian worship was patterned, of course, after the Jewish practice of donning sackcloth and marking oneself with ashes in order to show repentance and mourning.[2]

Remember how Mordecai's mourning in sackcloth and ashes moves Queen Esther deeply, thereafter she agrees to help out the Jews in Persia.

Job is the most famous person to sit in an ash-heap, as he mourns his ceaseless losses and endless streak of bad fortune. At the beginning of the book that bears his name Job "[sits] among the ashes."[3] In the midst of his harrowing struggle against the evil cast against him, Job says, "[God] has cast me into the mire, and I have become like . . . ashes."[4] And then toward the end of his incredible ordeal he says "I despise myself, and repent in dust and ashes."[5]

Job is actually quoting the oldest Biblical reference to ashes, Abraham's. In a match of wits with God, Abraham bargains with God in order to save the city of Sodom from utter destruction. God's original deal is plain. If Abraham can find fifty righteous men, then God will not destroy Sodom. Abraham whittles down the deal to a requirement of only ten righteous men. And he does so by an appeal to his humble status, pointing out to God that "I . . . am but dust and ashes."[6]

In this phrase we get to the point of the use of ashes by the Hebrew people and by Christians. It's all about humility.

Ashes of any kind are humbling. Look at a campfire the morning after it has warmed and charmed a gathering of campers, and no matter how high the flames licked the sky the night before, the embers and ashes smoldering in the daylight are indeed a humble residue.

Look at the devastation in Australia and California with their raging wildfires decimating thousands and thousands of acres of countryside and residential areas. The sight is harrowing. All that's left? Humble ashes.

And even with the palm crosses, branches, and fronds gathered over the last 20 years of Ash Wednesdays here at Community, this is true, as they've been rendered into three small bowls of ashes. On Monday when we gathered the left-over palm fronds, palm branches, and palm crosses which you had brought in from last year's Palm Sunday processionals, they initially amounted to about two, maybe three grocery sacks full. And what happened to them, once a match was set to them? Less than a mere handful of ashes. Humble ashes.

Ash Wednesday, in other words is all about humility. Not denigration and self-abasement. No, the world does enough of that to us that we don't need to do it to ourselves. Rather, Ash Wednesday is a time to echo Abraham's humble approach to God. "I am" –we are– "but dust and ashes." We know our connection with the majesty and the glory and the power of God. And in the face of such overwhelming experiences, we can never claim superiority or preeminence. Human beings are fragile creatures and need to treat one another that way. Humble ashes.

This is the kind of humility which New Yorkers shared on the island of Manhattan, on September 11, 2001, as they raced from the financial district, covered with ashes, wrought by the destruction of the World Trade Center's twin towers, humbled by their and our vulnerability, made one in suffering and ennobled by their similarly ash-covered faces. All divisive distinctions were covered with ashes. All manner of fear and hesitation about the differences that keep people distant from one another was made irrelevant by the commonality of their ashy countenances. Humble, humbling ashes.

Humility is what Ash Wednesday and Lent, and eventually Easter are all about. None of us are as invincible as we once thought we were. Thus, it behooves us to act with appropriate humility to care for one another and for ourselves, and to care for the entire planet and everyone on it. To be sure, the Psalmist is absolutely on target when he says, "We are fearfully and wonderfully made."[7] But the Psalmist is also right when he reminds us that

God has made us "little lower than the angels."[8] Even if you are fashioned in the image of God, if you are not God, humility is the order of the day.

I got to see what the embodiment of humility was all about when I met Dom Helder Camara, the Archbishop from Brazil, at a General Assembly of the Christian Church (Disciples of Christ) in St. Louis. The good bishop stood about five feet vertical, if that tall. Dressed in a full-length cassock, he seemed to levitate—as Yoda might levitate— when he passed across a room or walked down a sidewalk. At that General Assembly, which had gone to great lengths to secure his presence in St. Louis, this man who was hunted and targeted for assassination because of his work for the oppressed of South America; this man who said, "When I feed the poor, they call me a saint. When I ask why the poor have no food, they called me a communist"; this little, elfin figure had a constant twinkle in his eye and, like all saintly folks I've ever met, no little mischief in him. When I got to shake his hand and say how much I appreciated his sermon at the General Assembly and expressed my admiration for his work, there was more than the normal deflection of a compliment. When I offered my high praise, he laughed, chortled actually, and shook his head. The declaration in his eyes and the communication of his overall demeanor were obvious: "I am but dust and ashes. I simply do my part, as you do your part. And the quicker we figure that out about ourselves, the better off we and the world will be."

But there's another angle on Ash Wednesday and the mark we will put on our foreheads that needs illuminating. In addition to humility, Ash Wednesday is all about hope.

The book of Hebrews says that "Faith is the substance of things hoped for, the conviction of things not seen."[9] If Christian faith is worthy of anything, it's worth investing our best hopes and dreams and convictions into our daily practices. The 40-day journey of Lent is all about hope— from Ash Wednesday's smudge upon our foreheads to the brush of yellow pistils of the Easter lilies upon our arms when we embrace them on Resurrection Sunday.

Now this hope is actually crazy hope. What else could we call it in a world like ours? Paul admits as much when he describes the suffering of the church in Rome: "we also boast in our sufferings, knowing that suffering produces endurance, and endurance produces character, and character produces hope, and hope does not disappoint us, because God's love has been poured into our hearts through the Holy Spirit that has been given to us."[10] It's as if Paul is saying, "Just as you might put a dab of ashes on your foreheads to remind you of the call to humility, God is pouring a heaping portion of hope-filled love into your hearts." This is truly crazy.

Now let me explain a bit here. There's good crazy and there's bad crazy.[11]

Yesterday, American Century had their annual recognition celebration here at Community. All of the employees came over from the towers up at 45th and Main, and some came in from around the country for the occasion. They settled into the comfortable confines of our sanctuary for a review of their year's work. As you can imagine, recent months have not provided them rip-roaring, happy times. When I asked my friend Larry Pfaustch about the percentage of the company's losses, he said "About 40% from what it was a year ago." And even though that's better than most of the stock market has done, it's been devastating to so many, many people, including American Century employees. Still, on this particular day, there was something else in the air. In the wake of being utterly humbled by a ravaged economy, something else permeated the gathering. There were nominations from various American Century work groups and many accolades about award winners for performance and achievement over the past year. Top award-winners were announced. There was a stunning video that told the story of Jim and Virginia Stowers and the legacy of hard work they had bequeathed to all of the American Century team. What was amazing was how together and hopeful, actually joyful, the whole gathering was. Each award-winner was, at once, jubilant and humbled by their awards. And Mr. and Mrs. Stowers stuck around and greeted every employee who wanted to shake their hands. It was the craziest thing I'd ever witnessed in a business setting. It looked a lot like the *good* crazy hope that Ash Wednesday is all about.

So, allow me to heighten the distinction. There's good crazy and bad crazy.

A man erases the lives of his entire family with gun violence and then turns the gun on himself. That's bad crazy.

Mother Theresa salves the festering wounds of poor untouchables in Calcutta. That's good crazy.

Terrorists blasting away in the middle of Muslim high holy days in Mosul. Bad crazy.

Firefighters plunging into burning buildings time after time. Good crazy.

Mr. Madoff, bilking countless persons out their life savings— rich and middle-income alike. Bad crazy. A truly indiscriminate bad crazy.

Warren Buffet giving $50 billion of his fortune to the Gates Foundation for the benefit of the world. Good crazy.

Fred Phelps and his family yelling epithets at grieving folks at the gravesides of family members who fell in the war-torn provinces of Iraq. Bad crazy.

A cancer patient collecting a rainbow array of new hats to celebrate her new 'do' (or lack thereof). Good crazy.

The decimation of our public school systems over the past two generations. Bad crazy.

The hard, daily work of teachers and community groups who believe school systems can change for the better. Good crazy.

Thinking that traditional ways of worship will always connect with every forthcoming generation. Bad crazy.

Tom Haley and Melissa St. Clair and Kevin Snow and Donna Muiller and the team putting together the new 9:20 a.m. worship service, not really knowing exactly what we're doing, especially when it comes to technology. Good crazy!

The world thinking that it could kill God, so they put Jesus up on a cross on a shadow-filled Friday. Bad crazy.

Jesus bolting out of the tomb on a brightly lit Easter Sunday. Good crazy.

The betrayal and abandonment of the apostles in Jesus' hour of need. Bad crazy.

Jesus' entrusting the legacy of his love and his reconciling ministry to his fallen-away disciples. Good crazy.

Hope is crazy. It's good crazy. Manifested in Jesus Christ and granted unto us. Symbolized today by an ashy smudge on our foreheads.

So, when someone asks me, when someone asks you, "What's all this stuff about Ash Wednesday?", I suggest we offer at least one of two responses. First, it's all about humility. Secondly, it's all about hope, and a crazy hope at that.

Or we could provide a combo response: "It's about humility and hope, but I can't actually recall which one comes first!"

Let's have a great Lent, a Lent that's full of humility and hope, crazy hope, good crazy hope for us all. Let it be so.

Amen.

NOTES
1. Richard P. McBrien, ed. *The Harper Collins Encyclopedia of Catholicism* (San Francisco: Harper Collins, 1995), pp. 100-101.
2. Paul J. Achtemeier, ed., *Harper's Bible Dictionary* (San Francisco: Harper Collins, 1985), p. 75.
3. Job 2:8.
4. Job 30:19.
5. Job 42:6.
6. Genesis 18:27.
7. Psalm 139:14.
8. Psalm 8: 5.
9. Hebrews 12:1.
10. Romans 5:3-5.
11. I heard the "good crazy — bad crazy" dichotomy first from Dr. Joseph Lowery at St. Paul School of Theology, Kansas City, Mo., Feb. 17, 2009. The application to the theme of hope is completely mine, for good or ill.

20

I AND THOU

Text: Psalm 8

Welcome! Welcome to an Affirming Ash Wednesday Service.

For too many folks— those who were misused (and occasionally abused) by previously negative religious experiences— Ash Wednesday may represent something they'd simply prefer to forget or avoid: guilt, negativity and failure. That's not the purpose of Ash Wednesday at all.

There are other folks who regard most religious ritual as hocus pocus, who've maintained a safe distance from anything even remotely resembling religious faith because so much religious language has seemed to them like mumbo-jumbo. Some of you may have been insulted by some religionist somewhere who asked you to will your own schizophrenia and abandon your sense of reason. If you are in any of these camps, this service is definitely for you.

Ash Wednesday is the beginning of a great adventure called Lent. During this season that stretches from today's goodness to the glorious rise of Easter Sunday, there's a heightened sense of spiritual urgency and quickened appreciation of life's precious character.

At Community during this season— coinciding with the lengthening of our spring-time days, thus its name "Lent" — instead of stressing the twisted, stereotypical aspects of overwrought repentance, abject sorrow, and an overbearing kind of piety that disallows our full humanness, we stress the positive aspects of deepened prayer, glad and joyful worship, closer connections with God and neighbor. These are the dynamics that lengthen the quality of our lives along with the duration of the days.

So, welcome, and may your Lenten journey be a joyful, glad, and fulfilling experience.

Out text for today's service is a major affirmation of our human-ness, in all its grit and grandeur:

When I look at your heavens, the work of your fingers,
the moon and the stars hat you have established;
what are human beings that you are mindful of them,
mortals that you care for them?
Yet you have made them little lower than the [angels],
and crowned them glory and honor.[1]

In this text we see the dichotomy, the sacred tension, in which we live. The text, in various translations, says we have been created "a little lower than the angels."

A little lower. That pretty much sums it up fairly well, doesn't it?

When we know the crime statistics of our city, or any major city in America, human beings can certainly be described as "a little lower."

When we consider the crass expressions of some radio talk-show programs and the crude critiques that so-called media gurus apply to our political situations, we can easily say we are "a little lower."

Those who are older, who daily behold the creaks, the cranks, and the crevices in their bodies (and their personalities), can quickly confess that they are "a little lower." Those who are younger, who know their lack of experience and the frustration that sometimes ensues in their lives, can also say that they are "a little lower."

When we acknowledge the undeniable realities of the human predicament, which we can cite in every community, in every culture, in every country on the face of the globe, again and again and again— war, greed, enmity, recklessness, drunk-driving, child abuse— we must describe ourselves as "a little lower than the angels."

But before I lose my perspective and deny what I said about the affirming character and tone of today's service, let us also attend to the latter half of the phrase. Remember that Psalm 8 praises God's wondrous ways by stressing that we have been made "a little lower than the angels."

The evidence for the overall angelic tendencies of human existence is so very real and so very obvious when we have eyes to see and ears to hear and souls to receive such good news.

Listen to Beethoven's "Ode to Joy," or k.d. lang singing Leonard Cohen's "Hallelujah" during the opening ceremonies of the Winter Olympics or Louis Armstrong singing "What a Wonderful World" or Millie Edwards singing "If I Had My Way" or the Chancel Choir singing "River of Judea," and who wouldn't think of "angels"?

Your daughter dances in her first recital with grace and a tremendous smile on her face, and what else would you say but "angel"? Your son becomes an Eagle Scout, and, beyond all his blemishes and bungling, you say, quietly or loudly, "angel."

The agility of Doc Watson on a guitar, "angel." The musical enthusiasm of Scott Presnell, Gary Tannen, Nathan Kent, Davis Shafer, and Elizabeth Van Horn in our Journey music team, "angels."

The blessedness of home-made chicken soup, "angel." A Valentine made by a creative four-year-old, "angel."

The warmth of a grandparent's generous lap, "angel." The capacity to call a cease-fire in the midst of conflict, "angel."

Help in Haiti, "angel." Artistic expressions in all of their forms, "angels."

The ability to care for a child who is sick, a teenager who is struggling, a young parent who is sleepless, a middle-aged friend who is floundering, an elderly parent who is moving into twilight, "angel," "angel," "angel," "angel," "angel." Angels, indeed. Angels, all!

Oh yes, we can easily say "a little lower," but we must emphasize "than the angels."

The trick, of course, is the emphasis, isn't it? How do we maintain a proper emphasis on the "angel" side rather than the "little lower" side? In the face of all the forces that would persuade us that we are only "a little lower," how can we strike a saving balance and know, with consistency, the "angel" side to which our character aspires?

The way to a proper emphasis and a disciplined, saving balance can be found in Martin Buber's genius insight.

Buber was one of the intellectual and spiritual giants of the twentieth century, a philosopher, theologian and popularizer of the Hasidic movement within Judaism. By the time he was fourteen, he was multilingual, conversant in five languages, Yiddish and German (at home), Hebrew and French (during his childhood), and Polish (at secondary school).

He was born and grew up in Vienna but lived most of his early adult years in Germany. When the Nazis seized power in Germany in 1933, he immediately resigned his professorship at the University of Frankfurt, left Germany, and assumed a professorship at Hebrew University in Jerusalem. There he participated in the discussion of Jewish-Palestinian relations and was member of group which aimed at a binational state.

His greatest work, arguably, is *Ich und Du*, translated as *I and Thou*. In this book, and throughout his exemplary life, he stressed the I−Thou relationship as the ultimate expression and fulfillment of what it means to be truly human before God and in community with others. Rather than an I−It relationship, Buber would remind us, we possess the capacity to maintain an I−Thou relationship with God and our neighbors. In essence, he struck a chord with what Christianity is all about: God as a person. He said,

> The description of God as a Person is indispensable for everyone who like myself means by "God" not a principle . . . and not an idea . . . but rather . . . who− whatever else he may be− enters into a direct relation with us ... in creative, revealing, and redeeming acts, and thus makes it possible for us to enter into a direct relation with him.[2]

Buber believed that such a way of relating could be extended to all aspects of life, including the natural world. He was so sure of the I−Thou dimensions of life that he believed he could even enter into an I−Thou relationship with his cat![3]

Now, whether or not you have a cat to cuddle in your household, such an attitude and posture toward life can be achieved with God and our neighbors.

During this year's Lenten journey toward the good news of Christ's resurrection (and our own!), I encourage you to grow deeper into an I−Thou relationship with God. Such an attitude and orientation, according to scripture, tradition, reason, and our collective experience, is how God desires to relate to us.

Such an attitude, such an orientation, is the most intimate form of human connection. As Burris Jenkins, one of Community's great heroes, used to say (quoting Joseph Swain's hymn "How Sweet, How Heavenly is the Sight"): "We know each other, for we have drunk the cup of life together, 'Where sorrow flows from eye to eye, and joy from heart to heart.'"

I encourage us all to maintain an I−Thou attitude and orientation toward God, toward one another within our cherished fellowship of faith, and toward everyone we meet throughout this Lenten season, and indeed, throughout all of our lives. If we will do so, as consistently as we can, with as much joy as we are capable of, we will see, moment by moment and day by day, how the Psalmist was so very right in describing us as "little lower than the angels"! As you come forward for the time-honored and ever new and inspirational "Imposition of Ashes," receive the cross-shaped smudge as a reminder that you are "little lower" but also and always "a little lower than the angels."

Amen.

NOTES

1. Psalm 8:3−5.
2. Martin Buber, *I and Thou*, Second Edition, (New York: Scribner's & Sons, 1958), p. 135.
3. Ibid., pp. 96−97.

21

ASHES TO ASHES, HEART TO HEART

Text: I Peter 2:9—10

The season of Lent is an enriching stretch of time— from today, Ash Wednesday, all the way to Easter Sunday— during which we're invited to deepen our faith and broaden our spirits. It's chock-full of refreshing activities and interesting rituals and intriguing study occasions. Just as Advent prepares us for the splendor of Christmas, Lent prepares us for the glory of Easter.

And it all starts with the mark of ashes and a plain, straightforward statement: "Remember that you are dust and to dust you shall return." Such simple words, such a profound message. Now, many if not most of Community's family of faith treasure Ash Wednesday and the marking of holy time it signifies. Countless Christians welcome the seven weeks of Lent as a blessing for their faith. Prayer becomes deeper. Worship becomes more energized. The life of the Spirit takes center stage.

But there are some folks elsewhere— friends of yours and mine— who don't enjoy Lent and don't appreciate Ash Wednesday very much. I have some Protestant friends who cede Lent to Catholic Christians and can't understand why any Protestants should take after the practices of their Catholic forebears.

We all have other friends who – Protestant and Catholics and an array of curmudgeonly non-religious friends – who cast a caustic eye at Lent and consider it simply a guilt-relief machine: put in your penance for seven weeks, pull the lever of spiritual practices, and— *voila!* — you hit the jackpot of forgiveness. To this same curmudgeonly crowd, if you don't deposit the coin of your penance, then Lent becomes a guilt-producing mechanism.

Still other friends simply may not appreciate anyone, even a minister, imposing a smudge on their foreheads. "It's not seemly," these friends say, "it's obviously messy and definitely disturbing to one's normal appearance." Despite all these objections to Lent and Ash Wednesday, I love them both. Though I didn't grow up with much of an emphasis on the season of Lent or the day that launches it, Lent and Ash Wednesday have become— how should I put this? — precious to me.

I think this is so because of the simplicity of faith which Lent calls us to embody in our daily lives. And with regard to Ash Wednesday's emphasis on the simplicity of faith, it seems so right to quote Arthur Ashe: "Start where you are. Use what you have. Do what you can."

I have joined others in relishing the richness of Lent, also, because it never disappoints. For each year we have observed the Lenten season here at Community, blessings have poured forth: youth claim Christ's path as their way of life; young adults learn the advantages of prayer; senior adults come alive like spring flowers in the desert; those who never knew that a life of intimate connection with God was ever possible find that it's wonderfully, even occasionally stupefyingly possible.

So here we are, and Arthur Ashe is exactly right: "Start where you are. Use what you have. Do what you can."

Where we start is . . . dusty and ashy and earthy. It is a humbling moment where we are. It's humbling to note that though our bodies might be made up of 93% water, we all become dust one day. The ancient refrain reminds us to remember that we are dust.

But let us also recognize that we are magnificent dust! We are made of the very stuff of creation. We consist of the essential elements with which the world began. Scientists and poets alike tell us that our bio-chemical makeup reaches back to time's beginnings. Four and a half billion years ago, when the *chronos* of earthly time commenced and God said "Let there be light," the magnificent dust of God's creation was brought forth into being. Ever since then, elements have been building up and moving around, dispersing and carrying on, eon to eon to eon. From one generation to the next, the stuff of which we are made has been transformed from one person to the next. Ashes to ashes, indeed.

Compound the mysterious, wondrous journey of the ashes with the additional knowledge that the substance of the plants and the earth from which they emanate know no diminution. That is, all matter is bequeathed from previous matter, reaching all the way back to the earth's primordial beginnings. Meaning? Ultimately, the ashes we receive on our foreheads today connect us with all other followers of Jesus in all previous times.

It goes like this. The ashes used in today's service also have origins that are magnificent and treasurable. Just think of it: They not only come from the palm fronds and palm crosses of the previous twenty years here at Community. The ashes that touched the first forehead of the very first participant in the first observance of Ash Wednesday were eventually rubbed or washed away, falling into the confluence of a river that then deposited its residue into a silty plain. Or the ashy residue was borne by the winds to a farm a thousand miles away. In any case, perhaps we can say in all cases, the ashes from previous millennia then nourished the plants that then became the palm branches that were then cut and fashioned into palm crosses for more Palm Sunday celebrations, decade after decade, century after century, to this very day. [1]

Well-traveled, treasurable, magnificent dust indeed. Ashes to ashes, and, given their history from one penitent's forehead to another, heart to heart.

The epistle of I Peter had another way of putting this great claim about our magnificent dust:

But you are a chosen race, a royal priesthood, a holy nation, God's own people, in order that you may proclaim the mighty acts of him who called you out of darkness into his marvelous light. Once you were not a people, but now you are God's people; one you had not received mercy, but now you have received mercy.[2]

Where we are, and what we have at our disposal to use, and what we can do are all tied up in this simple, humble ritual with its powerful symbolic message. Hear now the traditional phrasing for Ash Wednesday with a new nuance: Remember that you are magnificent, holy, divinely touched dust and to such magnificent, holy dust you shall return.

Today, in the Imposition of Ashes, we are receiving a wondrous, mysterious sign, one might even say "God's fingerprint."

And the fingerprint's meaning? We are broadcasting to the world a very simple proclamation: We are claimed by God as God's beloved ones.

A month ago, my friend David Shirey, pastor of Coolwater Christian Church in Cave Creek, Arizona, reminded me of a portion of Matthew's gospel that reveals just what is going on today in our Ash Wednesday ritual.

The third chapter of Matthew depicts Jesus' baptism. As Jesus rises dripping from the waters of the Jordan, freshly baptized by the hand of his cousin John, a voice speaks from the heavenly realm: "This is my beloved Son in whom I am well pleased."[3]

His direction is clear. His path has been revealed. His destiny is assured. Jesus is God's beloved Son. His ministry will really be not so much about what he does as about who he is: God's beloved Son.

Two short verses later, Jesus is in the desert wilderness enduring the temptations of the Satanic One. And the first utterance of the tempter in the gospel of Matthew (and, of course, in the entire New Testament) is a dare: "If you are the Son of God, turn these stones into bread."[4] This is more than a mere appeal to physical gratification. It is more than a sneering taunt meant to ensnare Jesus in the performance of magic.

"If," the tempter says. It is a doubt-saturated rhetorical question. *If.* It is a profound attack on God's blessing.

We know the tempting, debilitating power of such an *if*, and how culture and the powers and principalities seek to constrain us and qualify us for special status.

- "If you're really smart, you'll choose this career path and thus be valuable and worthy."
- "If you're really a person of importance and prestige, then you'll wear this perfume, drive this car, drink this beer...."
- "If you're really a super-duper world power, if you are really the shot-caller of the globe, then you'll transform these pieces of bread for the poor into the stony implements of military weaponry."
- "If you're really a true patriot, then surely you can only vote for one candidate."
- "If you're really a Christian, then you'll express your beliefs in only one way."

Jesus resisted the debilitating power of such an *if*. He didn't yield to any doubting about the One who had blessed him and Whose he was. He didn't need to perform any fantastic feat to prove he was God's beloved Son. He rested comfortably and trusted unflinchingly in the status conferred upon him by God.

And the truth about Jesus is the same truth about you and me. God declares us to be beloved: "Once you were no people, but now you are God's people; once you had not received mercy, but now you have received mercy." We are beloved and made so— undeniably, unerasably, irrevocably— by God's blessing upon our lives. No malevolence can stunt it. No satanic force can erase it. No tempter can ever take it away. We are God's.

The message of the ashy smudge we receive today on Ash Wednesday? Two meanings which are eternally true: You are made of magnificent dust and you are God's beloved. No ifs, ands or buts about it.

I urge you to claim your magnificence this Lenten season. Throughout your prayer times and worship and study gatherings and service activities along the Lenten journey, remember the phrase "ashes to ashes and heart to heart." Allow yourself to be transformed by God's defining declaration: You are beloved. Let none of us ever forget that God's blessing can never be taken away.

Amen.

NOTES

1. The inspiration for this sermon came from my friend Bill Tammeus and his Facebook post from February 17, 2010, when he wrote: "As I get ashes on my forehead this evening at church I hope to remember to think about the fact that for millions and millions of years the molecules making up the ashes have been spinning about the cosmos. Maybe once before they were in Ash Wednesday ashes, and thus have gone from ashes to ashes."
2. I Peter 2:9-10.
3. Matthew 3:17.
4. Matthew 4:3.

22

STRONG AT THE BROKEN PLACES

Text: II Corinthians 12:7b—10

We begin the forty days of Lent today with an ashy smudge on our foreheads and something churning, burning, yearning within our hearts. That something within us has to do, I believe, with wanting to be made whole, needing to be brand-new and one with God and united with others, particularly those closest to us, including those within a body of believers that calls itself Christian.

Oh, we could be here because of habit, mere ritual, due to the rut of rote memory. "It's Ash Wednesday, time to get that ashy smudge on our foreheads." That kind of attitude. And while that's all right as a reason, I suppose, there's something else going on, something else brewing among us and inside of us.

I want to suggest that that something within us is something which is broken, something weakened. And in the face of that brokenness and weakness, I want to remind us of Ernest Hemingway's wonderful phrase from his novel *A Farewell to Arms*: "The world breaks everyone and afterward many are strong at the broken places."

The Apostle Paul called that something within us "a thorn in the flesh."

In his second letter to the church in Corinth, Greece, Paul the great apostle— the one who would write nearly two-thirds of what we've come to call the New Testament, the apostle who dared anyone to challenge his authority, the marvelous teacher who illuminated the cavernous gulf between grace and the law, the first grand theologizer of the Church, the premier exemplar of missionary zeal for the cause of Christ in the Church's first 1,000 years, the distinguished gentleman and scholar, the extraordinarily learned rabbi, the model convert to Jesus' path of love and mercy: *that* Paul said he was constantly afflicted, consistently harassed by "a thorn in the flesh." It was a point of utter vulnerability and pain for Paul. It was the sorest and weakest dimension of his life. "Thorn in the flesh." That's what Paul called it. Couldn't get rid of it, couldn't manage to have it leave him. "Thorn in the flesh."

What was Paul's "thorn in the flesh"? The short answer is we really have no idea. But many have postulated what it could have been.

Some say it was epilepsy; some say malaria; some say headaches, perhaps migraines; some say leprosy. Others say it was a speech impediment, a distinct, uncontrollable stutter that caused his hearers to regard Paul as a poor preacher. And yet others say Paul's "thorn in the flesh" was partial blindness or baldness, or bouts of depression, or a twisted physicality, or a limp.

Still others say that what Paul called his "thorn in the flesh" could have been a reference to his opponents, theological and otherwise, or to a nagging, insoluble question that assaulted his soul, kept him up at night and gave him grief. And yet still others have thought it could have been a pesky temptation that would never leave him alone.

Whatever it was, Paul recognized it as a harsh and unrelenting point of brokenness in his life. Paul's actual use of the word "thorn" references a stake that was used in military endeavors. Such sharp piercing must have felt like sheer torture. This is the kind of torment Paul is experiencing from the thorn in the flesh that refuses to leave him.

Paul appeals to the Lord to have the thorn in the flesh leave him. Three times he seeks God's powerful intervention in the matter. But the thorn remains. It is as if Satan himself is the cause of the pain and weakness in Paul's life. Despite his beseeching, his "thorn in the flesh" remains.

Enduring the thorn, abiding with the weakness is ultimately all right with Paul, since he learns from God that God's power is just the remedy for Paul's weakness: he is made strong at his broken places.

As I already mentioned, that's a phrase from Ernest Hemingway's *A Farewell to Arms*: "The world breaks everyone and afterward many are strong at the broken places." Like a bone that is healed to be stronger than before, stronger even than when it was unbroken. Like a sailing ship's mast which is scarfed and pressured and glued back together and becomes far stronger than a mast that had never been broken. "Strong at the broken places": this is Paul's declaration to the Corinthians and to us this Ash Wednesday.

I don't think I need to ask you if you've ever experienced a thorn in the flesh. Surely you have. Surely you can remember one at some point in your circuits around the sun.

It may be a dashed hope, a shattered dream.

It may be a persistent back pain, or incessant nausea.

It could be an ulcer or cancer or a heart murmur or migraines.

It could be a reckless teenager.

It could be a reckless parent.

It could be dyslexia.

It could be algebra.

Or it could be a cranky, crabby boss, who just won't let up.

In Jamaica it was a toothache that had persisted for a year in a man there until our Jamaica Partners Medical Missions Team arrived at the end of January and extracted it. And he was not alone. Hundreds of people, young and old, had been enduring great pain and suffering until Community's team got there. There were thorns in the flesh aplenty: pains in back molars, suffering in legs and arms and in chronic sinus conditions.

When I consider the phrase "a thorn in the flesh" I keep thinking about the Kansas City School District. What perduring failures the district has suffered. What lackluster commitment from all quarters. Definitely, thorns in the flesh.

And then there's the toxic mix of extremist radio shows and partisan politics. And that definitely makes for some undeniable thorns in the flesh of the body politic. When I think of how irritating some personalities can be and how rancorous campaign rhetoric can become, I'm reminded of Paul's torment in the book of Romans when he declares, to paraphrase, "For [we] do not do the good [we] want, but the evil [we] do not want is what [we] do . . . . Wretched [folks] that [we are]! Who will deliver [us] from this body of death?"

For Maya Angelou, her "thorn in the flesh" was a violation. As she relates in the first volume of her memoirs, *I Know Why the Caged Bird Sings*, she was eight years old when her mother's boyfriend violated her. She told her brothers about it and she named the man, Mr. Freeman, and the man was arrested. But he was only jailed for a day and then released. Four days after he was released, he was killed, very likely by Angelou's uncles. She thought her voice had killed Mr. Freeman, and so she did not speak for the next five years. Broken. Weakened. Muted. Thorn in the flesh, for sure. And yet she was able to overcome her brokenness. She knew, as Paul knew, the visitation of the Holy One who declared, "My power is made perfect in weakness."

One who had been violated, broken, and muted would go on to know an uncommon strength from God's generous hand. She became a dancer par excellence, and then an organizer and leader for the northern branch of the Southern Christian Leadership Conference during the halcyon days of the civil rights movement. She would become strong at her broken places.

She eventually would become, as we all know, a popular poet and memoirist and would stand in Washington, D.C., to give a dedicatory poem at President Clinton's inauguration. Strong at the broken places.

And Maya Angelou would go on even further, actually beginning in 1991 as the Reynolds Professor of American Studies at Wake Forest University and a spokesperson for Hallmark Cards. Strong at the broken places.

As you know, I returned last week from eulogizing my friend Denton Roberts in Los Angeles. For Denton, his very life was a thorn in the flesh. Denton was born three months before his father died in a tragic car accident. His birth and his life thereafter were initially surrounded by sadness. His oldest son Dane once heard Denton explain to a group of people "I just presumed as a child that I was the cause of all the sadness."

That was not Denton's only existential deficit. His mother was married a number of times, and Denton and his brother David moved constantly. At one point, when he was 11 years old, Denton decided that he had had enough, and he hitch-hiked nearly 900 miles, all the way from Midland, Texas, to St. Joseph, Missouri, to be with his grandparents. By the time he was in college, he had endured a perforated ulcer. All along his education he had been labeled a "slow learner." In Drake Divinity School he bore that burden all through his classes, even up to and including his last theology class with a "Professor Smith," in which he received an A. But he was still broken. He said to one of his good friends, "I really pulled a fast one on Professor Smith! I got an A. Can you believe it?" To which his friend responded, "You must be pretty smart to fool ol' Smith!" And at that remark Denton began to be healed of his slow learner status. He grew eventually to claim his intellectual capacities and began a turn that would render him strong at his broken places.

Yes, he had been broken and weakened, early and often, in his life, but Denton Lowell Roberts would become a leader in the International Transactional Analysis Association, and he would march for freedom with Dr. King in Selma, Alabama. His leadership would renew a struggling congregation in South Central Los Angeles and help to transform a community center into a vital center of hope, making the name "All Peoples" one of the bright, shining stars in the Christian Church (Disciples of Christ). Yes indeed, Denton Roberts was strong at the broken places.

I agree with Denton's sons that his most dramatic transformation and his greatest gift had to do with the fact that he was a tremendous father and uncle and grandfather. Again, Dane said it best: "Somehow, out of his own traumatic childhood and youth experiences, he was able to discern what sort of respect and love a child needs." By the all-sufficient grace of God, Denton became strong at the broken places of his life.

Are you beginning to get the picture? We are all of us strong at our broken places if we but allow God's grace to mend and mold and shape us. Grace is sufficient. Love conquers all.

So, now, the smudge you receive today can have new meaning on this Ash Wednesday. Let the horizontal smudge be a reminder of your oh-so-human, earthly weakness, your brokenness, your broken places. Let the vertical smudge remind you of God's blessings of strength and gracing love.

Ernest Hemingway was one hundred percent half right when he proclaimed, "The world breaks everyone and afterward many are strong at the broken places." Here's the better version of that phrase for this Ash Wednesday: The world breaks everyone and all are made strong at their broken places through the redeeming and sufficient power of Christ and Christ's gracing love.

Amen.

NOTES

For background materials for this sermon, please see the following:

Ernest Best, *Second Corinthians: Interpretation: A Bible Commentary for Teaching and Preaching* (Louisville: John Knox Press, 1987); M. Eugene Boring and Fred B. Craddock, *The People's New Testament Commentary* (Louisville, Kentucky: Westminister John Knox Press, 2004), pp. 572-573; *The New Interpreter's Bible* (Nashville: Abingdon Press, 2000), vol. 11, pp. 161-168.

23

WHERE YOUR TREASURE IS

Text: Matthew 6:9–21

Today's Ash Wednesday services are full of grand hopes and humble prayers.

The grand hopes are being expressed in the extraordinary music that is ours to enjoy and to be inspired by. Thanks to Tim Whitmer, Bill Langley, Kimi Yokoyama, and the Chancel Choir, under the direction of Kathryn Huey and with accompaniment by Jonathon Antle, our awareness of God's presence has been deepened and our hopes have been magnified.

And our humble prayers will be maximized in a few moments when we receive the sacred smudge of the imposition of ashes.

Surely among the premier reasons that energize our anticipation is this service's profound simplicity and astounding mystery. It is in this service — perhaps more poignantly than nearly any other service of the year — when we can come before God and utter all three of the "essential prayers," as Anne Lamott describes them: Thanks, Help, and Wow![1]

We say "Thanks" to God for granting us another year of living, breathing, hearing, seeing, caring, and considering.

We say "Help!" — without hesitation — because we know that we need God so direly, sometimes so desperately, and it is profoundly moving to have a mark on our foreheads to remind us of that need.

And we say "Wow!" because the gift of belonging to God is made plain after the service when we look in the mirror and see that God has a claim on us. On us! And on you! And you! And you! And me! The ashes of Ash Wednesday remind us that each and every one of us is the subject of the song that Kimi sang: "You Are Mine."

This year, the essence of Ash Wednesday is summed up for me in the word "treasure."

Beyond any monetary value in the secular marketplace, a treasure is a special window on the sacred, a sign and a symbol of the numinous. And treasures really are everywhere, around every corner, if we will but have eyes and ears and hearts and minds open and prepared to take them in:

- A sunrise brims over the horizon and, because of its beauty, you just know there's a God somewhere.
- A baby coos and then smiles at you, and your heart melts, and you just know the encounter is holy.
- You hear language spoken with felicity and flair, shared with artistry and utter integrity, and you are convinced all over again that eloquence is surely a sign of God's graciousness.

And they can even surprise us in the most unlikely of places, like on an airplane.

A good while back, on the backside of a three-legged trip from Puget Sound to Seattle to Phoenix to Kansas City, on America West Flight 596 from Phoenix to Kansas City, an epiphany happened right before my eyes.

During the pre-flight chatter proffered over the plane's intercom about the way to exit the plane in case of a catastrophe, I saw a pitiable flight attendant who was demonstrating the use of the oxygen mask and the lighted aisle markers and what to do in case of a crash. (You know that person, the one who looks like she'd rather be doing anything else in the world than withstanding the complete disregard of the 192 passengers surrounding her.)

This particular flight I decided to pay attention to the chatter and the flight attendant's requisite pantomime about the appropriate procedures for exiting the plan in the event of a premature descent and subsequent landing (in the middle of a cornfield, presumably).

I did so because there was something powerfully, mercifully different about this pre-flight routine. The flight attendant instructing us about what to do with the oxygen mask and where the flotation devices were stored in the event that we dropped down on a pond in a Kansas cornfield — she had a pin on her lapel. And the pin had some wings on it. And on that pin the word "Treasure" was clearly, visibly imprinted on it. *Treasure.*

What does this mean, I wondered. What is this? A new one-word mission statement for America West? Or a valuable gift? What kind of treasure?, I pondered. You know: "We treasure the opportunity to serve you with a treasurable trip aboard one of our airborne treasures." Was this some sort of highlighting of the frequent flights that this particular airline had scheduled to Las Vegas? Or was there a different explanation?

My mind and heart raced. Could it be a name she had given herself, as happens in our self-absorbed, self-locating, self-creating times? Could it be that this was an instance of someone daring enough to break through the limits of family and tribe, now subject only to her own preference, her own liking, her own self-naming?

Or could it be, I wondered further, that her parents had given her that name? If so, why? Was it a family name? Her mother's maiden name, given to her in Southern fashion to carry on a memory of matrilineal connections?

Perhaps she was the late-flowering child of some left-over hippies who wanted to give her a name to live into? (These kinds of namings occur more often than we normally hear about. Some friends of mine once named their new son, Funn, because, as Funn's mother said to me, "Well dude, we had so much fun making him!")

Or Treasure might have been the name that the proud and pleased parents gave to a daughter who was truly their actual treasure, way beyond incessant attempts to conceive, one unsuccessful try after another, until finally she was born.

No matter the reasoning behind the peculiar word on the pin on the lapel of the America West flight attendant's uniform, the word itself,

"Treasure," was an epiphany, a rare and fine gift for me on that plane ride and thereafter. "Treasure" was just the word I needed.

"Treasure" was exactly the charge that I required, require still, to see, to behold, to hear, to receive for the living of my days.

When this epiphany was granted to me, it was at first a challenge to figure out if the word was a verb or a noun. The answer that came? "Yes."

Treasure as a verb, yes: to hold dear, to be fond of; to be so glad in the presence of the treasurable that you would esteem it so highly that you would give anything in honor of the treasurable, maybe even— yes, quite likely even— your life. Treasure: to hold close and dear those aspects of your life that are far more precious, far more treasurable than any material thing. Treasure a seed falling to the ground in October's swirling air. Treasure the taste of an apple picked straight from a tree. Treasure the crinkle-crackle of Bible pages, particularly the Psalms. Treasure. Yes, a verb.

But also *treasure* as a noun as well. Treasure, as in something highly prized for beauty or perfection or both and more. Treasure, as in gift, as in valuable above almost all other valuables we might possess or know about. Something and/or someone appreciated above nearly all others. Yes, *treasure* as noun. Yes.

Both as verb and as noun, the word "treasure," as Paul Ricoeur would quickly remind us, had an autonomy of its own in that airplane.

Now, treasuring is what all of life is about fundamentally, when we get down to the bottom of the bottom of everything. And treasuring the life God gives us is our deepest privilege, our highest, our best purpose.

Beyond the ability to manipulate opposable thumbs, and beyond the finery and filigree of human language, our uniqueness as those who are "little lower than the angels" really has to do with our capacity to treasure the life that has been given into our hands.

Jesus preached about this reality principle in his Sermon on the Mount. Smack-dab in the middle of the collection of his greatest declarations— after the visionary grandness of the beatitudes and before the plain-as-day implications of his teachings on judgmental attitudes and being prayerful— there he is talking about treasures. What you treasure (the noun) and how you treasure (the verb) will determine the health of your heart and the integrity of your personality. What you treasure and how you do your treasuring will either shrink or enlarge your heart and your capacities for living.

If you believe that your stuff is the most important treasure in your life, your heart will shrink to the size of those things. And watch out when those things begin to fall apart!

I knew of a couple who loved what they called the good life, and they adored "the finer things" in life. They focused a lot of energy on getting things and treasuring them.

But when it came time for them to retire and move into smaller quarters, they were in for a rude awakening. They seemed to shrivel and to grow weaker and eventually more despondent as they tried to adjust to living without their stuff. Their hearts seemed to diminish. The horizon of their lives seemed to shrink. Life itself seemed to grow grim and dreary.

Contrast that with Fred and Nettie Craddock who desired to have a small ministry with the poor of Appalachia after Fred retired from his legendary career as a preacher and teacher of preachers. He and Nettie could have garnered all kinds of wealth to themselves, could have traveled the world in utter luxury. What did they do instead? Built a ministry among the poor of northeastern Georgia. Wrote newsletter articles about the ministry.[2] The great Fred Craddock, professor, preacher and teacher extraordinaire, whose books have never gone out of print, writing newsletter articles for the Craddock Center! And not only that but treasuring new vans, buying one van after another to take books to poor children. They know from personal experience that if children — no matter how poor — have books in their hands, those books can be a pathway to a new future. Fred and Nettie's hearts, like their true treasures, grow larger and larger every day.

In the end, Jesus declares that it's all a matter of what you treasure.

When I asked the flight attendant about the word "Treasure" on her lapel pin, it turned out it was her given name. I took great comfort in her telling me that fact. Other passengers on our flight and on previous flights, I imagined, had also taken comfort in this angelic message on the uniform of this cherubic flight attendant.

I was not only comforted, I was strongly encouraged. I wanted to call up her parents, or better, choose special, thick embossed stationery and write a note to them, maybe even a poem of praise, a missive of unabashed gratitude for the wisdom, for the saving, crazy wisdom, that possessed them to hang such a moniker on her and have her gladly live it out, embody it, in front of God and everybody, everywhere she happened to go.

I've waited until today to say to you what I wanted to say to everyone on that plane that day. I wanted to say to the people on Flight 596 from Phoenix to Kansas City, that the flight attendant's name had reminded us of the secret name God has given each and every one of us. We are all treasures in God's view.

We can see what and how God has treasured: the human family in all of our mysterious, miscreant, muddling magnificence. You remember it, don't you? For God so loved the world (God treasured us so much) that He gave his only son (that God's very heart of love came to dwell among us in the person and presence of Christ), that whoever believes in Him (whoever treasures Christ's way of life in all of its wondrous grace) should not perish but have eternal life (should inherit the great treasure of abiding with God forever).

Ash Wednesday marks the beginning of the Lenten season on the Church's calendar. While it doesn't have as many sparkling secular resonances like other special seasons do, Lent is surely one of the most important moments among the Church's ritual observances, because it helps us remember what we are to treasure.

In Lent we see the implications of the incarnation, as we behold the treasure of God's eternal hopefulness in response to humanity's persistent need.

In Lent we remember that Jesus was just like us, struggling in the wilderness of life to overcome temptation, to embrace firmly what is best and most noble, most treasurable in life.

In Lent we begin to see that, however dismal our attempts at the treasure of righteousness have been, we too can overcome and prevail.

At the conclusion of the Lenten journey, we will hesitatingly peek and then openly stare at the shimmering treasure of God's power to overcome all things harmful, crass, and destructive by the sheer force of divine love. As we launch what promises to be one of the most meaningful Lenten seasons ever experienced at Community, know this: This year's Lenten journey will be meaningful in direct proportion to how we treasure the ultimate gifts God grants to the world. May we treasure the grace of God more than any thing. And may our hearts grow larger thereby!

Amen.

NOTES
1. Anne Lamott, *Help-Thanks-Wow: The Three Essential Prayers* (New York: Riverhead Books. 2012).
2. Fred Craddock, *A Taste of Milk and Honey* (Suches, Georgia: Georgia Mountain Publishing, 2013).

24

CARDIAC CARE

Text: John 14:1 – 3

It makes my heart so glad that you're here, and I'm so glad to be here with you. Because of what we do today in our Ash Wednesday services, we can all be heartened and encouraged.

This service of worship marks the beginning of Lent, the forty days stretching from Ash Wednesday to Easter Sunday. (By the way, the figure of forty days is arrived at by subtracting the Sundays in between.)

The practice of imposing ashes has a long and varied history in religious traditions. Before the birth of Christ, various cultures, the Hebrews in particular, designated times of fasting, penance, and prayer by placing ashes on their foreheads.[1]

Sometimes in the fourth century after the birth of Christ, Christians made their penitence publicly visible by dressing in sackcloth and being sprinkled with ashes, as a sign of their resolve to live uprightly. At some juncture between the end of the eighth century and the middle of the eleventh century, it became a regular practice of the church for the faithful to receive the imposition of ashes at the beginning of Lent before proceeding toward the anticipation of Easter's resurrection celebration.

On our calendars and in our hearts, Lent is a period of the lengthening of days and a lengthening of our love for God and for one another. It is a time for enhancing one's flow of life with the rhythms of faith, a season for the passing away of the old and the welcoming of the new, for an intensified focus on renewed commitments and fresh, new covenants.

The Lenten journey provides Christians perhaps the richest seasonal opportunities for the deepening of our faith. There are more exciting occasions for enriching one's life during Lent than during any other one stretch of time on the church calendar.

I.

As we enter the season of Lent, I urge you to make a sacred covenant with the following as priority items of focus:

(1) Worship every Sunday you are in town, barring, of course, sickness or another emergency, and cherish the prayers, the music, the messages, and the fellowship you experience in each service.

(2) Partake regularly of the Wednesday worship events, at noon and 6:00 pm.

(3) Pray daily for the increase of Christ's love in the world, for the healing of our war-torn, strife-riddled world, for the health and well-being of all children of the world, and for the increase and growth of Community's congregation.

(4) Seek out a relationship in need of reconciliation and forgiveness in your life.

(5) Read the schedule of scripture texts in the gospel of John that are connected to the Lenten Sunday morning sermon series, *God's Love Letter to the World,* between Ash Wednesday and Easter Sunday.

(6) Learn something new by trying out a new class— Sunday mornings, Sunday afternoons, and Sunday evenings and Wednesdays, as well, at noon and in the evening— that will stretch your mind and your soul.

(7) Retreat from all media (television, radio, internet access, phone, and all social media) for at least one hour per day, allowing your soul to rest and be refreshed.

(8) Engage in acts of service for the benefit of others, doing at least eight hours of service over the course of the Lenten season, either through the various service opportunities at Community or through other volunteering avenues.

(9) Enjoy fellowship opportunities with others in Community's family of faith and invite friends to join you!

Allow these "Divine Nine" suggestions to suffice as a "Starter Kit" for your Lenten "Faith Tune—Up."

II.

Beyond these suggestions and the historical insights about Lent's origins and overarching meanings, I would direct your attention to the words from today's text in the 14th chapter of St. John's gospel. It's a simple declaration, a straightforward directive.

You've probably heard these cherished words more often at funerals and memorial services than at other times. That's likely because they are famously included in many funeral liturgies.

They are placed there, I believe, because they strike at the heart, so to speak, of the foundation of the human predicament: Too many hearts are troubled.

This was the situation of the disciples as they listened to Jesus final instructions, what Biblical scholars call Jesus' Farewell Discourse.

Beginning in the 14th chapter and stretching all the way to the 17th chapter, Jesus offers his longest and most extensive set of teachings in John's gospel.

Jesus is preparing his most devoted disciples for his absence. This is a parting bequest of his wisdom and his hopes for those he loved most dearly during the days of his flesh.

This is the stuff of ultimacy. This a matter of urgency and mystery and great grace.

Jesus has broken the bread and shared the cup of the Last Supper, and he is making ready for his final passion. He has said some things that he knows are troubling to his followers. And he will say more.

Jesus begins his final instructions with words of challenge and guidance. While we can regard this appropriately as an address by the historical Jesus, it is also the living Christ speaking to the Church about its (our) own situation.[2] And Christ is speaking about a problem that touches us all: our troubled hearts.

The litany of troubles with which our hearts of faith contend is woefully long and burdensome.

ISIS on the one hand, random slayings of Kansas City's children on the other. The death of a beloved family member, the death of a relationship. Troubled hearts.

Homelessness, challenges in our education systems, unemployment, underemployment, lack of integrity on the part of elected officials and television broadcasters. The mercurial advance of technology that has inspired some of the most savvy techies to yearn for the good old days of 2G. Troubled hearts.

Jesus was anticipating the predicaments in which his followers would find themselves. And so he declared, "Let not your hearts be troubled."

III.

This is a fitting mandate and metaphor for us. In more contemporary terms, Jesus is saying, "Take care of your hearts."

There are numerous heart problems in our physical lives, and there have parallels in our spiritual lives.

For some folks the heart of their faith is in fibrillation, twitching and sometimes skipping more than a beat and racing ahead. Doing too much, attempting too much, out of kilter with a natural rhythm. Do you ever feel like that? What shall we do? Let love be your guide about what's important, what's essential to do and to be. Move toward those who are loving and full of grace. Prioritize your tasks by focusing on the ones that will add the most love to the world.

The faith conditions of many suffer from a congenital heart disease known as cynicism. What shall we do? Practice hope by using a page from Ignatius' playbook, one of the rules from his *Spiritual Exercises*. This won't be the last time I ever proffer this guidance, but I'm urgently offering it today for your consideration for your Lenten journey this year: Exhaust all possible positive interpretations of every place, person, thing, encounter, event, before going negative.

If the heart of your faith is experiencing cardiac arrest, if your belief system has suffered a religious version of an acute myocardial infarction — let's call it a spiritual heart attack — there's still time and there's still hope. And your response can be simple and gentle: rest. Take it easy. Take a step back, or forwards, but only one small step. Take a breath. If your faith is in cardiac arrest, rest. Use this rhyming antidote: if in arrest, take a rest.

IV.

John's gospel then has Jesus proclaim the simple mandate of believing: "Believe in God, believe also in me." And while that seems plainspoken and may even have been crystal clear to the first disciples, living out such a mandate in our time has become much more complicated. I would do you and myself a great disservice to merely repeat those seven words as if they were a magical formula for the relief, restoration, renewal, and reinforcement of your faith.

A significant debate has raged throughout church history about the place of belief in the life of a Christian. But there really doesn't need to be one. Believing your way into a new way of life? Acting your way into believing? Both are legitimate. This is what I call the intertwining of the "Oath" and the "Path."

Recently I was sending an email to a friend about "The Path of Faith." When I looked over what I had written, I discovered a glaring typo. I had typed "Oath" instead of "Path." The typo became a moment of revelation, for I know that paths and oaths are intimately related.

Sometimes people declare an oath— a commitment, a faith position, a belief— and then walk down a path to live out that oath.

At other times, folks walk down a path— worshiping, practicing a discipline, engaging in service, enjoying fellowship with others— and then, and sometimes only then, come to the point of uttering an oath of faith.

However the process works for you, a shining reality abides: oaths and paths go together, whichever one precedes or follows the other. We need not beat up ourselves (or anyone else) over the order of the process.

V.

Then Jesus utters a wonderfully comforting promise as part of this first portion of his farewell address: "In my Father's house there are many dwelling places. If it were not so, would I have told you that I go to prepare a place for you? And if I go and prepare a place for you, I will come again and will take you to myself, so that where I am, there you may be also."

Could it be that what we need most to do and be at the outset of Lent is trusting? Trusting that God will take care of us, however befuddled we are in our understanding of how that care will take place? Trusting that Christ's promises of love and eternal life are true?

Could it be that simple? Just taking the hand of God, which will most likely involve taking the hand of a brother or sister in the faith, and walking out and on in trust, assuming we will have enough and we will be enough by God's grace, not only today and tomorrow, but in the long, long, long run of eternity as well?

Could it be that all we need to do is emulate Maya Angelou's grandmother and how she acted in a moment of crisis or danger or difficulty? In the middle of the degradations of the Depression in the segregationist South, Maya's grandmother, who she called Mama, would frequently declare, "I will step out on the word of God!"[3]

Increasingly, I'm discovering it is that simple, and I intend to put such simple trust to the fullest test I can during this year's Lenten journey. I truly believe it will lead you and me all the way home.

One final word. As you receive the imposition of the ashes, let the horizontal smudge remind us all to take care of our hearts. Remember that verse: Let not your hearts be troubled.

Then allow the vertical smudge to remind you to believe in God and believe also in Christ. To allow the oath and the path of faith to be intertwined in such a way that you will be filled with God's grace this Lenten season and always.

Amen and amen.

NOTES
1. See Esther 4:1-3, 2 Samuel 13:19, Job 42:6, and Jeremiah 6:26.
2. Fred B. Craddock, *The Gospels* (Nashville: Abingdon, 1981), p. 143.
3. Maya Angelou, *Wouldn't Take Nothing for My Journey Now* (New York: Random House, 1993), p. 74.

25

IN THE BEGINNING . . . LIGHT!

Texts: Genesis 1:1 – 5, Psalm 119:105; Numbers 6:22 – 26

Good morning! And welcome! And my, my, my, what a pleasure it is to be together! And, if we haven't said it already, it's so good to see you!

This morning we're launching our Lenten sermon series focusing on the theme "Let There Be Light!" In this new series we'll consider the abundance of meanings and metaphors that light has throughout the Bible. In both the Hebrew Bible and within the New Testament, light serves as a premier symbol of God's powerful presence and abiding grace. Over the course of the seven Sundays of the Lenten journey, beginning today and continuing through Easter Sunday, April 8, we'll explore the blessings and challenges that an enlightened faith can offer to all who follow the carpenter from Nazareth, "the light of the world."

But before we get to the light, a word about Lent. In the fourth century, the season of Lent became a period of forty days set aside for prayer, repentance, and fasting for all Christians. In the year 325 CE, the Council of Nicea designated Lent as the forty-day period that would precede Easter on the liturgical calendar. The number forty is significant in the Bible. Recall that the Israelites wandered forty years in the wilderness before settling in the promised land. And then there is the poignant remembrance of Jesus being in the wilderness for forty days, fasting and praying and resisting temptation, as he prepared for the launching of his public ministry.[1]

Now, about that light. Stanley Kubrick's epic movie *2001: A Space Odyssey* begins with Richard Strauss' fanfare tone poem *"Thus Spake Zarathustra,"* since the movie and the music both have to do with origins and the immensity of mystery in the universe. The fanfare was actually entitled "Sunrise" by Strauss, and that is where we are beginning today, at the rising of the very first sunrise as the Bible records it:

> In the beginning when God created the heavens and the earth, the earth was a formless void and darkness covered the face of the deep. . . .
> Then God said, "Let there be light"; and there was light.[2]

Light is the first agenda item on God's to-do list as God creates the island home for all the creatures and critters and for the most blessed creature of all, human beings. As if God were a cosmic movie-maker, before the cameras start rolling, before the command "Action!" is given, the divine director first says, "Lights!"

And that light — emanating from the greater light — will be what moves the seasons, as the earth hurtles through space around that greater light. Its heat will cause what we've come to know as photosynthesis, so that trees and plants and flowers will be able to grow and flourish. It is from that greater light that we even receive an essential vitamin, D, for the blessing of our health.

And the lesser light, also crafted by God during earth's Edenic beginnings, the light which we now call the moon in English, will influence the movement of the oceans, their ebb and flow, the rising of tides and the shifting of the seas.

I.

The light has to come first. And a powerful thing it is! This is one of the premier points of the Genesis account of earth's creation. Without light, nothing else can flourish, nothing else can develop, nothing else can be seen or revealed. But with light, oh what wonders can be wrought!

With the light of the sun, we can see the broad horizon of the land. And when the sun is situated just right in the sky, we can also see into the deepest canyon. It is by the sensing of light that a baby first knows they're not in the womb anymore.

And without light, we are stumbling in the dark, sometimes suspended into inaction, sometimes, completely immobilized.

A thousand theories can be marshaled for interpreting why the Bible depicts God as making light first in the overall scheme of creation. And nearly all of them have some plausibility. I'll tell you what my guess is. I think—no, better put, I *believe*—God made light first because it is the most beautiful and most fitting metaphor for God's very essence and nature. God repeats an emphasis on light when he sends Jesus to enthuse and redeem a world darkened by sin and death. You'll recall what many of us heard on Christmas Eve, when John 1 was read: "What has come into being through him was life, and the life was the light of all people. The light shines in the darkness, and the darkness did not overcome it."[3]

The essence of holiness is light. This is why our children served as acolytes this Sunday, to indicate that God's very presence is real and alive.

Dale Eldred was the light sculptor who finished Frank Lloyd Wright's vision for our sanctuary building by designing our Steeple of Light in 1993. When Dale and I were first becoming friends, he told me how he came to sculpt with light. While he was in Egypt, he had an epiphany within the interior of a pyramid. He was able to enter and proceed through the deepest recesses of a particular pyramid because his guide had caught the powerful light of the sun in a series of mirrors that reflected the light throughout the chambers of the pyramid. When he came out of the pyramid, he looked up in the sky and beheld the sun and determined that he had the biggest and most powerful generator in the world at his disposal for the making of beautiful, powerful art. After that he began bending, and reflecting and shimmering light everywhere.

As we got to know each other, Dale invited me to come to his Sculpture 101 class. He invited me to do a reading about the very first sculptor in the universe, greater than Michelangelo, grander than Rodin, better than all the sculptors throughout human history rolled into one. The text he invited me to read? The creation story found in the book of Genesis.

II.

Light is also a powerful metaphor for knowledge and wisdom. The one verse from the 119th Psalm that was read this morning says that God's illuminating word of truth and wisdom is "a lamp to our feet and a light to our path." Again, light is a fitting metaphor for our spiritual journey. This is especially true as we proceed through the season of Lent. The word "Lent" itself derives from Anglo-Saxon and Old English words that point to spring and the lengthening of the daylight hours. As we proceed through Lent, we are gathering more and more light, more and more insight and, hopefully, wisdom, for our journey along the path of faith.

Now, none of us should look into the sun, lest we go blind. We can see only so much light. And if we're following the metaphor of light closely here, we might chime in and say, "And we can stand only so much wisdom, so much truth." And we would be exactly right, to say that. But have no fear, it's all right not to know all truth and all wisdom all at once. In fact, we fool ourselves if we think we can. A humbler approach is always advisable and preferable. Our taking of the truth and our handling of wisdom is like what E.L. Doctorow said: "It's like driving a car at night. You never see further than your headlights, but you can make the whole trip that way."

III.

Light is also a fitting way to convey God's holiest blessing. According to the book of Numbers, God instructs Moses to tell his brother Aaron that when worship is over, he should give the blessing benediction upon the people this way: "The Lord bless you and keep you; the Lord make His face to shine upon you, and be gracious to you; the Lord light up his countenance upon you, and give you peace." The writer of Numbers visualizes God as somehow not unlike humanity, that is, with a face. Only God's holiness shines forth from his benevolent face: "make His face to shine upon you and be gracious to you." I like the way Eugene Peterson has this verse in his *Message* version: "God smile on you and gift you." That's exactly what we all want isn't it? God's smiling countenance to bless our days and gift us with what we truly need along our life's path.

IV.

One question remains: What shall we do with this light, the powerful light of creation, the illuminating light of God's word of truth and wisdom, the precious light of God's shining, smiling blessings on our lives?

First and foremost, remember the light! Remember that light is the given. It's the way God created the world. We all experience SAD sometimes — Spiritual Affective Disorder. But please remember, God intends us to have an abundance of light—astronomically, physically, relationally, communally—in all ways and from all perspectives. We may grow dim in our views, we may become sad and sometimes even depressed, but if you will seek the light long enough, it will appear and your path can be illuminated.

Secondly, celebrate the light the way God first celebrated the light. God didn't do a victory dance in the end zone of creation and shout, "Look what I did!" He simply pronounced creation good. Seven times a specific phrase is used in the first chapter of Genesis. You remember that phrase: "And God saw that it was good." A simple pronouncement, with a strong tinge of encouragement. This is what we are called to do during Lent: to pronounce creation, and the blessings we have received from God and God's creation, good. If we spent more time describing life and its countless aspects as good and less time abiding in the toxicity of negativity and condemnation, the world might be a whole lot better place to live in. If you're going to give up anything in Lent, I urge you to cast out of your life condemning expressions and negative attitudes, especially any that relate to your family relationships and closest friends and your connections in the congregation.

And lastly, share the light! God gives us the visual aspects of light for one and all to enjoy and live by. God gives us Christ, the light of the world, freely—liberally, unreservedly, indiscriminately, you might say, —to one and all, regardless of any deserving on our part. And we are to share the light in the same manner. In Samuel Green's book of poems, *The Grace of Necessity*, most of which was composed after he had visited New York City after the 9/11 attacks, he offers a poem with the simple title of "Oct. 18 New York City," whose concluding line goes like this: "No one . . . should be lost/ when someone else knows the way."[4]

Likewise, no one needs to suffer and stumble in the darkness when someone else has some light. Whether you're harnessing the sun in a sculpture like Dale Eldred did or you're simply lighting the candle flame of your own faith, share the light! Share the light! Share the light! Share the light!

And as I said at the outset of this word in this service, by the light granted to us by a gracious God, you look wonderful this morning, and it truly is so good to see you! I love you. God bless us all.

Amen.

NOTES
1. See Matthew 4:1—2 and Luke 4:1—2
2. Genesis 1:1—3
3. John 1:3b—6
4. Samuel Green, "Oct. 18 New York City," *The Grace of Necessity* (Pittsburgh: Carnegie Mellon University Press, 2008).

26

WANNA GET AWAY?

Text: Mark 6:30–34

Good morning! And welcome to the Sunday commencement of the Lenten season!

We're launching new sermon series this morning, *The Journey to HALLELUJAH!* Over the course of the Sundays of Lent, we will explore anew the paths that Jesus followed in his life and ministry on his journey to the resurrection.

As I said on Wednesday during our Ash Wednesday services, I am firmly convinced that this year's Lenten journey will be one of the most meaningful Lenten seasons we've ever experienced, if we will but have eyes and ears and hearts and minds open and prepared to take it in.

Southwest Airlines has consistently been about having fun—the chatter and the patter before your plane takes off, during the in-flight updates about the weather at your destination, and as you roll into the gate of your destination city.

I'll never forget the time when one Southwest flight attendant sent some snacks down the center aisle on take-off. As we ascended into the air, packages of pretzels and peanuts came sliding down the center aisle.

The Southwest folks have fun not only in the air but on the airwaves. In their television commercials they've been emphasizing for a while a certain extra-special promotion with the tag-line "Wanna Get Away?"

A humiliating experience happens at work, and the voice says, "Wanna Get Away?"

A stupid dance act results in a dancer wrecking a DJ's set up, his table, his CDs, his projector, and a voice says, "Wanna Get Away?"

A guy destroys a friend's big-screen television and the voice says, "Wanna Get Away?"

Southwest has gone so far as to create a fare known as "Wanna Get Away" fare, which is priced cheaper than all their other fares.

Now the "Wanna Get Away" invitation plays on our very human need to escape from hard predicaments, to evade certain embarrassing moments, to dodge the daunting and the exceedingly difficult, to avoid the awful dimensions in our human predicament.

Have you ever experienced this kind of situation?

- You let loose a slip of the tongue at a cocktail party, and you begin imagining the Southwest voice saying to you, "Wanna Get Away?"
- You have a wreck in your brand-new car during the first week that you're driving it, and you think you're hearing that Southwest voice say to you, "Wanna Get Away?"

- You spill mustard down your magenta-colored tie at a lunch function where you're to give an important speech, and you're sure the Southwest voice is speaking directly to you: "Wanna Get Away?"

We all have known the need to escape from such embarrassing moments.

This past week I had one of those "Wanna Get Away?" moments while attending a gathering of doctors and clergy at a local hospital. We were there to hear my friend Jeff Piehler as he spoke eloquently and forthrightly about his twelve-year battle with prostate cancer. It was a magnificent time of sharing, full of Jeff's quintessential humility, brilliance, and humor. Many stayed afterward to say how much they appreciated his presentation.

After the session was over, we walked through the hospital hallways and made our way to the parking lot. As we approached my Jeep, I bragged about getting to the hospital early to snag a prime parking space near the main entrance, a rare and fine treat for me. We said our goodbyes, and I got into my Jeep. Then I watched as Jeff walked to the far side of the parking lot to the spot where his car was parked. Then the clouds overhead seemed to pipe in that Southwest voice entreating, "Wanna Get Away?" And I did. Because I knew that Jeff had arrived earlier than I had and had intentionally parked far away so as to give others a shot at the prime spots. That's the kind of human being he is and seeks to be every day, not bothering with the shallow things of life like the presumed advantage of a close-by parking space, but rather focusing on being generous and thoughtful about the needs of others. "Wanna Get Away?" You bet I did.

Sometimes we approach our faith in general and the Lenten season in particular as occasions for such escape, such evasion, such avoidance, such dodging.

Now, Jesus knew trouble and daunting difficulties. But he never did yield to the siren sounds of "Wanna Get Away?" Instead of evasion and opting out of life's difficulties, he did something altogether different.

What Jesus does in our text from Mark's gospel is instructive and inspirational. It reveals Jesus' regular spiritual practice of "retreat and release."

Jesus has been healing and preaching and moving about from his hometown of Nazareth. He has been rejected there. He has called out the twelve apostles to come and follow him. He has commissioned them, and they've gone off and done ministry in his name. He has heard of the death of his cousin John the Baptist, and he has come to a resting place. Then he instructs the apostles to "Come away to a deserted place all by yourselves and rest awhile."

These are some of the most empowering words Jesus will ever proffer to his followers. He knows better than they do that they need rest. He has keener insight into their situation than they do about their need to retreat.

Jesus had already begun to refine this inclination toward retreat. Before every major move, before every crucial campaign, Jesus usually retreats.

Retreating on his boat allowed him to be ready to meet the madding crowd when he went back on shore. He maintained his capacity to see others in their human predicament. He bolstered his capacity to have compassion for others. And he was able to teach them many things.

By retreating he was able to release immense powers for the benefit of others.

As Jesus did, so can we:

- Consider regular worship—on Sundays and on Wednesdays—as moments of retreat and release.
- Consider daily times of prayer as moments for retreat and release.
- Consider just resting, taking a nap, slowing down, listening to the world, listening to your life, as times of "retreat and release."
- Take time to be with your family and regard it as retreat and release.

The season is really very simple and straightforward, as uncomplicated and elementary as our ABC's. Consider . . .

Lent is, of course, all about ashes. That's how the journey begins, with ashes of repentance and humility on the forehead. The ashes remind us of the dust-heaps of life which too many have known for too long. The ashes also remind us of the hollowness of our material possessions and how solid are the authentic and lasting verities of Christian faith. A dusty smudge on one's forehead rekindles in us an awareness that human life is as fragile as ashes hovering in midair, adrift and fleeting in the wind. The ashes remind us to be careful and to be kind and to be ever gentle.

Lent is a time for focusing on blooms and the event of blooming. Far from being a time to be driven down into the dirt of guilt and shame—a stereotype to which we should say good riddance, once and for all!—Lent is a time for the nurturing and nourishment of the latent capacity for blooming within the human personality. A new talent discovered. A new skill shared with another in need. A gift given for the betterment of the community. A graceful present offered for a child's maturing. A kind deed done for someone in dire straits. A cup of cold water. A word of healing forgiveness. An instance of comfort. All these are seeds of God's love, which eventually comes out blooming throughout a world in need. It is seasonally appropriate and historically understandable that Lent's culmination at Easter should parallel nature's verdant blooming in springtime.

And Lent is always an interval for proclaiming and reclaiming God's compassion for a world bruised, broken, and in need of restoration.

Recall Jesus' Sermon on the Mount. Compassion.

Recall Jesus' parable concerning the Prodigal Son and the Loving Father and his parable about the Good Samaritan. Compassion.

Recall Jesus' searing invitation to his disciples that "just as you did it to one of the least of these who are members of my family, you did it to me." Compassion.

Recall one of Jesus' most haunting pronouncements from the cross: "Father, forgive them, for they know not what they do." Again, compassion.

If Lent's meaning could be thematically distilled into one substance, it would be the clear, sparkling, unadulterated essence of God's compassion for a hurting humanity.

Let us learn our Lenten ABC's anew this year with a fresh and sure purpose.

But first, "Come away to a deserted place all by yourselves and rest a while."

Hungry parents can't feed children. A dry plant bears no fruit. An overused field finally fails. And a Christian who doesn't retreat lessens and sometimes loses the power to release good for others in the name of all that is holy and right and righteous.

This year I'm taking on a new Lenten discipline: securing the parking spaces that are far away from the entrance.

Amen.

27

HANDS ON THE TABLE
Text: Luke 22:14 – 23

My strong and sincere thanks to John Tamilio for the invitation to be part of your Maundy Thursday services here at Colonial United Church of Christ. Your fame as a congregation of courage and kindness has come over our way at Community, and it is a privilege to speak from this esteemed pulpit and share worship with this good, good pastor, and fine poet. With a pastor like John and given your shared work together as people and pastor, truly brightening this corner of Kansas and indeed the Midwest, your future shall remain promising and your ministrations to one and all true blessings.

And to Jimmy Mohler and Tom and Ivy Manning, Community members extraordinaire, let me say I am delighted to see you. And I would echo – once more! – the words of Psalm 139 and also say, "Whither shall I go from thy spirit? Whither shall I flee from thy presence? If I ascend up into the heavenly pulpit of Community Christian Church, thou art there. If I make my place in Washington, D.C., thou art there. If I take the wings of the morning and dwell in the uttermost locale of Colonial United Church of Christ in Prairie Village, Kansas, even there thy hand shall greet me and thy countenance shall meet me!"

Soren Kierkegaard tells a parable of a community of ducks waddling off to duck church to hear the duck preacher. The duck preacher spoke eloquently of how God had given the ducks wings with which to fly. With these wings there was nowhere the ducks could not go, there was no God-given task the ducks could not accomplish. With those wings they could soar into the presence of God himself. Shouts of "Amen" were quacked throughout the duck congregation. At the conclusion of the service, the ducks left, commenting on what a wonderful message they had heard – and waddled all the way back home. May such a fate for us be avoided here at Colonial United Church of Christ, in Prairie Village, Kansas, today!

Nearly two thousand years after the first Lord's Supper, we still break the loaf and share the cup in remembrance of the One who let himself be broken that we might be made whole. During the enriching rituals of Holy Week, real life is shared, actual agony is experienced, and the way is finally prepared for Jesus' crucifixion and resurrection. This being Maundy Thursday, the focus for the day is, of course, the Lord's Supper. In order to experience the sacred feast of the Lord's Supper with a new sense of vividness, I want to draw our attention to the words of Jesus at the conclusion of the Lord's Supper according to Luke's account.

Luke is alone among the gospels in telling of Jesus' after-dinner speech. Luke is a skilled writer and sets up the disciples (and us twenty-first century followers) by waiting until after the institution of the Lord's Supper for the shocking revelation he will share. The subject of his after-dinner speech? Nothing comical, entertaining, or sentimental at all. It's all about betrayal. About his betrayer Jesus says, "But see, the one who betrays me is with me, and his hand is on the table" (Luke 22:21).

These are hard words to hear. Hard because they are so intimate: "with me." Hard, too, because they are so personal: "his hand." Hard, as well, because they are so insinuating: after Jesus' declaration about betrayal, the text says, "they began to ask one another which one it could be who would do this."

But I suspect these words are hard for us to hear—as hard for us to hear as they were for the first disciples to hear—because they are also true—so applicably, directly true—about all of Jesus' followers.

So let us do as Jesus suggested and see the hands on the table. Obviously, Jesus refers to Judas, for he is the one who will turn Jesus over to the authorities. Yet are there not other hands on the table, the hands of those who will also abandon Jesus in his time of need?

See Peter's hand, apparently a strong hand that makes flamboyant gestures. Yet it will shrink away in denial three times before the cock crows.

See Thomas' hand, whose sense of touch is so acute that it will numb his heart's capacity to believe until he can actually put his hand into Jesus' wounds.

See the weary hands of the disciples when they fail to remain steadfast as Jesus prays. Indeed, in other accounts of Jesus' final hours after the supper, he states that the disciples "will all fall away" and that they "will be scattered . . . and leave me alone."

But we see other hands on the table as well. A question for anyone who breaks bread in remembrance of Jesus can be "What sort of hands do I bring to the Lord's table?"

Some of us have overly pious hands, so desperately clinging to heavenly religiosity that we can do no earthly good.

Some of us have anti-praying hands, so focused on the things of this world—and all of its attendant grime and grit and grunge—that we grow exhausted and dispirited because we have not taken enough time to be with God in quiet and stillness.

Some of us have cynical, all-knowing, condescending hands. With a flip of the wrist, we dismiss the world's grossness, our leaders' grievous mistakes, and all untoward actions with a simple, "Oh, I knew that. Yeah, I could have told you that would happen. They're all the same. It's all rotten. All the time."

Some of us have our-hands-are-the-best-kind-of-hands hands, defined by the illusion of supremacy—by melanin content (or lack thereof), by youthfulness (or lack thereof), or by wrinkles and age-spots (or lack thereof)—denying all the while the truth on which Paul and the members of the early Church would stake their lives, that in Christ we are all one.

On yet another hand, some of us have indifferent hands, overestimating the power of the shadowy places in the world, and underestimating our own God-given capacities, turning away from the world, and often our lives, with a woe-is-me, what-can-one-person-ever-do shrug of our souls. And when we do this, we neglect to respond to Christ's daring invitation to grasp the illuminating power of light and goodness and hope.

Now, before we grow despondent, please know there is good news about all this hands business. Yes, we agree that Jesus refers to Judas' betraying hands, and Peter's and Thomas' and the rest of the disciples' hands, and also our own hands. But let us also remember one other fact. All those hands, all our hands, are not set forth on the Lord's table alone. Remember, remember, *remember*—for that is what this day is for—our hands are with *His* hands on the table. While our hands can betray and doubt and be overly pious and anti-prayer and cynical and exclusive and indifferent, Christ's hands are there for us. As Jesus was "the man for others," as Bonhoeffer would describe him, His hands are for us. And how wondrous those hands are: healing hands, hoping hands, honoring hands, forgiving hands, encouraging hands. Hands of generosity and welcome, hands of hospitality and justice, hands of grace and faithfulness.

So faithful are Christ's hands that we come to a new understanding of the phrase "saved by faith": we are saved by God's faith, by God's continuously renewing, resurrecting faith in God's children. And God offers Christ's precious, saving hands on the table with an ultimate purpose and hope. As Christ's hands overcame excruciating loss and pain, so shall ours. As Christ's hands triumphed over the world's negative detractors, so shall ours. As Christ's hands rose in resurrecting power to bless the world once more, so shall ours.

Thanks be to God for Christ's hands—pierced and crucified and yet soon to be resurrected—which redeem all the other hands on the table.

Prayer: We give you thanks, O God, for the broken loaf that makes us whole, for the shared cup that fills us to completeness, for accepting us as we are, hands and all.

Amen.

28

MY GOD, MY GOD,
WHY HAVE YOU FORSAKEN ME?

Text: Matthew 27:46 (Mark 15:34)

Jesus' Fourth Word from the cross is a hard and haunting word. If you're keeping tabs, you will quickly see that Luke's gospel and John's gospel are each accorded three of Jesus' "Seven Last Words from the Cross."[1] But Matthew's singular word—which is echoed in Mark 15:34—is a necessary, essential proclamation for any holistic remembrance of the first Good Friday.

One could say the Fourth Word is saturated with Good Friday and that there's barely a hint of Easter in it. Jesus utters this cry from the cross at the nadir, the rock bottom, of his experience in the midst of the crucifixion. It is almost too brutal to recall, but I feel duty-bound today to say to you, we must remember that crucifixion was a sadistic form of capital punishment.

Look as hard as you might, you will not find crucifixion in the Hebrew Bible, the Old Testament. No, it was the Greeks and the Romans who would adapt from the Persians and devise this particular mode of cruel and excruciating death-dealing reserved for the lowest rung of the empire, those without the position or the privileges of citizenship.

Stripped and scourged, hung on a cross and left to die of exposure, hunger, dehydration, shock, and the gradual withering of breath from his body, Jesus cries out.

What he cries out is something he surely learned at the synagogue in Nazareth as a boy and later when he was taught to read Hebrew. What he cries out is the first line from Psalm 22. No other scriptural text will do for Jesus as he hangs on the cross. From his treasure-trove of memories of the Psalms, what Dietrich Bonhoeffer deemed "Jesus' prayer book," Jesus retrieves the harrowing eloquence of seeming despair, speaking in his native tongue, Aramaic: "'Eli, Eli, lama sabachthani?' that is, 'My God, my God, why have you deserted me?'"

And he speaks the truth, doesn't he? He has been forsaken, abandoned, deserted, "to the nth degree," as my grandmother used to say.

Gone are the religious leaders and teachers, most of his family, his hometown folks, and the clamoring crowds.

All those robe-wearing, palm-waving congratulators, who were so full of adulation just last Sunday are now full of condemnation.

Gone, too, are his disciples, his closest followers—one of them deserting him for money; another denying he ever knew him; all of them, just as Jesus had predicted, "falling away."

On the surface of things, Christ's expression of agony may seem like a declaration of abandonment. It is that. But it is more. So much more.

That day at Golgotha some people near the cross thought he was crying out for Elijah to come to his rescue. So, someone shoved a sponge soaked in sour wine at him, as if to stimulate him so he wouldn't expire, so they could see if, magically, Elijah would do the trick and take him down from the cross.

But that was not it at all. No, Jesus's cry was so much more.

If we listen closely with our sanctified imaginations, we can discover deep and profound truths with a multitude of meanings that this fourth of the Seven Last Words conveys:

- It is the cry of God's own Son in harmony with the anguished cry of God's own children — in all places and at all times everywhere — who have known pain, oppression, and lonely enduring.
- It is the cry of Willy Loman as he moves toward his self-demise in the second act of the play *Death of a Salesman* when he says, "After all the highways, and the trains, and the appointments, and the years, you end up worth more dead than alive."
- It is the cry of sorrow that we all know when a beloved friend or family member dies and leaves a phantom absence where once a relationship thrived.
- It is the roaring of Picasso's artistic anguish in his classic painting of war's hideous gore at Guernica.
- It is the cry of pain among those caught up in war and conflict and strife around the globe — in Myanmar and Syria, in our own times, and Buchenwald, Auschwitz, Dresden in other times.
- It is the cry of those at the Port of No Return, in the Middle Passage, and along the Trail of Tears.
- It is the anguished cry from the bloodied streets of our own country and our own city.
- It is the roaring silence which engulfs a person suffering from manic depression.
- It is the roaring landslide of desolation which smothers the schizophrenic.

When my dear friend the extraordinary sculptor Dale Eldred, died, I played a recording of Jessye Norman whenever I got in my Jeep. Now my Jeep's stereo system had a special repeat function, so I could listen over and over to any song I wanted to hear again. And what I needed to hear was Jessye Norman singing "There's a Man Going Round Taking Names."

There's a man going 'round taking names.
There's a man going 'round taking names.
He's taken my father's name,
And he's left my heart in pain.
There's a man going 'round taking names.

As you know, that spiritual goes on to talk about the singer's mother's name and the singer's sister's and brother's names which are taken by that "man going 'round taking names." In the end the song reveals that Death is that man taking names.

It is a full-blown Good Friday song with nary a hint of Easter in it. There was no better song than that for my grief. I needed that song, to lament, and weep, and to fully express and experience the loss of my friend.

And there are no better words than the roaring eloquence of Psalm 22 to sum up Christ's experience on the cross: "My God, my God, why have you forsaken me?"

But note with me that there is something more in Jesus's cry than the mere expression of personal desertion, something more than despair over abandonment. Using our fine-tuned listening ears, we can hear Jesus say the word "God."

In the midst of dereliction, he still can muster the name of God.

In the midst of seeming despair, he still can utter the name of God.

Though he might sense that he's been deserted by everyone, he can still cry out the name of the One who blessed him at his baptism as God's beloved Son in whom God was well pleased.

He can still cry out to the One who inspired him to pick up the Torah scroll and read from Isaiah's prophecy: "The Spirit of the Lord is upon me because he has anointed me to preach good news to the poor."

He can still cry out to the One who received his prayer in the Garden of Gethsemane, "Not my will, but Thy will be done."

He can still say the name of God.

And not only that, but he can say "My God." Twice! *My God, my God.*

Jesus knows with utmost intimacy God's purifying love and reassuring mercy.

Jesus knows with utter trust and confidence that God will finally, eventually lay waste to all hurt and pain and sorrow.

Jesus knows God not merely as a distant Master Designer, not merely an impermeable First Principle, not merely as the Unmoved Mover, not merely as that than which nothing greater can be conceived. No, Jesus knows God as My God. *My God.*

And what, we must ask, is God's response? If we listen closely, we can begin to hear the quiet quaking, the gentle thunder of God's reciprocating response. And it may also be a challenge. If we utter Christ's famous words, "My God, my God, why have you forsaken me?" on occasion, if we listen very carefully, we may hear God's holy plaintive reply: "My children, my children, why have you forsaken me?"

But I will not speculate further on that matter.

For we must go through the rest of the Seven Words, and then pass through the silent valley of Holy Saturday, and wait . . . and wait . . . and wait, even if impatiently, for God's answer. Which I assure you will arrive, come Sunday. Yes, God's answer to Christ's anguished cry and our own — "My God, my God, why have your forsaken me?" — is surely coming!

But for now, it is enough to know that even in the midst of Jesus' horrific death, apparent desertion, abandonment, and forsakenness, he could still cry out "My God."

We, too, can do the same. In the midst of desertion, when friends let us down and family falls away, we can say "My God. In the midst of abandonment, when you're a teenager and no one seems to understand, you still can say "My God." In the midst of forsakenness, when all your plans have crumbled, when all your dreams have been shattered, when all your hopes have been dashed, when you've been forgotten, or left behind, or run over by life's brutalities, you can still cry out "My God, my God."

And as that was sufficient for our Lord Jesus, surely it will be enough for us all, for now.

Amen.

29

FATHER, FORGIVE THEM, FOR THEY KNOW NOT WHAT THEY DO

Text: Luke 23:34

Jesus was consistently and enduringly focused on the power of forgiveness to transform human life.

Through prayer, contemplation, study, preaching, and the saving actions of his three years of ministry, Jesus drank deeply from the wells of a merciful God.

There is so much forgiveness recorded in the Bible that you could say that in the class called Human Existence God gives humanity a great big fat "F" — i.e., Forgiven:

- Adam and Eve, after their disobedience in the Garden;
- Cain, after he slew Abel;
- Jacob, after he hoodwinks his brother out of his birthright;
- The brothers of Joseph after they abandon him into utter desolation;
- Moses, after he commits a raging murder;
- David, after he arranges for Uriah to die on the front lines of battle and then takes Uriah's wife Bathsheba for himself.

Yes, the Biblical witness consistently shows God giving humanity a huge "F" (forgiveness) for our performance in the class called Human Existence.

Jesus, too, majored in forgiveness.

- To the woman caught in adultery, he asks, "Where are your accusers?" And when she sees there are none, that no one did as Jesus challenged them to do — i.e., pick up the first stone — she relates how they've vanished. "Neither do I condemn you," Jesus responds, in a heroically healing moment.
- To the question about how often a righteous person should forgive, Jesus uses hyperbole and says, "Seventy times seven," or in our more common-place American vernacular, a ba-jillion, zillion times.
- Jesus gets in trouble with the religious authorities of his day not simply because he does so-called work on the sabbath, but also because he dares to declare forgiveness of sins.
- And here — in this First of Christ's Seven Last Words from the Cross — Jesus mercifully, generously utters those sacred words, "Father, forgive them, for they know not what they do." (Luke 23:34)

Jesus, too, majors in the magnificence and munificence of merciful forgiving.

A question we can ask at this point is: Why did Jesus speak this word in the context of the crucifixion? And why did the church in its wisdom choose this saying as the very first one to be uttered in services like the one we're experiencing today?

Well, first of all, forgiveness is foundational! They needed to remember that he said it. Those who were nearby and those who would follow in the days and years and centuries thereafter would need to remember that the very first word of Christ's final sayings from the cross—uttered in the midst of his suffering and agony—was a word of mercy for those who were his out-and-out enemies and those who were his dearest followers.

Jesus knew that we would need to remember that he spoke a word of healing forbearance toward his powerful opponents—the religious authorities and the brutal minions of an evil empire—and also toward those who said they would be his faithful followers.

And why did they—why do we all—need to hear such a word?

- Because every child needs a do-over.
- Because forgiveness is the glue that holds any lasting marriage together.
- Because forgiveness is the stuff of which enduring friendships are made.
- Because forgiveness is the central dynamic that helps families abide their essential quirkiness. (Remember that Anne Lamott says, "If we can learn to forgive our families in all their craziness, we can learn to forgive anybody, including even ourselves.")

Secondly, let us never forget that forgiveness means equality.

Forgiveness puts us on equal footing with others.

When we receive forgiveness and when we forgive others—knowing that we are no better (and no worse) than anyone else—we participate in a great celebration of forgiveness that Christ intended for everyone to enact.

We are all equal at the foot of the cross. As the apostle Paul puts it so powerfully in the high summit of his profound correspondence with the early church in Rome: "All fall short of the glory of God."

Aware of that reality and wanting the best possible outcomes for our earthly journey, it behooves us all to engage in humility, a deep and abiding humility in all aspects of our lives.

Thirdly, let us recall that forgiveness makes it possible for all of us to know what each and every human being has always wanted to know. Reynolds Price has said it well: "[Strange] as it is in so many parts, [the gospel of John] says in the clearest voice we have the sentence that [humanity] craves from stories: The Maker of all things loves and wants me."[1]

This is the meaning of that portion of scripture that some have called the gospel in miniature, John 3:16: "For God so loved the world that he gave his only Son, so that everyone who believes in him may not perish, but have eternal life."

Somehow, deep down inside, we all of us want to hear a clear, saving utterance from God on high: "The Maker of all things loves and wants me." And this is what Jesus utters in the first saying among his Seven Last Words from the Cross. Oh, how we need to hear it, how we need to hear it so!

One final comment about this First Word. Perhaps I've not been careful enough in my exegesis of Christ's profound proclamation in Luke 23:34. Perhaps I have leaned too hard on the word "forgiveness," with its multiplicity of meanings and the overcoming power that Christ's forgiveness has meant and can mean for a world much in need.

Perhaps it would be better to emphasize the literal "first word" in this selection from Luke's great gospel.

Perhaps I should be so bold as to affirm with you the very first word in this First Word of Christ's ultimate sayings from the cross. And what is that word? You know what it is: Father. *Abba.*

Uttering such a precious word may be what we need the most during the current COVID-19 pandemic. Crying out the name of a parent and casting ourselves into their care may be exactly what we need during the crisis we are presently enduring.

For whoever among us can intimately address God as their ultimate parent, as Jesus did, will know not only the tender touch of forgiveness, for themselves and for the world. We will also experience the embrace of hope and grace and love. Whoever can address God as Jesus did will be in intimate communion with:

the Unmoved Mover,
the Creator of the Cosmos,
the First Cause of all Causes,
the Fundamental Ground of Being,
the Legitimator of Lazarus,
the Master Designer,
the Mysterium Tremendum,
the Foundation of all that is good and gracious and holy,
the One Who spoke at the dawn of Eden, when "all legion of possibility leaned forward to become."[2]

Jesus says, "Father, forgive them, for they know not what they do."

Hearing this saying from the lips of Jesus in the depths of our hearts ultimately makes possibility possible.

This is what makes generosity generous.

This is what makes new life new.

And thus we can know that our failures need not define our future, that our past deeds need not determine our destiny.

Let it be so.

Amen.

NOTES

1. Reynolds Price, "The Gospel According to Saint John: The Strangest Story," *Incarnation: Contemporary Writers on the New Testament* (New York: Viking, 1990), p. 72.
2. A description of the Genesis creation story which I heard first from Gardner C. Taylor. The original context in which he spoke these words is now lost to the bowels of mystery.

30

LOVE ALWAYS RESURRECTS!
Text: Matthew 28:1–8

Happy Easter! It is good to see you and it is exceedingly good to share this glorious morning together.

I love Easter as a person of faith because it is always so overwhelmingly positive and gracious and good and altogether lovely. I love Easter as a preacher because the Easter message is so simple, so straightforward. If we preachers stick to its simplicity and straightforwardness, there's a better than even chance that the Easter proclamation will come out just right.

Some sermons have three points. And some of those three-pointers also throw in a poem at the end. Other sorts of sermons have different moves and a host of complicated stratagems to make them ring and sing and zing.

But the Easter message really only has one point. One simple, single point. That's all. And that one point is more than enough. The one point is this: Christ is risen. I could just stop right there and sit down. I see some sneaky glances among some of you almost, daring me to do just that! But I think I'll continue just a little while, since you all went to the trouble of being here.

Juts one point: Christ is risen. And it's actually not merely a point. It's a whole sermon. In fact, it's the first sermon preached in Matthew's gospel in the aftermath of Jesus' death, burial and resurrection. An angel utters this first sermon.

Matthew waxes eloquent in the rich details of what happened on the first Easter morning.

It was early on the day after the sabbath. By the dawn's early light – with pink and azure and magenta and orange tinting the sky, the two Mary's approach the tomb. And then there's a terrible earthquake, and an angel descends from highest heaven and rolls back the stone covering the tomb. The angel's presence is arresting: the angel looks like lightning and dresses like the snow-capped mountains. And then, as if to enjoy a kind of taunting moment, the angel sits on the stone, one knee draped over the other, nonchalantly. The guards, who were about to be demoted because they let Jesus get loose from the tomb, are dumbstruck; they tremble when they think of what God-forsaken outpost they're going to be sent to when word of their failure gets to their boss. They even appear to be dead.

Then the sermon begins. The angel opens with a word of graceful introduction, which has come to be one of the hallmarks of the Christian faith: "Do not be afraid." And then the sermon, simple and straightforward: Christ has been raised from the dead. Christ is risen!

This is the gist of the Christian path: to imagine and then to believe that transformation and grace-filled power finally win out. In other words, resurrection, in all its mysterious and confounding and illogical and irrational ways, is true. The way a baby's trusting love is true. The way a grandparent's peacefulness in the face of impending death is true. It's a very simple sermon: Christ is risen. And the theological category undergirding the entire matter? Resurrection.

I've wondered, like you have on other Easter Sunday celebrations, what the first hearers of that first sermon experienced.

Were they surprised? Oh, don't you know they had to be! The text says that even after the reassurance that they had nothing to be afraid of, they left the tomb quickly, "with fear and great joy, and then ran to tell [Jesus'] disciples" what they had witnessed. Surprised? You bet they were.

You'd be right to assume that some folks this morning right here and now are also surprised. Surprised to see how grace has worked its way into their hearts and minds and souls. Surprised to know that—despite the paucity of scientific data—resurrection is real, has authentic purchase on our lives and our understanding of how the world works.

I once was seeking to portray my absolute belief in the resurrection and its reality in my life, and the friend who was listening to my portrayal responded by saying "Really? You really believe all that stuff about Jesus being raised from the dead." "Believe it?" I responded to her, "Believe it? I've seen it!" But still my friend was surprised.

The good news of the resurrection is certainly surprising. It amazes, it dumbfounds, it enraptures in nonsensical ways. It's almost undignified, it's so disruptive! How do we make God laugh? Show God your plans. You'll be in for a great awakening, a rude interruption. Surprising indeed!

That first sermon and the good news about the resurrection were also beautiful. "Beauty is truth, and truth beauty," said Keats. And in the truth of Jesus' resurrection there was, there is, rare and fine beauty.

Maybe this is why we are all here too. Because of the sheer beauty of Easter. I don't mean merely the lilies and the pastel colors and the blossoming of the whole earth in glorious splendor. I don't really mean to emphasize the redbuds in full bloom this year, along with the tulips and the daffodils and now the dogwoods in all their holy array. No, I mean something different. I mean maybe we like Easter so much because of the beauty of its assertion, namely, that love conquers death. I mean, as we frequently intone at the beginning of our services at Community, that "God loves each and every one of you, and there's nothing you can do about it." Maybe we come here because of the sheer beauty of the way love surprisingly transforms us all in the event of the resurrection.

Frederick Buechner didn't grow up very religious. He became an instant success with his very first novel, which became a best-seller. But after his second novel suffered through less than stellar reviews, and he was pronounced as being officially in a "sophomore slump," he started going to Madison Avenue Presbyterian Church in New York City and listening to a sandy-voiced preacher named George Buttrick every Sunday. And one Sunday, on the same weekend that Queen Elizabeth was experiencing her coronation, Buttrick proclaimed that Christ is crowned in the heart of every believer in the midst of "confession, and tears, and great laughter."[1] And in that phrase, Buechner, a man who loved beautiful, lovely phrases almost more than he loved anything else, except for God and his family, found himself cracked wide open, found himself weeping in the middle of worship. Because of the beauty and the reality and the power of the story of God's redeeming power in Christ. And because of that beautiful moment, he was never the same again. Oh, yes, we come on Easter sometimes because of beauty.

But there's something else about that first one-sentence sermon: "Christ is risen." It's a game-changer. In it's surprising, beautiful way, it transforms our world. It disrupts us into new ways of being, and we are never the same, the world is never the same again. Because, if we believe the resurrection is true for Christ, then it must be true for us. Jesus said, "I am the resurrection and the life; [anyone] who believes in me, though [they] die, will live."[2] Just as Christ was resurrected, we are slated for resurrection also. And that's a game-changer.

Whenever and wherever there is reconciliation between former enemies, there's a resurrection going on.[3]

Whenever a war-torn village comes to know real peace and the families of that village, especially the children, are provided consistent opportunities for growth and flourishing, there's a resurrection going on. Whenever a surgery patient receives a new lease on life, there's a resurrection going on. Whenever a dyslexic student masters a reading or math assignment, there's a resurrection going on. Whenever a family discovers a liberating way out of dreadful cycles of poverty and destitution and is liberated into a bright new frontier of security and sufficiency, there's a resurrection going on. Whenever a child with low self-esteem finds his or her true, high value, there's a resurrection going on. Whenever our elders are allowed to share their wisdom one more time, there's a resurrection going on.

"Christ is risen!" is a real game-changer.

Now, for some folks, maybe even for some folks here this morning, this is really not very new news. You've heard this all before. The word "resurrection" and the phrase "Christ is risen!" is yesterday's news, three-day-old bread, passé. Been there, done that, got the T-shirt. And for you, and maybe for everybody else who may be jaded about the resurrection, I want to offer you an equivalency, a fresh way of putting our traditional greeting, the first sermon after the death, burial, and resurrection of Jesus. The equivalency goes like this: "Love always resurrects!" Meaning Christ is love incarnate. And the is-ness of Christ's being raised from the dead means forever, always. And risen means resurrects, present tense, not only then and there for Jesus Christ, but also right here and now, for you and me. Love always resurrects.

I suppose I'm pulling back the curtain to reveal that I really only ever have one sermon to preach: Love always resurrects.

In your quiet moments and in your more boisterous times, say it: "Love always resurrects!" When you are cultivating your faith in private and when you're sharing it with others, say it: "Love always resurrects!" When you're seeking after things that you know won't save you and then you abandon those options, and you say, "Now what?" know that "Love always resurrects!" When you've lost one of the most precious persons in all your life—to cancer, to heart disease, to diabetes, to a tragic accident—say it: "Love always resurrects!" When the one you care about is in prison, and you don't expect her out for a long, long time, say it: "Love always resurrects!" When you're out of a job, or between jobs or you hate the job you have, say it: "Love always resurrects!" When your teenage children are rebellious and won't conform to what you wisely already know they need to do, say it: "Love always resurrects!" When your parents are rebellious and don't offer enough face time and intimate talk about the things that matter to you, say it, "Love always resurrects!"

"Not for just an hour, not for just a day, not for just a year, but always." Irving Berlin wrote those lyrics for a popular song once. He could have said, "Love always resurrects." But even if he didn't say it, we can. And we can proclaim that for which those words are an equivalency: Christ is risen. Love always resurrects.

Amen!

NOTES

1. Frederick Buechner, *The Sacred Journey* (San Francisco: Harper and Row, 1982), pp. 108-109. See also Frederick Buechner, *The Alphabet of Grace* (San Francisco: Harper and Row, 1970), p. 44.

2. John 11:25.

3. I have borrowed the phrase "there's a resurrection going on" from my friend Johnny Ray Youngblood, who used it in a sermon he preached at St. Paul Community Baptist Church, Brooklyn, New York. See Samuel Freedman, *Upon This Rock: The Miracles of Black Church* (New York: HarperCollins, 1993).

ADVENT AND CHRISTMAS

31

ADVENT: TIME FOR TESTIMONY
Text: John 1:1-14

Good evening. I'm so very glad to be here, so very pleased to be part of this Ecumenical Advent Service. Many thanks to the excellent committee which has overseen this service. Please know that I am honored by the invitation.

I thoroughly enjoy the season of Advent, nearly more than any other time on the church calendar. The color, themes, traditions, and heritage associated with Advent's journey of expectant waiting is rich with possibilities for the deepening of faith and the embrace of peace and goodwill among people of faith.

The season is replete with cherishable gifts. If one were to sum up what Advent is all about, one could say that it is about a particular dynamic, a specific reality. If I were to describe that dynamic and give a succinct summation of that reality, I could use the word . . . Adventure.

This really is the root of Advent: the coming of a great, adventurous gift to the world:

- The breaking out of old ruts.
- The striking out for new territory.
- The casting off of the tired, the clichéd, the hackneyed.
- The shedding of the over-bearing, overwhelming old.
- The gift of a very new in-breaking reality, which will knock our socks off, fill our sails, set us on the straight path, put our heads on right, put our best foot forward, and help us to sing the song in our hearts that most needs to be sung!

God knows we need some new adventures this Advent. What has passed for adventuresomeness has come back marked null and void:

- Our fleeting attention span that deflates the significant and inflates the superficial.
- The war in Iraq and its increasing death toll among our soldiers and the Iraqi people.
- Our adulation of celebrity culture instead of working for a culture worth celebrating.
- Our ability to become over-fascinated with the shallow until the next bauble comes along.

Oh, for an adventure that was about something! Like anticipating the arrival of a new way of being human, and a new way of forgiving, and a new way of beginning again.

But I didn't bring that word tonight.

I could have brought the word . . . Devotion. Now this is an excellent word for Advent. Devotion is what really matters. Devotion to ultimacy. Devotion to "the least of these," to whom Jesus called us to attend. Devotion to those for whom this season does not bring much cheer – the last, the lost, the left-out. Devotion to the little baby from a peasant family in Palestine who comes to let all of us peasants – poor ones and rich ones – know the open secret: "You need not be ashamed of who you are. I love you. And if you let me, I'll work on you until you and all of the children of humanity become the children of light."

Devotion, as well, to a gospel worth possessing and being possessed by and worth proclaiming:

- Not the gospel of you're-not-so-special (which is the shadow side of the ethic of humility).
- Not the gospel of Santa-Claus-is-coming-to-town (which is the shadow side of belief in miraculous rescue).
- Not the gospel of be-afraid-be-very-afraid (which is always the stimulus for and result of a scarcity mindset).

Devotion. Good word. Beautiful word. But I didn't bring that word.

I could have brought the word . . . Vitality. Surely this could be placed in nomination for an Advent word. We are really in need of the truly vital, aren't we, as opposed to the truly death-dealing or the unholy hum-drum which is equally death-dealing, lulling us into a false sense of aliveness?

When I say vitality, I'm thinking of what Maya Angelou calls "the life that is life" – that which quickens the pulse, jump-starts the soul, hastens our engagement with what is truly worthy of our highest fidelity.

When I say the word vitality, I mean the life that is life and the life beyond life, the life that rests finally in the One who raises us up for a divine appointment with each new day, the One who implants in us our autonomic capacities – our breathing, our heartbeats – without any conscious effort on our parts.

Vitality. A good word. But I didn't bring that word.

I could have brought the word . . . Enough-ness. Here we're getting down to the nib and the nub of what Advent and Christmas are all about.

For the world and all we know are both enough and not enough.

Not enough, in and of ourselves. Not enough, on our own steam. Not enough, if we depend on our own hard drives. Not enough, if we believe the world's reckless foolishness, namely, that we can keep on careening through history like we are. Not enough, in and of ourselves, for we are not now, nor have we ever been, our own.

But yet, also enough. Enough, because the gospel of God's love is enough. Enough, because D.T. Niles is right: "One beggar telling another beggar where to get bread" is enough gospel for everyone on the planet. Enough, because we truly have enough to go around if we will stop clutching and start sharing. Enough, because God is enough, more than enough, for this world and the next. Enough-ness. Yes, a good, good word, But I didn't bring that word.

Now, I could have brought the word . . . Numinous.

The numinous is essentially what we're after in Advent. Through all the hectic pace of the holidays, the shining presence of the best truths is what we yearn to learn and re-learn.

We yearn to be like the young man in the movie *A Midnight Clear*, who, when he hears that his country has called him to serve his nation, declares, "Now my life can be about something."

The numinous—the matters of deep spiritual concern, the reach to the highest tenets of faith—those traditional Advent themes of Hope, and Peace, and Joy, and Love, and Life. Those numinous values we broadcast in shining, luminous ways in our lights both humble and spectacular.

The Numinous. An absolutely necessary word for Advent. But I didn't bring that word.

No, now that I've exhausted the acrostic progression of the very word A.D.V.E.N.T, you can see what you may have suspected all along. The word I've brought for this occasion, the essential word for us this season, the most necessary word there is for Advent begins with a T.

And that word is . . . Testimony.

This is what John's gospel says Advent and Christmas are all about for those of us who receive the Christ child. Strange that a gospel that has no nativity narrative should be so on-target about what this season is for. When John's gospel describes John the Baptist, he also gives us our job description: "There was a man sent from God, whose name was John. He came as a witness to testify to the light, so that all might believe through him. He himself was not the light, but he came to testify to the light." And we? We have been bidden by God also to be witnesses, to testify to the light, so that all might believe through that One who is the light of the world. As much as we might like to fantasize that we are, we are not the light. But we are testifiers to the light.

Now, testimony and testifying can be greatly misunderstood.

To testify to the light that is coming is *not*:

- Exempting ourselves from embodied service to the needs of the world. Testifying is not a superior way of being Christian. We are still to feed the hungry, clothe the naked, visit the imprisoned, shelter the homeless, tend to the sick, comfort the lonely.

- Nor is testifying a matter of coming to God's defense as an expert witness.

- Nor is testifying merely a way by which we mean to convert unbelievers. I don't know about you, but I've grown weary of my friends and acquaintances who tell me, "Well, Rev., I really don't believe in the kind of God I see portrayed in some churches and by some so-called religious leaders." "Well John," I usually reply, "Fred Phelps is not a representative sample of what's best in the churches." Lately I've had another sort of response. I say, "Tell me the kind of God you don't believe in, and I'll bet I don't believe in that kind of God either. Then I will tell you about the God I do believe in."

- Nor is testimony to be restricted to trying to get other people to believe what we believe. As many of you know, Thomas Long has written a quite remarkable book entitled *Testimony*. I like his subtitle, *Talking Ourselves into Being Christian*, but I would have suggested another subtitle that would have been just as good. It really should be called *How to Talk About Your Faith Without Offending Others or Nauseating Yourself*. In Long's fine book, he says "Trying to persuade other people to believe what we believe, whether it's politics, parenting, or religion, is a classic device to shore up our own uncertainty."[1]

No, the testimony which I'm urgently suggesting for our consideration is something altogether different. The testimony I mean is talking about God and our beliefs and our lives as people of faith as if we truly believe what we say we believe. Dorothy Day says it well when she humbly declares, "If I have achieved anything in my life, it is because I have not been embarrassed to talk about God."

This kind of testimony would be in synch with living out our faith as if we enjoyed it, and not as if we dreaded it, as some folks apparently do. Have you noticed that some baptized believers go around living life with a sour expression on their countenances, as if they had been baptized in an acrid brine of lemon juice laced with garlic.

What I'm talking about is this: Let us offer our testimony to the world as Long suggests, "look[ing] for places in the world where God is at work and [then] join[ing] in the activity of God": on an airplane, in a classroom, changing a diaper, repairing a faulty faucet, making dinner, sharing in a concert. Let us declare with our lives what we have said with our voices: "This is the day that the Lord has made. Let us rejoice and be glad in it."[2]

Now, our witness does not have to be grand or grandiloquent, splendid or opulently resplendent. It can be as humble and plain as a simple greeting, one person to another. And a humble, plain greeting just may be a life-saving moment.

Doris Silver died in New Zealand on November 21. Janet Carter, her daughter, my friend, and our bell choir director at Community, had visited her many times over the past fourteen months, traversing the globe to be with her in her battle with cancer. And when I called Janet on that sad Wednesday afternoon, the day before Thanksgiving, she told me a story about her mother that gave her great consolation about her mother's passing.

When Doris was a young girl, she had a hard life. Neglected, left, abandoned it seemed. And then something happened in the school she attended. One day she heard another little girl ask the teacher for a pencil. The next day Doris asked the teacher for a pencil. And then the next day, she asked for another pencil, and the next day, and the next day, and for many days thereafter. Why did she ask for all those pencils? Not because she needed them. She kept on asking for all those pencils because she wanted to hear what the teacher had said to the other little girl. "Can I have a pencil?" asked Doris Silver's classmate. "Yes, you certainly can have a pencil, my dear." Doris Silver had never had anyone say those precious words to her: "My dear." So, she asked for all those pencils and heard the teacher repeat that phrase each time, never hesitating, knowing, somehow, what Doris truly needed: to hear herself claimed and proclaimed "My dear."

When Doris heard that phrase, she was hearing one of the greatest testimonies about how God relates to the world. *My*—you are mine, you are mine. I claim you, no matter what. I will not leave you. I am here. You are mine. This is what "the word made flesh" says to the world, and this is what Doris heard about herself.

And *dear*. You are precious to me. If I define you as dear to me, it is a definition that can never be denied. You are dear to me.

This is the testimony Doris Silver heard about herself and about God. With such testimony, Doris Silver would eventually become a Christian. And she became such a believer in Christ that she would offer herself for missionary work and service to countless others. For nineteen years she was a missionary in India, always conveying to others what she had received: "My dear." She would give birth to Janet and speak that same blessed testimony to her: "My dear." Then she would adopt a little girl who had been like she had been as a little girl, left and bereft of hope. And she would bring home the little girl as a sister for Janet, and you know exactly what she said to her, don't you? Yes, that's right. "My dear."

May this Advent season be a blessing to you as you hear God declare to each and every one of us here tonight: "My dear." And may we give testimony to what we believe, as we address and engage and relate to and struggle with and care for and love each and every person we meet, with the simple salutation: "My dear."

Amen.

NOTES

1. Thomas G. Long, *Testimony: Talking Ourselves into Being Christian* (San Francisco: Jossey Bass, 2004), p. 116.
2. Psalm 116:24.

32

SHEPHERDS:
WAKING UP TO A PRECIOUS GIFT
Text: Luke 2:8 – 12, 15 – 20

Today we begin a new sermon series—*Meet Me at the Manger!*—as we consider the cast of characters who were part of the first Christmas experience. The narratives that relate the Christmas story are not uniform or in agreement. Our first message in the series focuses on the shepherds, based on Luke's account of their participation in the Nativity drama. Let us see the kinds of lives that shepherds led at the time Jesus was born and the parallels between their existence and our own contemporary experiences.

The theme of God's presence—as we find it in the shepherd's journey to behold the promise in the manger—is so obvious in Luke's nativity account. But we are rushing a bit too quickly and theologically into Luke's ultimate meaning. Let's consider the shepherds first.

Nearly 75 years ago Scribner's publishing house issued a book about Christmas entitled simply *Christmas: A Book of Stories Old and New*.[1] The stories, selected from a broad range of cultural sources, were edited by Alice Dalgliesh and illustrated by Hildegard Woodward. In the important section called "The First Christmas," Ms. Woodward depicts three figures looking upward toward a brilliant star.[2] At first glance one would think that this is the stereotypical view of the three magi "following yonder star." But closer inspection reveals that the figures are actually shepherds keeping their flocks by night, as one clearly discerns from all the sheep situated around the shepherds. And this is as it should be, and exactly as Luke's gospel has it: the first Christmas definitely had shepherds as central players in the drama surrounding Jesus' birth.

It's appropriate that a word about Jesus' birth should come to the shepherds. Surely Luke knew (and he wants us to recall) that Bethlehem is called the city of David, and David was himself a shepherd.[3]

In the stories about David's origins in the book of I Samuel, David is identified as a shepherd.

David is tending sheep when the order from Saul comes down that the king desires David to play some soothing music for him.

The story of David slaying the giant Goliath begins among the fields where David is tending his sheep.

So, the shepherds play an important role in the Christmas drama, echoing Luke's understanding of what is happening in the birth of Jesus. As Geza Vermes points out, "Luke's low-key birth narrative depicts a simple . . . rural event."[4] Luke's account of the shepherds' activities related to the birth of the

144

Savior of the world is not the sweet, romanticized image we've been led to believe.[5] In the days of Jesus' birth, shepherds had a hard life and a bad rap among folks.[6]

- They almost always lived outdoors with only a camel-hair cloak and a head veil to guard them against the weather.
- They ate only what they could carry—bread, cheese, olives, figs, dates, raisins.
- Their sole focus was the sheep: protecting them by day; rescuing them when they got lost or stuck in a dried-out gully; binding up their wounds; watching out for them at the sheepgate; keeping the sheep safe from predators.
- They not only had a hard life but a disreputable one as well. They were considered nomadic lowlifes and worse. And they were often regarded with suspicion, distrust, and dislike.[7]

And besides, they weren't very religious. Shoot, they wouldn't have known a protocol in the cleanliness code to save their lives! They had no in-depth knowledge of the intricacies of ceremonial life. And they had slim ideas about the rules, regulations, and meticulous observances required of good Hebrew folks to call themselves righteous and good.[8] In short, they were rather lacking in religious flair.

Shepherds even today are similarly cut down to a debased level, even in the collected wisdom of theological textbooks. If you try to discover what *The Interpreter's Dictionary of the Bible* has to say about shepherds, lo and behold, in all 3,954 pages of that text, you find no definitions or descriptions, only a scant reference: "See SHEEP"![9]

Yet, still, God comes first to and through the lowly shepherds.

In the first decades of the thirteenth century a strange and eccentric man created a way of life and a name for his ways in the world. His name was Francis and before too long, he would even create a movement that followed after him and his spiritual disciplines. Today, seven centuries later, we use the description "Franciscan" for those who pattern their lives after his.

It was Francis who created the very first living nativity scene (or Christmas crèche, as it is sometimes called). And it was Francis who would lower himself to the degree that succeeding generations of evangelists (including Billy Graham) would follow his example: by preaching to the animals in the field and the birds in the air. If there ever was a shepherd's" perspective on what it means to be a priest, Francis had it. In one of his early rules for his religious order he insisted, "[the brothers] must rejoice when living among people considered of little value and looked down upon, among the poor and powerless, the sick and the lepers, and the beggars by the wayside."[10]

And as the old adage goes, "God must really love poor people since he made so many of them!"

Yes, God comes to and through the lowly—to Mary and Joseph, peasants both of them, and then to those lower still, the shepherds.[11]

That the incarnation of God's very essence is coming to and through the lowly means also that God's way is a bottom-up operation and that God comes to the whole human family and not merely to a privileged few.

Because God makes the first public announcement of Jesus' birth to peasants, we know something about whom God wants to bless.

Remember that while Matthew's gospel has Jesus preaching "Blessed are the poor in spirit" (5:3), Luke's gospel records Jesus as saying "Blessed are you who are poor." (6:20)[12]

According to Richard Rohr, "Shepherds were people outside the system . . . associated with bandits, conformists, boorish and dirty folks."[13]

And please note with me that while legend has bestowed the Magi with special names (Gaspar, Melchior, and Balthasar), the shepherds don't even have Larry, Curly, or Moe! They're simply anonymous shepherds.

The word that comes to the shepherds is a divine reassurance that bolts across the entire span of human life and human history: *Do not fear.*

This is a word that we all could welcome down into the deep recesses of our souls these days!

- Retirees—Do not fear!
- Parents sending three children through college at the same time—Do not fear!
- Fans of losing professional football franchises—Do not fear!
- Those who believe they've been marginalized, stigmatized, compromised, or demonized—Do not fear!
- Those who've been devastated by hurricane after hurricane in Jamaica and Haiti and Cuba—Do not fear!

This is how we know what Christmas is really about. Henri Nouwen put it this way:

Somehow I realized that . . . good feelings . . . nice presents, big dinners . . . do not make Christmas. . . . Christmas is saying "yes" to a hope based on God's initiative. [14]

The shepherds, in their simple shepherding, were humble enough to move beyond their own fear and their own elation and to say "'yes' to a hope based on God's initiative." That's why they run to Bethlehem to see the sign they've been promised. Stuart Briscoe has correctly noted, "A shepherd has nothing to lose in recognizing his need of grace; the proud must first overcome their pretentiousness and the pull of their possessions."[15]

Because the shepherds were humble enough, they were able to wake up to surprising gifts in their lives, and they never were the same again. What were those surprising gifts? It's impossible to say for sure, but we can make some educated and imaginative guesses:

- You have to think they went back to shepherding with a different spring in their step. Maybe they even pondered what the child in the stable would become. Maybe some of them, if they were young enough, heard about how he grew up and took off his carpenter's apron and then one day took up preaching, even referring to himself as the "Good Shepherd." Perhaps they even wondered if he knew that it was the shepherds who were the first public witnesses of the good news that Jesus himself would eventually preach.

- You also have to think that, regardless of their intellectual clarity or denseness, they went back to their shepherding with a greater inclination to gaze upward at the heavens. Looking for another visitation of the heavenly host? Perhaps. Or maybe they were simply looking up at the vast canopy of the sky and seeing what scientists calculate as the 62 quintillion, 500 quadrillion stars that have been spewed across the universe. That's enough stars, you know, for each of earth's inhabitants today to have 10,416,000 stars![16]
- You'd like to think, wouldn't you, that they began to live a little more alertly, with a quickened heartbeat and a fresh engagement with their everyday lives and a keener sense of God's surprising presence made available to them and to everyone else in the world.

What were the surprising gifts to which the dumbfounded shepherds awoke?

God's presence, to be sure, in the form of a little baby who would bless humanity from the bottom up, starting with the shepherds.

That they didn't really have to fear for their lives because their lives were held in the palm of the hand of the One who made all life, who was and is and will be the real security system, the real spiritual security system, which nothing can ever disrupt, interrupt, or bankrupt.

That all those miraculous stars above their heads, above our heads, too, numerous ever to count, except by a physicist's measuring calculus—all those stars can lead us to wondering instead of wandering, to love instead of lifelessness, to the freedom of merciful joy instead of an acrid bitterness because of a lack of justice, to a fullness of the soul instead of over-eating our way to satisfaction, to the grace of each new day instead of the futility of "waiting for Godot," to future projects and dreams and journeys that make our hearts sing like the first day of creation instead of languishing in regret over what might have been.

May it be so for all of those who are shepherding their lives and the lives of others along the human journey, whether or not they know anything about sheep.

Amen.

NOTES
1. Alice Dalgliesh, ed., Hildegard Woodward, illus., *Christmas: A Book of Stories Old and New* (New York, Scribner's, 1934).
2. Ibid., p. 85.
3. Richard A. Jensen, *Preaching Luke's Gospel* (Lima, Ohio: CSS Publishing Co., 1997), pp. 30–31.
4. Geza Vermes, *The Nativity: History and Legend* (New York: Doubleday, 2007) p. 92
5. Richard Rohr, *The Good News According to Luke* (New York: Crossroad, 1997), p. 84.
6. Kaari Ward, ed., *Jesus and His Times* (Pleasantville, NY: Reader's Digest, 1987), p. 23.
7. Stuart and Jill Briscoe, *Meet Him at the Manger* (Wheaton, Illinois: Shaw Books, 1996), pp. 99–100.
8. William Barclay, *Luke* (Philadelphia: Westminster Press, 1975), p. 23.
9. George A. Buttrick, ed., *The Interpreter's Dictionary of the Bible,* (New York, Abingdon, 1962), vol. 4, p. 325.
10. John V. Kruse, compiler, *Advent and Christmas: Wisdom from St. Francis of Assisi* (Liguori, Missouri: Liguori, 2008), p. 88.
11. Marcus Borg and John Dominic Crossan, *The First Christmas: What the Bible Really Teaches About Jesus's Birth* (New York: HarperOne, 2007), p. 48.

12. Ibid.
13. Rohr, p. 84.
14. Henri Nouwen, *The Road to Daybreak*, quoted in Judith A. Bauer, compiler, *Advent and Christmas: Wisdom from Henri J.M. Nouwen* (Liguori, Missouri: Liguori, 2004), p. 50.
15. Briscoe, p. 100.
16. I'm grateful to Forrest Church for first guiding me to this overwhelming fact.

33

WHAT THE MAGI SAW
Text: Matthew 2:1–12

Welcome, travelers! And even though the big day is ten days away, because you are here tonight and may not be here on December 25th, Merry Christmas!

And even if you are here on December 25th or tomorrow and every day thereafter, even if we see each other multiple times a day, as the Community staff will, it's still meet and right and good to say, "Merry Christmas!" and to say it often and with glorious holiday gusto. We really can't get enough of Christmas, of the Christmas music, of the Christmas cheer, of the Christmas story, of the Christmas love. So, "Merry Christmas!"

But a special "Merry Christmas" for all of you who are here this evening because you're going to be traveling away from Kansas City in the next week or so.

The story of Christmas is really a story about travelers.

Mary and Joseph traveled from Nazareth to Bethlehem and eventually all the way to Egypt to flee Herod's minions.

Herod's minions traveled from Jerusalem to pierce through every new baby crib in Bethlehem and all through Judea to slay the little one they had heard would de-throne King Herod.

The shepherds traveled from their places in the fields to a feeding trough in a stable cave so they could witness what a traveling multitude of the heavenly host told them would happen.

And the multitude of the heavenly host? Just think of how far and from whence that band of angelic voices traveled!

But I suppose the Christmas Eyewitnesses who are the most famous travelers are the Three Magi, the Three Kings who, "bearing gifts . . . traverse afar." They account for the origins of our gift-giving traditions and, one can suppose, the idea of traveling great distances to see family and friends, as well as the theological tenet of inclusion, namely that Christmas was and is for everybody.

Not much is really known about the actual magi. They weren't kings, though "We Three Kings" is one of our favorite songs of the season, particularly when we get to that big turn in the road and sing "Ooooooohhhh, star of wonder."

They have been described as Zoroastrian astrologers, as wise men (which is pretty much what *magi* means). They have been granted legendary names: Caspar, Balthasar, and Melchior. Some commentators have speculated that they came from different homes of origin. In Spain it's understood that each one represents a different continent: Caspar Asia;

Balthasar, Africa; and Melchior, Europe. They're almost always depicted in paintings and drawings as riding on camels. How else would great men of prestige and supposed wealth come to lowly Bethlehem but by revving up their camels and putting them into fifth gear? Even though the number of magi are not specified, we usually say three wise men because of the three gifts they present to the Christ child: gold, frankincense, and myrrh.

But I've often wondered, what did they see as they came from such great distances, possibly over a stretch of two years, to stand illuminated underneath that strobing star of wonder? What did the eyes of these Christmas Eyewitnesses really see?

Surely they saw the sign of a star. The star is almost a Christmas character itself, isn't it? It's a light of beauty, not unlike the beams we're going to see at the conclusion of this service, as we celebrate the 16th anniversary of the Steeple of Light being fulfilled here at Community. Mysterious beauty. That's surely what they saw and what kept them traveling in the beam's glow. It was a star of wonder, too. Wonder and awe, the kind that causes your body to slip into endorphin rush and your pulse to quicken, all at the same time.

But, most surely, they saw the star as a sign of some significant thing that would happen in their lives and in the life of the world.

Like the Wise Men of the nativity, we, too, are steered according to certain gatherings of holy light. But whereas they had one, we have several. Within the constellations of our skies, there are at least the following.

The Star of Beauty. In a world which is frequently full of ugliness, cruelty, and the unseemly, there is need for an affirmation and appreciation of that which brings a touch of the beautiful to our lives. So, linger a bit more at the site of beautiful Christmas lights, stay a little longer by the crackling fire at your hearth, rock a bit longer in the rocking chair with a child, squeeze a little longer the hand of the one you cherish, stay a little longer at the dinner table when the conversation sparks warm memories and hilarious laughter.

The Star of Wonder. In a world which is frequently full of the dull, the mundane, and the cynical, there is a need for cultivating the capacity for wonder. Wondering does not mean reflecting superficially on strange occurrences, or walking around in a haze, or gazing blandly off into the wild blue yonder. Rather, wonder consists in those poignant moments when mystery is made plain, when your heart is broken and made whole in the same instant, when the mystique of birth and the mystery of old age cause a smile to come upon your face.

The Star of Longing. In world which is frequently full of resignation, dolor, and apathy, there is a need for the experience of longing. Desiring, yearning, striving, hankering, wanting, craving—all these are moments of longing. And yet the experience of longing is so much more. Longing is that feeling you get when you know you need a place to go home to, when you see the world as it is and imagine the world as it could be, when you posit possibilities for growth and change in your life and you begin to see some of them come into being, when you wait to hear about a new job prospect, when God is coming to visit you, when God's love is about to be born within you.

Like the magi, we are all looking for a sign. But sometimes we aren't as daring or as bold as the magi were in seeking after it. This Christmas, I urge you to risk looking for a sign of God's grace—a sign of beauty, wonder, longing—in your life. Risk the possibility that God will discern your wish, your wanting, your unspoken desire for a sign of something holy and good and altogether precious to be revealed to you.

Surely the magi also saw each other. Now, that might not seem like a lot, but when you travel together over such a long distance, the sights you see the most are the persons you're with. And seeing each other for so long, with such forbearance and still maintaining a focus on your ultimate mission, may just be an occurrence approaching the status of miracle.

Now, seeing each other can be difficult. It was so on a mission trip once between two folks I'll call John and Tom. I was preparing coffee on a Tuesday morning, the second day of the trip, when John announced to me, "If you don't take care of Tom, I'm going to bust! I just might explode! And not in a Christian way!" John and Tom couldn't see each other. They really couldn't. Sometimes it's extremely difficult simply to see each other when you share close quarters on a long trip together.

Seeing each other, truly seeing each other, can be a gift of the first magnitude. And this the Magi gave to one another, and to the Holy Family, along with gifts of gold, frankincense, and myrrh.

The Gobledales gave this kind of gift to the people they served. Disciples of Christ missionaries Ann and Todd Gobledale and their two children, Thandiwe and Mandla, once served fourteen rural congregations in KwaZulu, in the former Natal province of South Africa. When they first arrived, the novelty of their white features drew interest and curiosity from their black parishioners. After a while, the Gobledales wondered how they were being received as the new pastors among the KwaZulu congregations.

One of the elders told the Rev. Ann Gobledale, "The people here like you, because you see them."

"What do you mean? How do we see them?" asked Ana.

"You don't regard them as invisible," replied the elder. "The people of these KwaZulu hills know that you see them as real people, because you wave to them as you walk among them and when you pass along the road in your car. Rarely, if ever, have the white people who have lived around here done that."

"You see them." This is what the magi did. They saw each other. They beheld the precious nature of the other magi and continued on their journey. They saw the Holy Family for the precious trio it was. They saw Herod and his legions for the fear-saturated murderers they were.

What if we saw each other, I mean really saw to the core of one another's essence, in all our glorious variety and splendor? It surely would be a blessing to each of us and to the world.

Surely the magi saw God doing a new thing in another way, by another power, according to another plan, different from any other they had ever beheld before. Isn't this the gist and grit of Christmas, that God is doing something new, not only in a manger in Bethlehem, but in our hearts and souls and among us and between us? What might God be doing to us, to us fifty here or to 700 million travelers around the world, coming from the east and the west and all points in between? Could it be that God is always right there on the edge, in other places and other realms, always waiting for us to go by "another route"? That's the way Eugene Peterson translates the final verse of the magi's story in Matthew's gospel: "So they worked out another route." Or, as the Revised Standard Version has it, "they departed to their own country by another way." Another way: that's God's way.

Instead of any old normal way, another way: peace.

Instead of hunger, another way: fullness and satisfaction for every child upon the face of the earth.

Instead of lack of imagination, another way: creativity and strange new ways of doing things.

Instead of the same old rut (which is really just a grave you walk around in), another way: doing something brand-new.

Instead of hackneyed triteness, another way: profound truths spoken boldly and powerfully.

Instead of violence, and the silence that reinforces and allows violence to continue, another way: voicefulness and courage to speak truth to power and to say what needs to be said.

Now of course, the main questions for us travelers do not merely pertain to what the magi saw when they traveled. Rather the main questions are: What will we see? Will we see a sign? Will we see beauty, wonder, longing? Will we see each other? Will we see another way by which to make our way home?

A big part of my heart has every confidence that those kinds of sightings are exactly what we—each and every one of us—not only need to see but want to see and will see in our lives and in the world this Christmas. May it be so!

Amen.

34

JOY?
Text: Psalm 30:5

Today is Gaudete ("Rejoice") Sunday on the Christian calendar, and thus we have lit the Joy candle on our Advent wreath.[1] But neither a candle nor a traditional distinction for this day can erase the immense grief that courses across the land this morning. It seems somehow out of place, surreal almost, to rejoice on the Sunday after the tragedy in Newtown, Connecticut, just a mere two days ago, when twenty children and six adults were gunned down by Adam Lanza, who also killed his mother before turning one of the three guns he was toting on himself.

Instead of rejoicing, a more appropriate focus for this day could be the traditional expression of sorrow originally from the book of Jeremiah: "A voice was heard in Ramah, wailing and loud lamentation, Rachel weeping for her children; she refused to be consoled, because they are no more." This is even appropriate in the telling of the Christmas story in Matthew's gospel, as Matthew uses that quote from Jeremiah to describe the response to Herod's murderous ways "in and around Bethlehem" after the birth of Jesus, "kill[ing] all the children . . . who were two years old or under."

And if we do express lamentation then perhaps let's say, at least, "Lord have mercy."

Lord have mercy upon the families of the twenty children and six adults who were killed by Adam Lanza, who earlier killed his mother, before also killing himself:

Charlotte Bacon, age 6
Daniel Barden, age 7
Rachel Davino, age 29
Olivia Engel, age 6
Josephine Gay, age 7
Ana Marquez-Greene, age 6
Dylan Hockley, age 6
Dawn Hochsprung, age 47
Madeleine Hsu, age 6
Catherine Hubbard, 6
Chase Kowalski, age 7
Jesse Lewis, age 6
James Mattioli, age 6
Grace McDonnell, age 7
Anne Marie Murphy, age 52
Emilie Parker, age 6
Jack Pinto, age 6

Noah Pozner, age 6

Caroline Previdi, age 6

Jessica Rekos, age 6

Avielle Richman, age 6

Lauren Rousseau, age 30

Mary Sherlach, age 56

Victoria Soto, age 27

Benjamin Wheeler, age 6

Allison Wyatt, age 6

Plus the gunman's mother, Nancy Lanza, age 52

Plus the gunman, who killed himself, Adam Lanza, age 20

Lord have mercy on the rest of the children in Newtown and all of our children, here and everywhere, as we seek to console them with the reassurance that life is going to be all right, and we will do all in our power to protect them and keep them safe.

Lord have mercy on the first responders, normally police officers and firefighters and other service personnel who consistently and compassionately put themselves in harm's way on our behalf; in the case of Newtown, it was the principal, Dawn Hochsprung, and Mary Sherlach, the school psychologist, who proceeded toward Adam Lanza seeking to stop him. Who knows how many lives they saved by their sacrifice.

Lord have mercy on all our communities and our nation as we grow weary of the seemingly incessant onslaught and too-frequent expressions of ravaging violence in our culture. Statistics may show a rise or a decline in the number of violent deaths caused by murderous rampages by persons with twisted minds and broken souls who have succumbed to the more horrific demons of their nature. But it is sheer willful ignorance to evade the violence over which we exuberate in our media, our entertainment, and social fabric. Lord have mercy on us as we seek better solutions than we've achieved up to this point.

Lamentation and "Lord have mercy." Both of these are right and meet to do, as we express our sorrow and as we try to relieve the pain visited upon our American family once more through mass violence enacted by a deranged person whom we could not stop in time before his raging rampage caused (and still causes) so many tears.

And there is another response we can have as well. It is to remember that the God of our lives is not unfeeling or distant from our pain. Psalm 30:5 reminds us: "Weeping may tarry in the night, but joy comes with the morning." Even in the midst of horror, God hopes that we will reach out with courage for the joy that awaits us.

And so, even though we are contending with the ravaging horror from Newtown, let us note that we are approaching the fulfillment of Advent's expectations and the arrival of Christmas, including the joy that awaits us. One could say that it is a moral duty to cling to the possibility of joy for our children, indeed for all children, and for ourselves, for our world. In response to that moral-duty claim, allow me to suggest the following emphases for joy in your life and the life we share together:

- Look at the faces of children as they joyfully play at school or at home or frolic in the stores looking for presents for parents and grandparents and siblings and friends.
- Look at the faces of our elder friends as they remember Christmases past and the treasure that family gatherings are for them.
- Look at the faces of new parents as they bring their newborn children to worship services, particularly on Christmas Eve this year. They truly bear an objective-correlative experience of what the Christmas ideals are all about.
- Look at the faces of friends and family — and imagine what your own face is like — as you join together for the singing of some of the most inspiring music ever composed in the history of humanity.
- Look at the faces of strangers you see — at work, at play, at school, in stores, on the street — and no matter how dire their struggles, deep beneath their facades, they will show a hunger for the same joy which you too desire.

Frederick Buechner put it this way: "God created us in joy and created us for joy, and . . . even when we cannot believe . . . even when we feel most spiritually bankrupt and deserted, God's mark is deep within us. We have God's joy in our blood."[1]

If we look and see and appreciate and exult in all the hope and gladness and hunger for joy which all of those faces reveal, then we can answer the daunting question of how to affirm the theme of joy in the face of the tragedy at Newtown. "Weeping may tarry in the night, but joy comes with the morning." May that morning come, full and shining and soon. Let us cling to that hope, that promise from God's generous heart of grace.

NOTE
1. Frederick Buechner, The Longing for Home: Recollections and Reflections (New York: HarperCollins, 1996), p. 128.

35

A CHRISTMAS OF FIRSTS
Texts: Luke 2:1 – 20 and Matthew 2:1 – 12

For many folks this will be an unusual Christmas. This year's holiday season will mark a "first Christmas" sort of Christmas experience for them.

For some folks we know, this will be the first Christmas they've spent away from that place they've normally and traditionally called home. For our clergy residents, Melissa St. Clair and Kevin Snow, this will be true, and it will be interesting to hear about how they will experience Christmas here in their new home in Kansas City.

For some folks we know, this will be the first Christmas they've spent in a new place, even if they've lived in their new place for several years. This will be true for Trent and Jan Jones, who, for the first time ever in their married life, and in connection with their family of faith here at Community, are absent from this service this evening. As Jan said to me a couple of weeks ago, "This will be the first Christmas I will not wake up in the home I grew up in, in Anthony, Kansas. This will be the first Christmas we've ever attended Community's Christmas Eve services on Christmas Eve. This year, for the first time, I will wake up with Trent and Ella on Christmas morning in our home in Lee's Summit."

For others we know, this will be the first Christmas after the death of their beloved or after a lost friendship or a divorce.

For some, among the families within Community's family of faith, this will be the first Christmas they will not have to worry about the fate of their sons and daughters because they've come home from Iraq and Afghanistan. For others, here and in countless other places across the country, this will be the first Christmas that such worry has set into their souls because, for the first time, their sons and daughters are not here, not home, and not nearly safe enough to satisfy their families.

For some in our congregation, like the Cychols, the Greenwoods, and the Kays, this will be the first Christmas they wake up – in an intentionally leisurely fashion, I might add – with a baby in the home.

For some folks we know, this will be the first Christmas they can ever remember when they didn't have a job, having recently been laid off, or let go, or whatever euphemism companies use to describe what they do in their downsizing actions in this tough economy.

On the more pedestrian side of things, this will be the very first Christmas without Carl Peterson at the helm as president of the Kansas City Chiefs. Whether you are experiencing ultimate glee because of this fact or this fact escapes you altogether as important or significant, for many Kansas

Citians this will be the first time in twnety years when the future of their hometown football team is even more uncertain than usual.

For Republicans this will be the first Christmas season in a while when they are not anticipating one of their own reascending the heights of power in Washington D.C., but instead, will join Democrats and Libertarians and Green Party folks and the ever popular "None of the Above" in anticipating the swearing in of the first African-American, President-Elect Barack Obama, as the holder of the most powerful office in our nation and indeed, at this time in global politics, in the world.

As I said, this year's holiday season will indeed mark a "first Christmas" experience for many.

You'd think that such was the case with the actual first Christmas in Bethlehem. To our modern ears, without knowledge of similar stories from that time and before, it sounds as if the shepherds were the first ones ever to wake up to the surprising gifts of God's grace. But other shepherds, like David, had known of God's merciful character and saving power.

We assume that the magi were the first to ponder curiously after the meaning of a bright star and that the bright light as described in Matthew's and Luke's gospels was the first to ever guide searchers and seekers after the divine. But ancient history, not to mention legend and lore, speaks of untold legions of soothsayers, necromancers, and wizards who have sought after something holy by lights from above and beyond.

You'd think it would be a safe bet that the weary world of Palestine was the first and premier place awaiting the long-expected Messiah. But other places and times and peoples have also cried out plaintively "Is this the one? Is this one going to be the saving presence? Could it be that this one will bring us deliverance?"

So where is the sense of "firstness" in the first Christmas? What's so distinctive and special about Bethlehem's babe for religious-leaning residents of the twenty-first century?

The "firstness" of God's gift of Christ to the waiting world is found in how so many "firsts" accrue to Christ's identity, life, and mission.

In Christ we will see for the first time how a Messiah subjects himself to be baptized, to bear in his own life the humbling ritual of submission to a set-apart way of life.

In Christ we will see for the first time a Messiah and his cousin conjoin to do ministry together.

And it will be in Christ that we behold for the first time how all demographic groups and all age groups and all ethnicities of all sorts of folks are unconditionally loved.

It is in Christ that we hear how the "firstness" of life is not all it's cracked up to be: "[the] first shall be last, and the last shall be first."[1]

It is in Christ's challenging teaching to James and John that we see that "firstness" has to do with being supreme in service, highest in helping others, the pinnacle of proffering one's life for another in need.[2]

And it is in Christ, year after year, season after season, here and elsewhere, whether in a new first home or a tired old one, that we see that the real Christmas "firstness" has to do more with the gifts of God's love in Christ and what it will first do with and to us.

Could it be that this is why we clamor eagerly back to the manger each year, to see if God can do a miracle in us, in the manger of our hearts, and make us brand-new, and that we will know it for maybe the very first time in our lives?

Could it be that we'd like to see God touch us with mystery and help us to know life at its savory best, in all its splendor and wonder, like we once did? Like we did when we took our first steps, or tasted barbecue for the first time, or were baptized, or tasted the sacrament of communion for the first time?

Could it be that we hover over a manger not only to reaffirm that Christ is born in the world once more, but to welcome the birth of God's love in our lives, awaking us to the "real reality" and a non-hackneyed understanding of "the first day of the rest of our lives"?

So, let us consider how this year's Christmas can be a first-time encounter. Or at least as we'd like it to be. Because we all want to be, we all need to be, made brand-new. And we all are seeking some new first-hand manner and method by which to head out into some fresh new existential territory, not to secure first-place status, alluring as that might be, but to know the truth of T.S. Eliot's words in "Little Gidding" at the end of his monumental *Four Quartets*:

> And the end of all our exploring
> Will be to arrive where we started
> And know the place for the first time.

May we each know Christ's loving presence in a first-time way this Christmas, and in the midst of a Christmas of firsts may the first thing that leaps from our lips be that which God pronounced in the form of a little baby in Bethlehem: "I love you."

I love you, and may God bless us all this Christmas. jmAmen.

NOTES
1. Matthew 19:30.
2. See Mark 10:35-45.

36

THE ANGELS' JOURNEY OF LOVE
Texts: Luke 2:1–14

There is something about angels that is absolutely comforting and reassuring to us all. While we can never give an adequate report as to how angels do their work, or the ontological essence of angel-ness, there is something reaffirming, one could almost say sheer grace, whenever we see them depicted.

No one can ever forget the bumbling Clarence in *It's a Wonderful Life.* In this sentimental favorite by Frank Capra, you'll recall that small-town banker George Bailey (portrayed by James Stewart) considers ending it all as his life lurches toward financial ruin. But he finds a reason to live when Clarence, his guardian angel, shows him what the world would be like if he'd never been born. Now, there's something in it for Clarence, too, since if he can save George, Clarence will get his wings, and a bell will ring.

Neither can anyone forget the specter angel in Tony Kushner's *Angels Over America* who compels our compassion and a holy rage about what is happening to those affected by HIV and AIDS.

At our house, the Christmas tree is not completely trimmed until the cardboard angel sits atop our green beauty.

Angels, angels, angels, everywhere. And of course, they're here on Christmas Eve. Our text from Luke declares that angels made a journey of love. And within Luke there is once again something about angels that is absolutely comforting and reassuring to us all.

The Psalmist had hinted at these angels when he declared: "[W]hat are human beings that you are mindful of them . . . . Yet you have made them a little lower than the angels" (Psalm 8).

The New Testament book of Hebrews inspires us always to show plenty of hospitality to strangers because, who knows, we may just "entertain angels unawares."

I believe that the most comforting and reassuring aspect of Luke's angels, and the angels that come and visit the magi and Joseph in Matthew's account of the nativity, is the announcement they bring about God's gift to the world. It is all about love.

Love truly is at the heart of Christmas. Love compels the church's great music to gravitate toward expression at Christmas time. Love moves us to coo with warm affection when parents bring their babies before the congregation for blessing and dedication during this precious season. Love inspires us to act in congruence with our best selves, causing even the crustiest souls to become kind and gentle and generous.

159

Love is the motivation and destination behind all our preparations and traditions during this sacred season. Love is what warms our homes and our hearts even in the middle of winter's icy chill.

Love is tough resistance in the face of any thing or force which would bruise or hurt or harm. Love is the peace that abides when we let go of old habits and outdated conventions that hinder creative growth in our individual and collective lives.

Love is baking a pie, writing a note, praying a prayer, organizing a worthy project, sitting in silent vigil at the bedside with patient, earnest hope. Without love, such caring acts become mere drudgery.

Love makes all things complete. Love is telling children of your joy in them, complimenting someone about a new haircut, expressing thanks for someone's unique talents. Without love, such transactions are mere rote rituals or, worse, sham-filled facades.

Love abides when we vigorously challenge one another to live out our highest ideals. Love is made manifest in the zip of an octogenarian's steps as she paces the mall with gladness and glee. Love is undeniably front and center in the face of any child of God who is unafraid to tell the truth.

Love is generative, moving us to seek and to offer forgiveness when estrangement has occurred.

Love is supportive, prompting us to provide sheltering kindness for the least, the lost, and the lonely among us.

Love can be discovered in the midst of everything the church does during Christmas time:

- in the transcendent music of the choir as it proffers magnificent, healing presentations;
- in the words of scripture, which prompts contentment, remembrance, and earth-shaking insights about the possibilities of new life;
- in the prayers of elders at table;
- in the sharing of communion with friends, family and strangers;
- in the sacrificial giving that is rendered for a world in need.

Love, God's love, love as it has been given to the world through the birth of a baby in Bethlehem long ago, love as it is being given to new hearts even now this evening—all this love constitutes the reason for the season.

Now the love which the angels foretell has three wondrous and yet strange aspects. It is first and foremost an extravagant love.

The angels proclaim the good news of great joy to the shepherds, one of the least prominent, least significant, least prestigious groups of Judean culture at the time. "Unto you," the angels proclaim.[1] And of all the people in the world to whom they could announce the "good news of a great joy," their offer of the grace of God's gospel of love is to the shepherds.

As Hal Luccock used to say, "The best gifts of love, are those that show a lovely lack of common sense."[2] And this gift of the Messiah for the likes of shepherds is totally lacking in common sense.

I once heard a comedian speak about Christ's extravagant love, that which Christ would show in his adult years, particularly at the crucifixion. The comedian said that Christ's being born, and then living, teaching, healing, and then being willing to die for all the sins of the world was truly extravagant. The comedian said, "That's what I call picking up the tab for the whole table." I think the comedian would agree: God's extravagant love in the birth of Christ is totally lacking in common sense.

The angels also tell about a love that upsets our expectations. This is the heart of the Christmas message about God: "The essence of God is not power but vulnerable love."[3]

This is what the angels declare to the shepherds: "This shall be a sign for you: you will find a babe wrapped in bands of cloth and lying in a manger."[4] Nothing like what they may have been led to believe a Messiah should be like. Nothing like what the traditions had taught them and countless others in Israel's tradition about how ultimate power is given expression.

Lastly, note with me that this love of which the angels tell is a reassuring, unconditional love.

The angel begins the heavenly declaration with the words, "Be not afraid."[5] The same as the angel Gabriel spoke to Mary. The same as the great "I Am" would have us hear and receive this evening.

The multitude of the heavenly host closes the proclamation with the words "and on earth peace good will among those whom he favors."[6] Peace.

And please see that there are no conditions, no qualifications no hair-splittings about the announcement. It is proffered straightaway, with reassuring unconditional love.

Two great, loving, unconditional reassurances: "Don't be afraid." "Peace."

Whenever Christmas comes around, I go to the Blaisdells. Maybe not literally, but figuratively and imaginatively and spiritually, at the very least. Their home became a welcoming haven, and ultimately my home, at various crucially significant stages of my life, and most especially at Christmas.

I recall spending several Christmases in the warmth of their home in Ft. Worth during the halcyon days of college. And I can remember like it was yesterday, one holiday time during my graduate school tenure, driving in the dead of night from Nashville to Ft. Worth, through wretched weather, enduring one of the wheels literally falling off my car, just so I could be in the Blaisdell's living room on Christmas morning.

Chuck Blaisdell remains one of my dearest friends on the face of the earth. We've known each other since the topsy-turvy days of high school CYF conferences. When I arrived at TCU in Ft. Worth, it was through Chuck that I met his parents Hazel and Dick, and their home would become a joyful dwelling place for me.

Sunday afternoons at the Blaisdells meant the Dallas Cowboys and brisket. Thanksgiving meant turkey (and at least a week's worth of turkey soup) and games of Risk and Monopoly until the wee hours. And Christmas meant grace and comfort and cherry tarts. (To this day, cherry tarts are a necessary portion of my personal Christmas rituals.) And the blustery days of the Super Bowl weekend meant chili and a persistent debate about which of the Cowboys teams was the greatest of all time.

In time, Chuck's brothers Jim and Greg would also become like brothers to me. And despite time and distance, I cannot imagine anything I would not do for Chuck or his brothers if they asked me. (I would echo Jacob's sentiment when he embraced Esau: "Truly to see your face is like seeing the face of God, with such favor have you received me.")

It was Hazel and Dick, as I said, who provided the strong, mysterious, and lasting attachment to Christmas for me. Among all the wonderful people whose hosting I have been privileged to enjoy, the Blaisdells were and remain the ultimate expression of what Christmas is all about: a treasuring of simple, lastingly good relationships, good events, good food; mercy and jubilation at the daily gifts life brings to one and all; and warm, unconditional love.

Their affectionate affirmation was always abiding and gracious. Their joyous gratitude was always deep and profound. And their hospitality was irrefutably genuine.

I guess the way I would put it these days is as follows: the Blaisdells made a place for me in their hearts and their home, and because of their tender mercies, I was born anew.

How was and is that possible? Because of the blessing of unconditional love.

What I received from the Blaisdells I would call "Blaisdell Blessedness" —as beautiful as new fallen snow, as exquisite as a baby's smile, as essential for a fully developed life as the air we breathe. Whatever you name it— Brown Blessedness, Driscoll Blessedness, Muiller Blessedness, Allen Blessedness, Thomas Blessedness, etc. —I know it surely must be as blessed and crucially essential to you as the Blaisdell Blessedness was and is to me.

I hope and pray that everyone here this evening—as well as all our friends and visitors and acquaintances, too—may experience some good portions of Blaisdell Blessedness. For me, it is one of the best ways I know of to get close to a certain manger in Bethlehem.

And now, because Reinhold Niebuhr is right[7]—that on Christmas Eve we want poetry more than we want prose—allow me to offer the following gift, as my custom has been for the past fifteen years, a new poem entitled "Decembered Mercies."

On Januaried ground we stand
with twin-faced hesitation:
to return to the other pasture
or to plow new ground ahead.

A Februaried love is followed quick
with the ides of March and Marched ideas
that then birth cruel Apriled new growth and
and its unrepentant rains.

We swing around poles Mayed with ribbons and
revel in Juneteenthed freedom.
Our summer lows are summer hot,
accompanied by the fires of Julyed skies.

The Augustian days bring new resolve,

just as Septembered school days
lead into Octobered frosts, followed by
the deeps of Novembered nostalgia.

Then the best, the healing, the most pristine comes:
amidst landscapes of blue-tinted ice and snow,
silenting all but the fall of more snow, snow on snow,
and the gift of vulnerable love in the straw.

This is the time for Decembered mercies –
a baby born, instead of the boots of the tramping warrior;
a new light of peace when all was thought to be forsaken;
fresh furrows for any who had quit the cultivation.

This is the season for Decembered mercies –
forgiveness for what was thought to be unredeemed;
the taste of fresh bread and new wine;
a sprig of hope on a stump left for dead.

This is the moment for Decembered mercies –
embraces instead of harming,
kisses instead of wounding;
love made real, undying, without qualifying,

This is the song for Decembered mercies –
angel voices to shepherds' ears:
morning by morning new mercies to see;
blessings all yours, with ten thousand beside.

May you know an abundance of "Decembered Mercies" tonight and
every moment hereafter. Merry Christmas! I love you. AMEN.

NOTES
1. Luke 2:11
2. As cited by John Buchanan, "Extravagant Love: Vulnerable Love," *The Christian Century,* December 11, 2007, p. 3.
3. Ibid.
4. Luke 2:12
5. Luke 2:10
6. Luke 2:14
7. Reinhold Niebuhr, "A Christmas Service in Retrospect," in *Essays in Applied Theology* (New York: Meridian, 1959), p. 29.

MYSTERIOUS STRANGER IN THE STRAW
Texts: John 1:1–14

Welcome! And Merry Christmas! We're so glad you're here tonight.

If this is your first time to be in Community's sanctuary, we're so glad you chose to be in this place. We hope we'll see you again

If you're a newcomer to the city or the state or tonight's state of being, please know that you are welcome; you are among fellow-seekers.

And to Community members and long-time friends, welcome and abundant blessings on you as well.

You've all braved the cold and gathered your selves and your souls together with others in a community of wonder. I join you in believing that there's really no better place in the world to be than right here, ready to receive the blessings from the manger. *Borta bra men hemma bäst*—"Away is good, but home is best"—goes the Swedish proverb that you can behold at almost every turn down in Lindsborg, Kansas. But tonight "away" and "home" are synonyms, or, at the very least, nonsensical, for we stand closer together as siblings in the human family than ever before.

Tonight is that moment when all faces are beautiful and welcome and all of our souls are clarified. This is that time when we embrace the gifts God has for the world in all of its complicated, joyous, invigorating, inspiring messiness, when we watch in wonder at all the beauty, particularly the crystalline beauty brought by the snow.

We are here for the carols and the lights and the feelings that abound in this service. But those facets of our experiences are tied to the core of our hearts' desires: we yearn to listen to the story once again, to hear the accounts of Jesus' birth, and to bring our awe and reverence in response.

And accounts of Jesus' birth and our responses to it have to do with a Mysterious Stranger in the Straw.

Christmas defies any sort of final calculus. It can never be put into propositional form that demands a thumbs-up/thumbs-down vote. God's mysteries are immense. Babies and music and the world's befuddling ways are like that.

Poet and children's author Madeleine L'Engle has it just right:
This is the irrational season
When love blooms bright and wild.
Had Mary been filled with reason
There'd have been no room for the child.[1]

The apostle Paul offered equal eloquence when he said to the church at Corinth, "I tell you a mystery! . . . we will all be changed, in a moment, in the twinkling of an eye."[2] He reminded his protege Timothy, "the mystery of our religion is great."[3]

There's certainly a mystery about the dating for Christ's actual birthday, by the way. Up until the fourth century, the nativity of the Lord was celebrated on January 6, what we now call the feast of Epiphany. And while Eastern churches—Russian, Greek, Serbian, and other Orthodox congregations—would still maintain this ancient observance, the rest of the Church, by the year 336, had somehow moved its celebration of the birth of Jesus off of a day that focused not only on the birth but on other activities associated with Jesus' childhood and growth into his mission as the Messiah. And thus the majority of the Christian world has its Christmas observances in December.[4]

Mystery also surrounds us on this particular Christmas Eve in the form of the weather. As we gather for Christmas Eve services, Kansas City is blanketed with snow. If you're not driving or at a bus stop, the fluffy gift from the sky is beautiful. If you're a child or a teenager skimming down a hillside, the blanket of snow is a thrilling adventure. If you're simply inside, watching and wondering, you receive yet another sign of God's grace, another angle on a wondrous mystery: rounding every corner, smoothing every edge, quieting the din of our busy-ness, softening every footfall, hushing (even if only for a moment) the crash of the world's brutality, covering every trash heap and dumpster (everywhere!).

The graceful mystery of snow reminds us of the graceful mystery of God in Christ that makes everything brand-new. We are reminded, again, God will never give up on you and me. God loves us forever, and wants us to follow Christ's example of love and forgiveness.

Because the manger holds a great and magnificent mystery that cannot be defined by mere human talk, we must sing. Because it cannot be defined by loveless logic, we remember Einstein's keen insight that imagination is more important than knowledge. And because it cannot be contained by any formulaic recipe or dismissive dogma, we open our hearts to the stunning revelations of prayer.

But also note with me that this mystery is strange. Christ is not only mysterious, he is a stranger.

This is why the opening words of John's gospel are so appropriate for tonight and why the Church has always seen fit to include in its lectionary a reading from John 1:1−14 for Christmas Eve and Christmas Day. These words about the logos—the Word of God made flesh (and sinew and tendon and blood and tissue)—are more than mystical incantations. They are passing strange, and they resonate with the passing-strange portions of our souls that know there is something beyond ourselves that we must have or we will be spiritually dead. On Christmas Eve we give voice to a daring, undaunted declaration: there is something more to our fate than mundane struggling day after day; we are destined, as we always have been, to be God's children and not petty blobs of protoplasm randomly spotted on a small blue ball hovering in the midst of a ceaselessly expanding and altogether indifferent universe. We are here on purpose! The Word made flesh offers this strange, abiding truth: "God became like us so that we might become like God."[5] Not to become God. No one can do that. But to become like unto the divine. To come into a true claim upon the status God gave us when we were born: divine dust.

This is what is at the heart of what we call the Incarnation. "Because God took on human flesh, human flesh is made holy. Even lowly and dusty feet, if they carry God's message, are beautiful. . . .Things that we would prefer to keep separate — the holy and the profane — have come together in a . . . smelly stable."[6]

Ephraem of Syria, early church poet and preacher, described by the folks within the Syrian Church as "The Harp of the Holy Spirit"[7], says that Christmas is the day when "the creator of all things became the restorer. He gave them back their former beauty."[8]

And behold how the beauty is made real. There is a mystery. And it is passingly, wondrously, beautifully strange. And it happens in the middle of the straw!

Instead of a palatial domicile, a stable serves as Jesus' birthing room. Instead of a fire-and-safety-certified, hazard-free, officially-approved baby bed, a manger serves as his resting place. A manger. Not ethereal, set upon a cloud — why does divinity always have to repose on clouds!? — but tethered to the earth. Not some indistinct idea of some uncertain principle, but crudely, impertinently placed in a rough manger full of crude straw. The One who would become the very bread of life for a world spiritually famished is placed in a feeding trough for animals.

And, if you will pardon a stinker of a pun, this just may be the straw that breaks the camel's back of our petty presumptuousness. For if God can do this — make the strange mystery of love become real in the middle of the most humbling and rude circumstance — then God really can do anything, even change us, even move us to some new plain of caring compassion for the world, inspire us to some new depth of tenderness with one another, lead us to some new heights of understanding about ourselves.

This past July, one of the great preachers of America, Dr. Caesar Arthur Walter Clark, at the young age of 93, took his last breath. You probably will not find his picture or his obituary in the special end-of-the-year edition of *People* magazine. But rest assured, we shall not see the likes of Dr. Clark for a good long while. He was a preacher's preacher, a true prince of the pulpit. At the physical height of about 5'6" (at his tallest!) he still stood tall and regal as the pastor of the Good Street Baptist Church in Dallas, Texas, for more than 50 years. During that time, he was released by his congregation for 25 weeks or more each year to preach elsewhere in revivals across the land. During his preaching career he became, next to Billy Graham, in terms of sheer numbers, the greatest, most prolific revivalist this nation has ever known. And yet, and yet . . . and yet, Dr. Clark knew something of the astoundingly strange mystery of Christ in the straw and of preaching about Christ. Many may be shocked to hear a statement he made into the maturity of his preaching career. Dr. Clark wondered, he said, if all his preaching and proclamations, what others would call his monumental ministry, would really only amount to "an embarrassed stammering."[9]

Yes, the Mysterious Stranger in the Straw causes us to stutter and stammer in the face of the stunning realities which God in Christ has come to establish in our hearts:

- You really can be made whole.
- You really do have a high, beautiful, important purpose on this earth.
- There really is more forgiveness in God than there is sin in the world.

Now, in response to the mysterious stranger in the manger, whatever we do, we surely must do the following:

(1) Like we are doing now, gather in the bonds of a caring community. Ultimately, human life is a "we" proposition. The human condition is always moved forward in concert, together. We are strongest, healthiest, most mature, most empowered, most tender, most creative when we are together.

(2) Let wonder loose in your life, risking the world's scoffing if need be. Liberate your capacity to be full of awe and reverence. Laugh and love and do so through your mouth and your heart — wide open in gawking delight. And when you let wonder loose in your life, don't be surprised if you liberate some wondering in someone else's life as well.

(3) And rejoice! Rejoice! And rejoice again. For we were made for rejoicing and the mysteriously strange and astonishing event of singing. Rejoice in your singing and rejoice in the candles and rejoice in the closeness of those next to you. Rejoice even in this poem, which is another way for my soul to sing and rejoice with you on Christmas Eve:

Mysterious Stranger in the Straw

The mystery —
a holy conundrum,
a magnificent puzzle,
a sacred enigma,
beyond all finite reckonings —
is here.

Strange in its beauty,
reflecting the strange light
in our eyes,
the mystery now in our hands
to share amidst rough straw
and the rude blessings of love
and the crude caress of human flesh
upon the earth and
throughout all the mansions of
God's heart.

Forever and ever
and ever,
it is so;
and so let it be,
until grace is no longer a stranger
and love comes home for good.

Amen. Merry Christmas, and may God bless each and every one, here and everywhere!

NOTES
1. Madeleine L'Engle, *Glimpses of Grace: Daily Thoughts and Reflections* (San Francisco: HarperCollins, 1996) , p.103.
2. I Cor. 15:51-52
3. I Tim. 3:16.
4. See Greg Pennoyer and Gregory Wolfe, eds., *God with Us: Rediscovering the Meaning of Christmas* (Brewster, Mass.; Paraclete Press, 2007), p. 124.
5. The original phrase is from Athanasius.
6. See Isaiah 52:7 and *God with Us*, p. 127.
7. Joseph F. Kelley, *Origins of Christmas* (Collegeville, Minn.: Liturgical Press, 2004), p. 115.
8. *God with Us*, p. 127.
9. *The Times Picayune* (New Orleans, La., 1972), quoted in Eddie S. O'Neal, "An Embarrassed Stammering," *The African American Pulpit*, Winter 1999-2000, pp. 83-87.

38

THE FIRST CHRISTMASES

Texts: Isaiah 9:2−7, Luke 2:1−14, John 1:1−14

Merry Christmas and a special greeting to you and you and you, to all of us, on this the very first Christmas of our lives. Yes, you heard right. This is a first Christmas for all of us.

I

By first Christmas I don't mean the first historical Christmas that surrounded Jesus' birth, according to the scriptures . . . in a humble stable, which was actually very likely a rough and rude cave-like structure, where domesticated animals were kept and secured . . . in the midst of a tax season, or at least in the census-taking time leading up to the tax season . . . in Bethlehem, a forgotten town in a backwater province of a vast empire, with *Bethlehem* meaning the "house of bread," thus making it so fitting and right: the House of Bread welcoming the very Bread of Life into the world.

Now, never mind that our picturesque combination of shepherds (from Luke only) and magi (from Matthew only) is a logistic and theological conundrum, a conflation spanning over two years of time. This first Christmas—hovered over by angels, guarded by peasants, covered with astrologers' gifts, suffused by the devotion of Mary and the loyalty of Joseph—is precious. Despite all disputes, something happened there in Bethlehem and in the contiguous world that surrounded Bethlehem and Nazareth and Jerusalem and the wide, waiting world. No ordinary baby was born but rather One who would be proclaimed Messiah, Savior.

There is that first Christmas, the so-called historical first Christmas. And there is generative power in that foundational event beyond anything we can imagine. But there is more.

II

There are the personal first Christmases that we recollect from childhood and family get-togethers and our own personal journeys. Many of these first Christmases are lost to memory. But the feelings—profound and deep, resonating over the years, as we entertain them unawares—remain. Like a cascading waterfall they come back every year in our hearts and minds and souls:

The first Christmas we recall opening presents. The first Christmas we knew about the difference between Santa Claus and a baby named Jesus. The first Christmas we heard "Silent Night" sung by a choir. Or the first Christmas we heard "O Holy Night" sung in the original French. Or the first Christmas we saw snow. Or the first Christmas we tasted eggnog. Or the first Christmas we heard "Grandma Got Run Over by a Reindeer." Or the first Christmas we remembered to have enough tools (and the right tools!) to assemble all the toys. Or the first Christmas we went to a midnight service. Or the first Christmas we realized the whole operation hasn't ever been about the magi giving precious gifts but about them being humble enough to kneel and receive a gift—the gift of a new life, a new direction home, forever.

There are among those first Christmases, to be sure, the personal first Christmases recollected from the treasured halls of memory. In this gathering tonight, there are as many of those first Christmases being reprised in our minds as there are Christmas lights on the Plaza. But there is still more.

III

There is also tonight's existential first Christmas.

For some this is the first Christmas when all the family has been together in a long time. Or it's the first Christmas for you as newlyweds. Or it's your first Christmas at Community. Or it's your first Christmas with a new baby in your home. Or it's the first Christmas you can recall when the word "Occupy" was associated with a protest movement. Or it's the first Christmas when your loved one is home at last, no longer in uniform.   Or it's your first Christmas without your beloved. Or it's your first Christmas sober. Or it's the first Christmas you've ever heard "Sweet Little Jesus Boy" or it's the first Christmas you've ever seen a drum set as a part of a Christmas Eve celebration. And still there is more!

IV

For all of us, this can be a first Christmas spiritually. For all of us this can be a first Christmas to know and receive the warming truth, the blunt fact that we can really be human after all.

This is the message from the manger back then which is the same message to our hearts now.

Tonight, Christmas Eve, December 24, 2011, we really can be real, we really can be human, after all. No need for sham or pretentious supposing. We can be open and receptive and honest with God and with one another. And being open and receptive to what God desires to give us, all of us, we can be made whole.

And for all of us this can also be the first Christmas to be brave enough to share Christmas with others, those who wonder if it's true, if they too can be enrolled, like Joseph and Mary, in a holy census and the sacred story of God's healing gift for a wounded world.

My prayer tonight is that this Christmas will be so for you and yours.

I urgently hope and trust you will let this be a first Christmas moment for your own life and that you'll share it with others so that this Christmas will be for them, for us all, the first of many to come, a continuous first Christmas of hope and love and peace and joy.

As has been my practice each Christmas Eve here at Community, ever mindful of Reinhold Niebuhr's caution that what folks want most of all at Christmas are not lengthy sermons but the compelling comfort (and succinct mystery) of poems, and thankful for your kind reception, I'd like to offer a poem, "Remember the First Christmas."

Remember the first Christmas,
amidst phantasms of empire,
at the crossing of time and treasure,
redefining what power is.

Recall the prophetic anticipations,
the solace of grizzled men
annealing every bruising;
think of stumps greening with new shoots.

Retrace the shepherds' vigil,
the magi's trek, the angels' hovering
at the stabled crèche;
and honor Mary's assurance: "Fear not."

Recollect the Herod-haunted world
and its colossal mistaking,
confusing promise with threat,
blood with dominion.

And yet, remember, still,
that the boots of the tramping warrior
did not snuff out the light,
could not stifle love's perduring.

Reprise the first Christmas then
with your own first Christmas now,
among sheltering love and guiding lights
and surprising gifts.

Remember, now, this first Christmas
beyond palaces and palisades,
when prose cannot suppose,
and only poetry will do.

Remember this first Christmas
of your own journey —
when you, a holy child, too,
find your own song and let it loose upon the world.

Relive the first Christmas of hope's arriving,
with new life rising in you and then
rejoice that this Christmas
is the first of many to come, tonight and forever.

Merry Christmas, everyone! I love you. God bless us all. Amen.

39

THE ULTIMATE CHRISTMAS STAR
Texts: Luke 2:1—14, Matthew 2:1—12, John 1:1—14

The ultimate star of the Christmas story is a baby. For the entire season of Advent, leading up to Christmas Eve, we've been guided by the Christmas story as conveyed through the great carol "The First Noel." And while the astronomical star that guided the wise men has a prominent role in the carol—being mentioned four different times, completely overshadowing Mary and Joseph, who aren't mentioned at all—the ultimate star is the one proclaimed in the refrain that concludes every verse: "Born is the King of Israel."

The ultimate star of the Christmas story is a baby. A real baby. A baby wrapped in swaddling clothes, Luke says in his version of the Christmas story. A real live baby with a real family looking into a real roughhewn manger after the miracle of a real birth, never imagining, never able to imagine the miracles that are to come.

A real baby with a real name, according to Matthew's version of the original Christmas pageant. A squirming, charming, blinking, gurgling baby, whom a teenage maiden and a dreamy father will bear into Egypt to avoid the murderous hands of Herod's minions.

Beyond the harried and hurrying crowds, beyond the tinsel on the trees and the tempests of family gatherings, beyond the presents and the pablum, way beyond all of our devices and devising, we come to this Christmas Eve moment to know once more it's all about a baby.

This is what John's gospel declares in his glorious first chapter prolegomenon, which is so perfect as a text for Christmas Eve: "And the word became flesh and dwelt among us." Which means that the gift of Christmas itself, the gift that God gives us at Christmas-time is a real and tangible gift: human flesh. The theological term for this is *incarnation*. The word-on-the-street term for this is . . . *It's all about a baby.*

And if in the beginning Christ is a baby—truly, fully human—then he can hurt like us, hunger like us, dream and hope like we do, experience suffering like we do. And, in turn, if he can be resurrected after his suffering and pain, then so can we be redeemed and so can the world.

This is John's genius insight, his spiritual nugget: "God so loved the world that He gave" not a philosophical dissertation, not a theological exposition, not a technical treatise, but rather a baby, love wrapped in human flesh.[1]

As long as the story of Christmas has been told and retold, as long as people have stood agog at a stable in belief and bewilderment, as long as

173

songs have been sung and candles have been lit, this truth has been unavoidable: Christmas is all about a baby.

Last Sunday evening, just three days ago, in one of the most beautiful Christmas pageants we have witnessed at Community in quite a while, our children portrayed the drama of the Christmas story with affection and enthusiasm. When the presentation was complete and the shepherds and the magi and the sheep and Mary and Joseph were correctly, beautifully in place, one of the sheep, portrayed by Auben Ward, provided us a parable of what Christmas is all about.

Auben was out of place. Instead of being with the other sheep all in a line over to the side, she found her way to the middle of the drama, right in front of the manger. She drew back her sheep-head hood, because, I suspect, it was too hot for her comfort. Then she simply plopped down in front of the manger. And she stayed there, in her kneeling position, gazing intently at the little baby Jesus in the Christmas cradle. She was transfixed, mesmerized. It was so very plain that she truly believed the story that had been narrated and of which she was a small part.

Whether Auben will ever remember her sheep role in her first Christmas pageant is hard to know. But I know I will never forget the sermon which a two-year-old spoke to my heart and to the hearts of those gathered in this sanctuary then. It was—as the Christmas story is itself—an enfleshed sermon: a two-year-old kneeling before a manger cradling the "new-born king" given to the world, given to her, given to us all. (And, by the way, Auben truly lived out her middle name that evening: Noelle!)

I hope you are comforted by the truth that God has given you a gift wrapped in human flesh, has given the world a gift that is made real in a baby.

And I hope and trust you are comforted by the truth that such a baby "dwelt among us, full of grace and truth."

This is the other side of the coin, so to speak, about Christmas. The ultimate star of Christmas is a baby. But this baby is not merely animalistic in nature. This baby comes to remind us that we babies are not merely animals either. Jesus is given in order to portray and provide grace and truth.

Grace and truth—meaning a life touched with wonder and wonders, both daily and extraordinary.

Grace and truth—like drops of dew in a desert.

Grace and truth—like the fond caress of a grandmother's hand.

Grace and truth—like the song that causes your soul to soar.

Grace and truth—like the squeeze of a hand in a circle of care.

Grace and truth—like the unforgettable smile of my dear friend and friend of countless other grateful souls in Kansas City, Fr. Norm Rotert, now of blessed memory.

Grace and truth like Charlie Gaines, a friend down in Fort Worth, Texas, discovered once more, last Sunday, at about the same time we were enjoying the Christmas pageant here at Community.

Charlie was stuck in an elevator between the fifth and twentieth stories of his building . . . for two and a half hours! He sat in the elevator—a space measuring five feet by six feet—all alone. "The first hour and a half there," he said, "was with zero communication other than a short call to the emergency operator." His enforced solitude offered him a chance for meditating on an important truth of the Christmas message. "It was interesting," he said. In his reflection, he concluded: "I'm fine. The truth is, my friends, we're all fine. We have much to be thankful for and much to look forward to. Don't . . . fall into line with the naysayers and negative among us. The world is good, and nearly all the folks in it are fine people. Those that are not so good, need our example to show them the way. . . . Take in the day you're living right now and know how good it really is. Life's too short to waste a minute of it."[2]

We need to hear that again—whether we're striving for justice or recovering from an injustice, whether you've been down so long it looks like up to you or you're soaring higher than the treetops, whether you're among the Ph.D's or the no-D's. We all need to hear that again: "The world is good, and nearly all the folks in it are fine people. Those that are not so good need our example to show them the way."

The gift of a baby leads us to the teaching-preaching-wonder-working gifts of an adult who leads us to the gift of a way of life. And—oh!—that way of life is the ultimate gift that keeps on giving, beyond our wildest imaginings. It's a gift freely given—which no one can ever purchase at Best Buy or Costco or via Amazon—without any cost on our part except the cost of being humble enough to receive it.

The gift of Jesus' way of life is resplendent with possibilities for hope, joy, justice, peace, love, mercy, and reconciliation. And it is finally a gift which Jesus bids us to give away to others freely, joyfully, without restraint or hindrance.

This is what I came by this Christmas Eve to convey to you:

(1) Christmas is all about a baby.
(2) There is a grace and truth which that baby made possible for you and for everyone.

And so, as has been my custom over the past several years, this morning I wrote a poem, "The Stars Conspire Tonight," and want to share it with you now.

The stars conspire tonight in humble hues
to shine and show a graceful face
whose love will guard the certain hearts
of shepherds and wandering, wondering kings.

Here more than memory is going on
and on and on in the clutch of a baby's grasp:
what the angel did say in genial glory
is in fact and faith our own story.

Our winter's night is not so deep or cold
that we cannot thrill to sounds of "Noel, Noel."
We would dare the darkness to quit its quest,
to leave well enough alone, to leave us well together.

All shadowed and shivering souls have been
by Bethlehem blessed under a gleam
that does not rest or stop or stay just there
but everywhere fills opened hearts full out.

By that same star we guide our feet
and homes and work and words
and say a pledge of grace and truth:
you can be free; you can be made whole.

This premier star, the brightening nova
declares what we also say·
You, we all of us, are enough, now, always,
and loved beyond reasoned reckoning.

What stars conspired in humble hues,
at the love-lit dawning and beyond time's passing,
we receive as the new birth, there and then,
and here, even, ever as our own.

Merry Christmas. I love you. And may God bless us all!

NOTES
1.   John 3:16
2.   https://www.facebook.com/charles.c.gaines.3?fref=ts

40

YOU HAVE FOUND FAVOR WITH GOD

Texts: Luke 2:1ff, John 1:1ff

Merry Christmas!

It is a sweet delight to say it once more. So, why don't we? Merry Christmas!

We are gathered to hear and to receive what the angels first proclaimed — to the shepherds, and to Mary, and to Joseph, and to the magi — and proclaim still to the world that gathers eagerly at Bethlehem's manger: "You have found favor with God!"

It really is that simple. You, and you, and you, and you, and me, and we all have found favor with God!

Because of our own innate denseness, and the complications of history, and our devisings and divisions, we complicate such a gift and haven't yet fully taken it in. Thus, our rituals and traditions, the supreme, exquisite joy in singing the songs of this season, and our gladness in gathering.

The best we can do beyond the poetry of the songs and our sacred texts, something we all need to do, is to clarify what such favor can mean.

So, what can it mean, this favor from God?

First, a quick word about what the favor is NOT! The favor God is giving to us and the world through Christ is not the following:

- NOT that you have been elected to an exclusive club!
- NOT that you have found an advantage unavailable to anyone else!
- NOT that you have earned a special privilege from God that God will not grant to your neighbor, or your competitor, or your enemy!
- To repeat, God's favor is:
- NOT about privilege but about empowerment,
- NOT about advantage but affirmation,
- NOT about favoritism but faith,
- NOT about the exclusive but the universally inclusive!

What can such favor mean in the positive? God's favor is really about these affirmations:

#1 — You are accepted as you are. And our job, to use Paul Tillich's fetching phrase, is to accept that we are accepted — wrinkles and warts and hitches in our get-along and all. You are accepted, blemishes and bruisings and brokenness and all. And not only that but this too! — you are accepted in all of your brilliance and beauty and boldness! You are accepted as you are!

And there is a second positive declaration:

#2—You are being attended tb y God. You've got God's attention! God is giving you full, undivided attention, today and in all of your days. "All day and all night, angels watching over you and me," beyond our normal reckoning. We are not alone. Though we may be afraid from time to time, God's presence and the presence of God's spirit through and with angelic presences in our lives will see us toward completion and fulfillment.

And there is a third and ultimate positive affirmation:

#3 – God believes in you. God is the original believer. And this is what God believes: You can be made whole, it's all right to be human. Beyond all the tensions and toxicity, beyond all of our acting out and addictions, it's OK to be human, to claim and be claimed by the *Imago Dei* (image of God) in which we were created. We have been blessed with capacities and talents and pleasures and treasures beyond anything that we can ever know.

And now what to do with such favor?

In response to God's favor, God desires a favor in return, only not to God, but to others. There are countless friends and family members and strangers who yearn for encouragement. There are others who desperately need to know they're loved, others who yearn to know they have been granted grace, others who want to know the truth of what Ann Weems says: "It is not over, this birthing. There are always newer skies into which God can throw stars. When we begin to think that we can predict the Advent of God . . . that's just the time that God will be born in a place we can't imagine and won't believe."[1]

There are others who, like ourselves, need to believe—really believe—in the possibility of goodness being realized in all our lives, to know Todd Davis' soaring, searing insight, that "the only corruption comes/ in not loving this life enough."[2]

And, now, as is my practice, I want to bring this sermonic moment to a close and conclude this proclamation with something less prosaic and more poetic, my gift to you this Christmas Eve.

Send On the Song!

Who knew that God would seek
The favor of our company?
Who could ever tell that angels
Would want to bend near this earth?
There's enough cynic in our finest
To exclude such supposing.

But the supernal light did come
And comes again this night.
Peace on and in the earth is bestowed
In a time blunt and unpoetic.
Songs from on high recall for us
Our nature's better angels.

Our task beyond this time of receiving?

To will goodness for neighbors, to send back the song,
Echoing in concrete canyons, sweeping over the plains,
Whooping down in the bayou, resounding across the seas,
Saying and singing beyond all the fears of all the years
And fulfilling every enduring hope.

Where to send such a love-graced song?
Oh, we know, we know for sure—
To Sandy Hook and Portland and Oak Creek
To Joplin and Blacksburg and Columbine,
And to Kabul and Damascus and Cairo,
And here and there, wherever Babel sounds are rising.

And what song to sing, what melody to intone?
A child-like song that God first sang in the manger child:
You can be made whole, it is all right to be human,
You have found God's favor, tonight and forever,
And this, too: we are now the angels watching over you,
And we will sing the song until we all sleep in heavenly peace.

Amen.

NOTES

1. Ann Weems, "It Is Not Over," *Kneeling in Bethlehem*, (Philadelphia: The Westminster Press, 1980), p.85.
2. Todd David, *The Least of These* (East Lansing: Michigan State University Press, 2007), p. 7.

41

A TIME FOR SINGING

Texts: Isaiah 9:2, 6–7 and Luke 2:1–14

Merry Christmas! It's Christmastime and that means it's time for singing!

We've now reached the culmination of our *Christmastimes* series.

Four Sundays ago, we began the series by considering the theme of hope as "A Time for Letting Go of the Past."

Then we looked at "A Time for Being at Peace."

In a brief communion meditation, on our special Music Sunday, which was also *Gaudete* Sunday, we celebrated "A Time for Real Joy."

Then last Sunday, we explored love as "A Time for Second Chances," a phrase which capture's Jesus' life and ministry and what he proclaimed about the possibilities of love among us.

This past Wednesday, during our Traveler's Christmas Eve Service, we illuminated Christmas as "A Time for Light."

Ultimately, in each of our four beautiful candlelight Christmas Eve services, we shared with great feeling and poignancy what it means to celebrate our "First Christmases."

Now on Christmas morning, it truly is "A Time for Singing" as we continue to enjoy some of the greatest music in the Christian music repertoire.

Singing is surely the best way for proclaiming "Merry Christmas." Whether in dulcet, whispered tones or with bold blasts of gusto, singing helps when spoken words fall short. Not that saying what we feel about God and faith aren't important. They are. But in expressing what's deepest within us, music, more often than not, elicits our grandest affections and our strongest adorations.

This morning, very briefly, I'd like to amplify four specific Christmastime songs and highlight their special significances.

I

Four Sundays ago, we began our journey to the Christmas cradle with "O Come, O Come Emmanuel," and last night at the "midnight mass," as it's commonly called, the Chancel Choir's opening Introit was also "O Come, O Come Emmanuel," ushering in our blessing of the Christ Child.

"O Come, O Come, Emmanuel" is one of our oldest Christmas songs, with words dating back to a twelfth century gathering of seven antiphons that employed seven Old Testament names for the Messiah. Its music dates back to a fifteenth century funeral processional used by French nuns as a devotional hymn.

All of which conveys the power that Christmastime music possesses to transform even something associated with death into something life-giving.

II

"Joy to the World," which culminated three of our Christmas Eve services and commenced this one, is the most popular hymn among Disciples of Christ. Did you know that? On July 27, 1992, at Walden Inn in Greencastle, Indiana, the Chalice Hymnal Development Committee cast its very first vote for the new hymnal they were creating. The first song for inclusion in the new hymnal was "Joy to the World." According to a denomination-wide survey the committee had used, it was recognized as the most widely sung hymn by Disciples congregations.

"Joy to the World" is without a doubt, the most popular of the six hundred hymns composed by Isaac Watts, the father of English hymnody. You should also know that "Joy to the World" was not originally a Christmas song but rather a hymn giving voice to Psalm 98:4, 9 ("Make a joyful noise to the Lord, all the earth . . . . for he is coming"). Don't be surprised if we sing it before next Christmas, say in April!

All of which conveys that Christmastime is not to be kept only to December 25 but truly can be celebrated at any time.

III

There's a Christmas carol that's not in our hymnal, and its absence is a shame.

I first heard "In the Bleak Midwinter" as a cut from an album by insanely talented guitarist John Fahey, who was probably more famous for influencing Leo Kottke. After turning the corner at Westport Road and Broadway, I literally had to stop my Jeep and park it in order to hear the entirety of the tune.

"In the Bleak Midwinter" is one of the loveliest songs ever to express the Christmas story. The words are by the English poet Christina Rossetti, who died ten years before her poem was given a musical setting by Gustav Holst, now known famously for his orchestral suite *The Planets*. The words describe the needfulness of the world, the great and simple grace of the nativity, and the exquisitely plain and genius response we can give to the gift of Christ.

In the bleak midwinter, frosty wind made moan,
Earth stood hard as iron, water like a stone;
Snow had fallen, snow on snow, snow on snow,
In the bleak midwinter, long ago.

. . . .

What can I give Him, poor as I am?
If I were a Shepherd, I would bring a lamb;
If I were a Wise Man, I would do my part;
Yet what I can I give Him: give my heart.

"Silent Night" is without peer or competitor as the most popular Christmas carol in the United States. The words, by clergyman Joseph Mohr, and the music, by organist Franz Gruber, made their debut on Christmas Eve 1818 in the Austrian village of Obendorf, at, appropriately enough, St. Nicholas Catholic Church. Legend has it that the organ at the St. Nicholas Church broke down, so Gruber provided guitar accompaniment for the song's debut. Whether sung in the original German ("*Stille Nacht*") or proffered by a group of eight-year-olds in a Christmas pageant or sanctified beyond imagining by Millie Edwards, "Silent Night" maintains, year after year, its capacity to swell our praise, expand our wonder, and magnify our awe in the presence of God who would deign to stoop low and grace us with unconditional love.

So, Merry Christmas! And let's keep on singing! And let us know the gifts that singing provides at all times, including at Christmastime.

(1) As we attempt to describe an event beyond description — the birth of divinity in a child — nothing is better than music.

(2) Music — all kinds of music but especially music at Christmastime — will increase your peacefulness. Music, better than almost anything else (except for maybe the euphonic waves at a beach), increases endorphin rush in our biochemical make-up and therefore our equanimity and sense of calmness.

(3) Singing is egalitarian. That is, music always is an equal-opportunity occasion for blessing. Everyone can sing, even if you can't carry a tune. You can take your instrument everywhere. Everywhere you are, there your voice is, too! And because of this mobility, you can sing everywhere — at home, in the shower, at the kitchen sink, in your car, on a walk, in your own mind and heart and soul!

(4) Music helps us reclaim our childlikeness. Music at Christmastime has the power to transform the crustiest, sometimes even the most hardhearted, among us into the children we once were. Becoming like a child is as close to the holy as we can possibly manage. Like our "Song of the Christ Candle" proclaims today:
Grace is a gift that dwells in our souls,
Jesus comes home and makes the world whole.
When God is a child there's joy in our song
The last shall be first and the weak shall be strong,
And none shall be afraid.

So, again, Merry Christmas! And let's keep on singing!

NOTE

I'm grateful for Bill Henderson's *Simple Gifts: Great Hymns: One Man's Search for Grace* (New York: Free Press, 2006) and for our Disciples' *Chalice Hymnal: Worship Leader's Companion* (St. Louis, Missouri: Chalice Press, 1998), which supplied background information for some of the songs described in this sermon.

JUSTICE, JUSTICE, YOU SHALL PURSUE

42

REMEMBER THE DREAM!

Text: Daniel 2:1 — 6, 10 — 12, 16 — 23

Good morning, and please know what a pleasure and an honor it is to be with you this Sunday morning! Greetings from the brothers and sisters at Community, who will welcome Rev. Cleaver and the Daybreak Choir and any and all St. Jamesians in our 10:30 service. We also invite our guests, if they are able and willing, to our luncheon, at which one of our members, Marva Eberhart, will be sharing her mission experiences from her time in Ghana last summer. We would cherish the opportunity to welcome any and all of the members of St. James to share worship with us.

I must also extend these introductory remarks by telling you how blessed I have been to know both Rev. Cleavers who have blessed you and are blessing you anew with their mighty ministries. The past twenty years of this pulpit exchange have blown by like a shooting star. It seems like only yesterday when I met "Dr. III," who was then simply "E III," in the old sanctuary. And now here he is, beyond merely the cusp of a great consummation, but fully involved in the transformation of St. James into its next glorious chapters of ongoing excellent witness. And while Rev. Emanuel Cleaver II will be with us this morning, we look forward to greeting you, "Dr. III," next year, as the torch will be fully passed to your hand.

And to my dear friend and colleague Rev. Emanuel Cleaver II, all I have to say to you is "I don't know how you've done it, being a Congressman and pastor here at St. James!" As the mantle is passed fully come June, please know that you'll always have a pulpit away from your home pulpit, if you so choose, at Community Christian Church.

This morning I want to offer a brief word centering on the thought "Remember the Dream."

I.

All doctors, and especially psychiatrists and psychoanalysts, will tell us that dreaming is important.

Sigmund Freud and Carl Jung, the major driving forces behind modern psychology, both agreed that dreaming is important for human functioning, for overall human health and well-being. Each in his own way held to the notion that dreaming is the working-out, in an unconscious state, of unresolved issues from our waking hours. Freud stated pointedly that dreaming fully, and not remembering what you dreamed about, was perhaps the best kind of dreaming, helping us to bring closure to unresolved matters from our daytime lives.

Each person here this morning, I am sure, can recall when they had a dream, whether or not they recollect all the definite contours or detailed story lines of the dream, and it left them refreshed the next day. Dreaming is important—in fact, it is crucial for human health and well-being.

For example, I'm still dreaming of wearing my wedding ring. Seven months after shattering my wrist in a bicycle accident, I still can't put my wedding ring on my ring finger. And while that doesn't bother Priscilla, I don't quite yet feel right. I keep dreaming of the day when I can return the ring to its rightful place on my ring finger.

The dreams of our childhood, which we work out in our waking hours, are also extraordinarily and excruciatingly important. When I was a tow-headed boy growing up in Brownsville, Texas, I had two dreams: to play centerfield either for the San Francisco Giant (like Willie Mays) or for the New York Yankees (like Mickey Mantle) and to have a Zippo lighter like the pachucos did in my neighborhood. Imagine my satisfaction, then, when, lo and behold, I had achieved half of my life goals by the time I was eighteen!

Dreaming has been important, metaphorically and poetically speaking, for countless folks involved in faithful struggles for liberation and freedom's fulfillment. We are here this morning, in fact, engaged in this pulpit exchange, because of the dreaming activity of our respective congregations. Leaders among both of our families of faith have held fervently to the dream that we are, as Robert Putnam puts it, *Better Together* and that we'd rather not be *Bowling Alone.* [1]

Carl Sandburg understood the importance of dreams for human personality and as one of the significant forces that drive human progress when he said, "Nothing happens unless first we dream."

Thoreau knew the importance of dreams when he declared "Do not lose hold of your dreams or aspirations. For if you do, you may still exist but you have ceased to live."

Howard Thurman would give a shimmering description of the nation of Israel and its monotheism when, in his very first book, *The Greatest of These,* a gathering of dreamy meditations on the thirteenth chapter of I Corinthians, he described the Israelites as the "keepers of the one-God dream." [2]

And during this past week, as Caroline Kennedy withdrew her name from consideration for the open Senate seat for New York and Sen. Ted Kennedy was whisked away to the hospital in the middle of the celebratory luncheon in Statuary Hall in Washington, who could not have recollected the renowned aphorism from George Bernard Shaw made eternally famous by Bobby Kennedy more than a generation ago: "Some men see things as they are and say, 'Why?' I dream of things that never were and say, 'Why not?'"

Yes, dreams are so very, very important—biomedically, physically, developmentally, poetically, politically.

We realized the importance of dreams once again this past Tuesday, when the inauguration of Barack Hussein Obama as the 44th president of the United States of America was happily and joyfully accomplished. At that dramatic moment, the long-awaited fulfillment of a million dreams over the past 233 years of our nation's blemished and yet beautifully blessed experiment with democracy had arrived. The hopes of so many—those who voted for President Obama, along with all those who yearned for America's promise to be realized more completely—had come upon a threshold of attainment.

It was a moment when the dreams of so many who died were satisfied. These were the dreams of those "who more than self their country loved, and mercy more than life" and fell on fields of battle in defense of our nation; they were the dreams of those who never tasted freedom's full savor and suffered death by exhaustion or an assassin's bullet along the highways and byways toward freedom.

It was a moment in which the dreams of common Americans— particularly those born without privilege or position, those launched on their paths without monetary advantage, those without famous family names or the highest political pedigree—were rekindled.

Yes, many said, the dream has been realized, at least partially, in the parading arrival of President Barack Obama, along with Michelle, Malia, and Sasha, as residents at 1600 Pennsylvania Ave.

And yet, and yet . . . I have come by here this morning to remind us all to "Remember the Dream." For too many folks, I'm afraid, may be prone to believe and then act as if the dream that Dr. King dreamed about so eloquently in 1963—and that had been borne so nobly by the likes of A. Phillip Randolph, and Howard Thurman, and Marcus Garvey, and Frederick Douglass, and Sojourner Truth, and Abraham Lincoln—had been fully accomplished. We still need to keep on dreaming!

Just this past Wednesday, two things happened that are quite notable. One was a sign of the fulfillment of Dr. King's dream, and the other a sign that we need to keep on dreaming.

The first was a phone call I received from a Community member who happens to be African American. Forty years ago that kind of interchange might not have taken place at Community.

The second thing was the report from that same member that one of his children at a Johnson County middle school had been placed on a two-day in-school suspension. The reason for the suspension? He had been shoved that day by a white student—two days after the Martin Luther King holiday and the day after the inauguration of President Barack Obama—and when the shoving took place, the white student said "Move n_ _ _ _ _!" "What in the h _ _ _ did you say," he replied. The white student shoved him, and then the young man shoved back. And then they were in the principal's office. Now the father of the young boy who suffered from the racial slur did not take kindly to his son's use of the H-word, but he was wounded in his heart at the idea that something so pathetically puny as a racial slur could be slung at his son. Of course, the utterance by the young white boy, "Move n_ _ _ _ _!"—the result of a wretchedly stupid teaching and because the boy was flippantly caught up in saying something he heard someone else say—is bonafide evidence that we need to keep on dreaming. And the lackluster punishment for the offenses—the racial slur and the physical altercation—

was further evidence of the need for all of us to remember the dream and not be satisfied the dream has been achieved. A golden opportunity for teaching was missed. The white boy could have been instructed to write a 500-word essay about the dangers of the hurtful, hate-filled language of racial epithets. And our member's son—a young man whom I hug every Sunday after services—could have been instructed to write a 500-word essay on how Dr. King would have handled the situation differently than he did. Instead of a learning opportunity, only a two-day suspension. We still need to remember the dream!

II.

The book of Daniel tells a story about the importance of dreams and their interpretations. Dreams and dreaming are mentioned more in the book of Daniel than in any other book in the Bible. The book of Daniel tells the story of Nebuchadnezzar, the king of Babylon during the sixth century BCE who was visited by dreams he could not understand and had somehow forgotten. Nebuchadnezzar calls forth the magicians, the enchanters, the sorcerers, and the Chaldeans to divine his dreams and their meanings and none can perform the impossible tasks—except for Daniel and his cohorts, Hananiah, Mishael, and Azariah, later to be known as Shadrach, Meshach, and Abednego. Daniel is one who can divine dreams and offer interpretation. Unlike Nebuchadnezzar, Daniel sees and remembers the dreams that have been visited upon the king and can offer interpretation. And best of all, he remembers from whence Nebuchadnezzar's dreams come: "Blessed be the name of God for ever and ever . . . to whom belong wisdom and might . . . . [H]e gives wisdom to the wise and knowledge . . . . He reveals deep and mysterious things; he knows what is in the darkness, and the light dwells with him."

To wit, he knows not only the substance (the *what*) of Nebuchadnezzar's dreams but also from whom all holy dreams come. Daniel stands in a long line of dreamers, dream interpreters, and dream rememberers.

You know them too. Can you recall? Remember Jacob, who dreamed of a ladder leading up to God and—in a dream-like state—wrestled with an angel and was given a new name, Israel.

Daniel stands also with Joseph, who had magnificent and powerful capacities when it came to dreams and helped to bring stability and hope to Egypt when it was assaulted by famine.

Daniel stands as well with Amos, who dreamed of a new ethic of holiness for all of God's people and declared, "let justice roll down like waters and righteousness like an ever-flowing stream."

And Daniel stands with the prophet Joel, who proclaimed that young men (and women) shall see visions and old men (and women) shall dream dreams, a proclamation that Peter would later use as his text in his Pentecost sermon.

Daniel stands also with Joseph, the carpenter, husband of Mary, who listened to the dreams that visited him and thereby secured the baby Jesus' safety so that he could grow up fully into his Messiahship.

And he stands with other dreamers like the apostle Paul, who dreamed in his first letter to the Corinthian Christians of "a more excellent way," love, that "bears all things, believes all things, hopes all things, endures all things;" and then, in his second letter to the church at Corinth, Paul told them of the dream of God "no longer counting their trespasses against them" and of the beautiful green dream of "reconciliation."

Daniel ultimately stands in the line of witnesses that leads straight to Jesus who dreamed of salvation for all: "For God so loved the world that he gave his only son, so that everyone who believes in him may not perish but have eternal life. Indeed, God did not send the Son into the world to condemn the world, but in order that the world might be saved through him." (John 3:16-17)

Yes, Daniel reminds us all that it is not merely the REM (rapid eye movement) observed by medical dream researchers that is important for the well-being of humanity and the world. It is also the REM (Righteous Energizing Mystery) that quickens the soul and inspires actions of justice and mercy and love and that matters most to God.

III.

In short, Daniel reminds us that the ultimate dreamer is not Daniel or Nebuchadnezzar or Jacob or Joseph or Joel or Amos, or any of the other prophets. The premier dreamer of all time is not the apostle Paul, or any of the twelve. The ultimate dreamer is God Almighty, who stepped out on the nothing of all emptiness and said, in the words of James Weldon Johnson, "I'll make me a world." He might as well have said, "I'll dream me a world."

So, remember the dream! Remember that it is God's dream that we are called to remember, a dream of wholeness and wellness and care and compassion, a dream of love and mercy and full righteousness. Remember the dream.

God's dream is a dream expressed in the American dream but not bound to it, for there are others who are also God's children, "who are not of this flock." Remember the dream.

God's dream is for every child to have sufficient food and proper shelter and excellent education. Remember the dream.

God's dream is for Uzi machine guns to be beaten into fuel-efficient cars and nuclear weapons into college educations. Remember the dream.

It is God's dream that the earth be preserved and honored instead of being exploited and despoiled. Remember the dream.

It is God's dream that all people — black folks and white folks, Jews and Gentiles, Protestant and Catholic, Israelis and Palestinians, Northerners and Southerners, Kansas City Chiefs and Oakland Raiders — grow up into a mature humanity and sing together and work together and play together and share together. Remember the dream.

So, God bless Martin Luther King! And God bless President Barack Obama! And God bless our pulpit exchange this year and every year! But praise be ultimately to God, who is the original dreamer of a world come of age in peace and grace and truth. Remember the dream! Remember the dream! Remember the dream!

NOTES

1. Robert Putnam, *Better Together: Restoring the American Community* (New York: Simon & Schuster, 2003). Robert Putnam, *Bowling Alone: The Collapse and Revival of American Community* (New York: Simon & Schuster, 2000).
2. Howard Thurman, *The Greatest of These* (Mills College, California: Eucalyptus Press, 1944), p. 1.

43

HEALING A VIOLENT WORLD
Text: Isaiah 2:1 — 14

On June 16, 1963, Rabbi Abraham Joshua Heschel sent a telegram to President John Kennedy, commending him for a meeting the president was convening the next day to address the issues of poverty and civil rights in the U.S. Among the pleasantries and politeness that "Father Abraham" expressed so freely and naturally was a challenge to President Kennedy to compel all clergy to commit their "personal involvement [and] not just solemn declaration."[1] Rabbi Heschel's imagination was powerful, and so he also urged the president to call upon all clergy to donate one month's salary to back up their words with actual support for programs of social betterment and justice. The telegram ended with this profound, benedictory sentence: "The hour calls for high moral grandeur and spiritual audacity."

Today is such an hour.

Moral grandeur and spiritual audacity are certainly our high calling in a world such as ours. And this is especially so in a world as saturated with violence as ours is.

Today, it may seem audacious and morally impossible to take on the subject of this sermon: "Healing a Violent World." Healing is all right as a point of focus when it comes to medical situations, including both the physical and the psychological aspects of healing. Such healings were paramount in the ministry of Jesus. And it's equally plausible, imaginable, possible, to take up the matter of healing in our families as we did last week. I'm appreciative of the positive feedback and affirmations I've received for last Sunday's proclamation.

But healing . . . violence? Isn't it the height of presumption, edging on arrogance, to think that the healing of violence is even effectively possible? And healing a violent world? You're thinking surely I jest. Browning was right to say that "a [person's] reach should exceed his [or her] grasp." But healing a violent world is going way too far!

This morning, I want to declare that it is not the height of presumption, nor is it an edging toward arrogance, to think that healing our violent world is possible. It is not only possible, it is a tenet of our faith and a mandate by the God whom we worship.

I.

Four Sundays ago, before the sermon proper, I offered in each morning service an unrehearsed and extemporaneous statement in light of the tragedy at Sandy Hook Elementary School in Newtown, Connecticut, and in response to the disturbing reactions many had made, nationally and locally, in the days that followed the heinous acts that left twenty children and six adults dead and their families bereaved beyond description. My sentiments from that day remain steadfastly the same: my heart is broken. And I know your hearts are broken as well by that senseless tragedy. And I would not be worthy to be called your pastor if I did not share and confess this broken-heartedness with you and tell you that we as a country, we as a nation, must be transformed. Since December 16, I've been even more heartbroken as colleagues and I have been ensnarled—and too often stymied—in discussions about the array of responses by various organizations and institutions to the situation in Newtown, Connecticut.

This morning I want to say again that we surely must protect our children. But I must also say that I do not believe that we have to have guards posted at the doorways of our congregations or elementary schools to keep us safe, inside or outside!

And hunting rifles are far different from assault rifles, with their high-capacity magazines intended for military purposes. I do not believe it is the inalienable prerogative of citizens to have such military-type weapons in their possession.

The topics for possible discussion on this crucial issue are wide-ranging and difficult: weapons buy-back programs, the banning of armor-piercing ammunition, and the gathering of facts and figures of gun violence in our culture. But make no mistake about it: we must have the conversation and move our country forward as we do something far different than what we've done (or failed to do) in the past. It is unconscionable to continue letting more and more guns saturate our society.

Community and St. James are places that function well as open forums for the discussion of ideas and for hearty engagement with the issues of our day. To engage in such a discussion and to presume that people of faith can do something meaningful about our violent world puts us in good company.

Isaiah, son of Amoz, prophesied some 2,800 years ago about a time when people would declare, "Enough is enough," and thereafter they would say "let us go to the mountain of the Lord . . . that he may teach us his ways and that we may walk in his paths." And among the nations and the collective peoples, swords would be beaten into plowshares, and spears into pruning hooks, and nation would not lift up sword against nation, and neither would they be at war with one another anymore.

Isaiah's "word from the Lord" is our word this morning, if we will have the openness—and the moral grandeur and spiritual audacity! —to hear it.

In order to hear this powerful word in the service of healing a violent world, I want to suggest that we understand the nature of violence itself. In our coffee-shop conversations and dinner-table talk and fellowship-hall sharing, we need to affirm an engagement with the following issues:

1. An assault weapons ban (and high-capacity magazines along with them);
2. Mental health reform,

3. The reduction of the amount of violent content in our video games and movies.

We really must engage all three of those issues together!

II.

And we must begin to understand the root emanations of violence in their various guises.

We do violence to others when we blithely take up swords and spears and AK-47s and AR15s and treat other human beings as invisible. The violence of invisibility is what Martin Luther King fought against all his adult life. The violence of invisibility is what ended the life of Marvel Johnson on the night of December 30, in the 1300 block of E. 81st St. in Kansas City, Missouri. He was asked by a young man if he had a light. Marvel didn't, but he asked the young man if he knew anything about the car prowlers that had been seen on the block where they were talking. The young man somehow became so angered by Marvel's question that he pulled a pistol and, telling the two kids with him to run, turned to run himself and then fired back at Marvel, hitting him in the abdomen. The young man who killed Marvel has not yet been apprehended, but he and those around him who know what he has done have committed the foundational violence of treating Marvel as if he were invisible.

They do not know what our own Jean Sailors knows, namely:

- that Marvel was a graduate of Truman High School in Independence;
- that he had been part of the Cornerstones of Care program that provides foster care for children whose parents cannot;
- that he had enrolled in business school;
- that he worked in a restaurant;
- that he could sing, and that he was pursuing a recording contract;
- that he was funny, and that he liked to laugh;
- that he was baptized and a member of Blue Ridge Church of Christ;
- that he had a girlfriend, and that he had a mother and friends and people who loved him and cherished his smile and his hugs.

Had the assailant known about Marvel's sterling qualities and characteristics, perhaps he wouldn't have shot him in such a devastatingly cavalier way.

II.

Let us also understand that violence emanates from ignorance. The people whom Isaiah described in his prophecy faced this dilemma. To say "Come, let us go to the mountain of the Lord . . . that he may teach us his ways and that we may walk in his paths" is to admit that one needs to know some new knowledge, that one has some learning to do in order to overcome an ignorance that may do them harm if they do not dispel it.

Howard Thurman knew intimately and wrote persuasively all of his adult life about the violence of ignorance. He received one of his first lessons about it when he was a boy.

When Thurman was growing up in Florida, a young white girl for whose family he worked was bothering him one day as he raked leaves. He would rake the leaves together, and she would scatter them. When he cautioned her that he would report her to her father for what she was doing, she stuck him with a pin. In response to the pin-pricking, Thurman naturally flinched and protested. But the little girl was not moved. In fact, she was taken aback and said, "Oh Howard, that didn't hurt! You can't feel!"[1]

She didn't really regard Thurman as human. She was ignorant to the utmost degree about the common humanity they shared. By such disregard, by such willful ignorance, she could arrogate to herself the right to inflict violence upon him.

Are we not willfully ignoring the humanity of others when we set the prerogative of owning an assault weapon (along with a high-capacity magazine) above the right simply to live?

IV.

Note with me now the nefarious sort of violence that comes from indifference. If famed Nobel Peace laureate Elie Wiesel only spoke the following quote, that would be sufficient for us to remember him with hushed awe and quiet revering forever: "The opposite of love is not hate. The opposite of love is indifference."[2]

Indifference is a plague of our current times. The ennui, the I-don't-care-ness, the solipsistic idolatry of one's self, all of which goes into a collective glob of indifference, is a horrible burden we have heaped upon ourselves.

And underneath the indolent sense of indifference that plagues our times is, I believe, an assumption that sixteenth-century philosopher Thomas Hobbes was right to assume that the state of nature is absolute evil and that human life is "solitary, poor, nasty, brutish and short."

But as people of faith, we know that exactly the opposite is the case: human life and the life we share with the rest of creation are:

- Communal, as we remember the African proverb: "If you want to go fast, go alone. If you want to go far, go together;"
- Enriching, as we see what gifts are ours from God's very generous hand of grace;
- Lovely, especially when we gaze into a child's eyes;
- Humane, in fact, more humane than you may have ever dreamed possible for human beings to be humane;
- Full, as long as love can bear us along on its long, long, long line of care.

In Anthony Lane's brilliant *New Yorker* reviews of two movies, *Gangster Squad* and *Jack Reacher*, he asks some powerfully pertinent questions: "What does it mean for the majority of us, the nonviolent millions, that, year after year, we should observe such a rising flood of savage fictional acts that, after a while, we scarcely notice or mind? And is there anything a filmmaker could or should do to stem the flow?" He then goes on to challenge "the reflex assumption that we can somehow have thrills without spills."[3]

He is adroitly describing the burdensome violence of indifference that we must transform if we are to have any hope of a more peaceful world.

V.

If I were asked what the principal mode of violence occurring in American culture today is, I would quickly respond and say the violence of invective.

The use of abusive, attacking, critical language does untold amounts of damage to us all.

Barking accusations at one another is fit for dogs but harmful to humans.

Slinging snide remarks at others, even in the guise of and for the sake of comedy, doesn't push the ball down the field of human endeavor one inch. It only slimes us all.

When invective reigns, master poet William Butler Yeats becomes a prophet once more:

> Things fall apart; the center cannot hold;
> mere anarchy is loosed upon the world,
> the blood-dimmed tide is loosed,
> and everywhere the ceremony of innocence is drowned.[4]

In sounds and images, countless dehumanizing, hate-filled invectives assault our senses and our sensibilities. In movie theaters and music halls, on DVDs and CDs, we have permitted the violence of invective to prevail. Rarely does anyone claim or employ the chief tool for resisting such invective and making change happen: the boycott of a business. But they could. And given how broken our public discourse is and how tacky and brutalizing our various media are (particularly radio culture), perhaps such boycotts, whether officially or unofficially organized, are just the strategy to employ right now.

Whatever we do, transforming and changing the violence that is involved in our invective-laced culture would be an awesome—and many might say, welcome—revolution.

VI.

All the violences we've examined this morning have an antidote, you know.

The ways of God and the path that we may walk after God's example and leading, the key to overcoming all invisibility, ignorance, indifference, and invective all depend, of course, on love.

How do folks beat their swords into plowshares and their spears into pruning hooks? How does any one of us ever not learn war anymore? By love — plain and simple and, in the end, a joyfully daring thing to do.

If I were asked to speak a word on your behalf to the families who lost their little ones in Newtown, Connecticut, I would simply say this:

I love you. We love you. You are loved by God and by your community and by a nation that will continue to love you in and through your loss. I don't know how you will ever get over such a devastation, but I know you can get through it. And we promise to keep you in our prayers and to go on loving you until life rights itself, and you can walk without being hobbled by paralyzing anguish. I, we, will help you hang on.

But we will not only love you with our hearts; we will also serve the cause of justice on your behalf with our minds. We will work and discuss and gather information, and we will begin to transform the policies of this land regarding violence, and gun violence in particular, so that children are not riddled with bullets from semi-automatic assault rifles with high-capacity clips.

Now, that's what I would do if I were asked to offer a word to the Newtown residents. More importantly, on a personal level, I'm obviously sharing this word with those I care for deeply — all along the years of the rich tradition of this pulpit exchange — with you all. May the discussions we have in the coming months, may the prayers we offer for the sake of transformation, may the public forums we share with the wider reaches of Kansas City be a part — a spark — of a new revolution in our personal manners and our public lives. And may that transformation, that revolution begin today, with Isaiah as our guide!

And remember: Isaiah did not say *if* it would happen or that it *might* happen or that it *could* happen or that it is merely *supposed* to happen. No, Isaiah declared in the imperative tense:

They shall beat their swords into ploughshares, and their spears into pruning hooks. Nation shall not lift up sword against nation, and neither shall they learn war anymore.

In our day and time that translates as:

They shall beat their assault weapons into textbooks, and their high-capacity clips into art supplies. Neighbor shall not lift up weapon against neighbor or stranger, and neither shall they learn bloody violence anymore.

And it can mean:

They shall beat their violence-laced hate-radio programs into musical concerts, and their slew of invectives into affirming messages of hope.

And further, it must mean:

Political parties shall not lift up sword against one another,
and neither shall they learn the idiotic intrusion of the filibuster anymore.

And:

They shall beat their hate speech into scholarships and nutrition for all children, and all harmful words into a cascading waterfall of grace! One group shall not lift up accusation and condescension against another group, and neither shall they learn division anymore.

God didn't ask our opinion about whether we thought that was practically implementable, nor if we liked it. The divine mandate communicated through Isaiah simply declared, "they shall . . . they shall . . . they shall."

Amen.

NOTES

1. Howard Thurman, *With Head and Heart: The Autobiography of Howard Thurman* (New York: Hartcourt Brace Jovanovich, 1979), p. 12.
2. Elie Wiesel, interview with Alvin P. Sanoff, "One Must Not Forget," *U.S. News & World Report,* October 27, 1986, p. 68.
3. Anthony Lane, "Violent Screen," *The New Yorker,* January 21, 2013, p. 79.
4. William Butler Yeats, "The Second Coming," *The Collected Poems of William Butler Yeats: New Edition,* Richard J. Finneran, ed. (New York: Palgrave Macmillan, 1989), p. 187.

44

BUT ONLY SAY THE WORD

Texts: Matthew 8:5–13 and Philippians 4:8–9

I want to say a word of thanks to your pastor—and my friend and colleague—the Rev. Laura Ann Phillips, for her gracious invitation to fill this pulpit this morning. (I'm humbled beyond measure that she would regard me as "mentor." Her words in the introduction are true gifts that I will cherish from this experience this morning.)

I also want to say a word of thanks to Peggy as well. It is so good to be with you and share in this service with you, in this congregation that you have loved and served with such constant devotion for so long.

You all are to be commended for this sermon series during the month of February. The Rev. Dr. Sarah Lund, who authored the book which has served as a book-study focus for you all, is a dear friend of mine, and she would be extremely gratified to know that you have journeyed through the worship/sermon series entitled *Blessed are the Crazy: Breaking the Silence about Mental Illness, Family, and Church.* I have heard from Laura (and Peggy) that you have already considered the issues of anxiety/depression, suicide, and addiction. It is my privilege and challenge this morning to take up the concluding themes of moral Injury/PTSD. But first, let us consider the scripture text from Matthew's gospel.

I.

In our central text for this morning, we have the first narrative of Jesus performing his first specific, public miracles.

After his baptism and then a time of temptation in the wilderness, after beginning his ministry in Galilee and the calling of his first disciples, after ministering to crowds of people, including offering healing to all sorts of afflicted folks, he delivers his most famous oration, the Sermon on the Mount, proclaiming mandates and guidance on a lifetime's worth of issues and topics: from adultery to loving our enemies; from anger to almsgiving; from anxiety to asking, seeking, and knocking; from prayer to the fulfillment of the law and the prophets; from the beatitudes to being salt and light.

Descending from the mount, Jesus acts in power for the marginalized and the excluded.

First, Jesus cleanses a man afflicted with leprosy. Then, entering Capernaum, Jesus meets a military man.

There he is. A centurion of the Roman occupying forces. A man of power and prestige. A man with one hundred soldiers under his command (thus, his distinctive rank of centurion). A man adorned with a distinctive helmet, armor, sword, and medals indicating his service and valor, and an intimidating cudgel staff. In today's military parlance he would likely be a captain.

This military man, this centurion, this captain of the Roman Empire has great capacity, as he represents Roman control of taxes from the famed fishing and transportation in the region. Yes, a man of power and high rank and control. But there is one thing he cannot do.

One of his servants, a man in his charge, a person for whom he feels responsible, is paralyzed and "in terrible distress." We do not have the particulars of the disease or distress that has caused the paralysis. We don't know the exact diagnosis, only that the paralyzed servant's situation is so dire that the centurion has come to seek a word from Jesus, whose fame as a healer and wonder-worker has already spread throughout Galilee.

We should also note that we have no indication of the centurion's religion or faith. We cannot see any book of holy scriptures — whatever they may have been — under his breastplate of armor. We don't know what kind of prayers — if any — he may have spoken to any sort of deity. We only know that he is seeking a word from Jesus.

Jesus offers to go to where the paralyzed servant is laying in distress, but the centurion says no, he is not worthy to receive such a powerful visitation under his roof. The centurion has a connection with Jesus. He knows how, as a centurion, he has authority to command actions among his soldiers and those actions simply happen. He has abiding faith that a mere word from Jesus can compel the healing his servant so desperately needs.

II.

We often hear this story told, about the great faith that the centurion has in Jesus. "Not even in Israel" has Jesus witnessed such profound faith. It is a profound and seemingly miraculous faith.

But please see with me how overwhelmingly distinctive the centurion's faith is: the simple trust in a mere declaration from Jesus. Not a touch. No healing ointment. No formulaic ritual. Just a word. That's all the centurion asks, because he believes that is all that his servant needs.

This centurion, this military man, this captain of the Roman Empire knows, with almost premonition-like wisdom, how powerful Jesus's words can and will be.

And you know how powerful Jesus' utterances will and can be, too.

- Remember how he enlists the participation of the disciples in his movement of grace and love: "Come, follow me."
- Remember how he calms the storm on the raging sea: "Peace, be still."
- Remember how he includes the little children within his embrace, when the disciples want to keep them away: "Let the little children come unto me."
- Remember how he speaks the great commission: "Go, therefore and make disciples of all nations."

The centurion has a trust in Jesus' powerful way with words. All this military man asks is this: "But only say the word."

Such a singular request, such a simple ask is informative for us this morning. And it should be. Beyond being a sweet, nice-and-neat story about Jesus and a distant Roman centurion, Matthew's gospel has a powerful message for our lives and especially for those who serve now and who have served in the military forces of America.

The situation is a bit different, of course, but the parallels and the fit with our own lives is undeniable.

There is no centurion here this morning, asking for Jesus' healing touch for a servant, someone in his or her charge,

No, it is the modern-day American centurion, or should I say the many centurions, indeed the millions of soldiers, who wait silently—sometimes desperately—in need of a word of healing. Too often, tragically, our modern-day centurions, suffering from post-traumatic stress disorder or moral injury, do not seek, do not ask for, do not express a need for such healing. But they stand in need of that healing, as do their families, nonetheless.

III.

Post-traumatic stress disorder became part of the collective American vocabulary in the 1970s in response to the situations of veterans of the Vietnam War. It became part of the official diagnostic language of the American Psychiatric Association in 1980. PTSD occurs as a disorder after we are exposed to a traumatic event, including war, car accidents, sexual assault, and child abuse. Symptoms range from disruptive dreams, conflicting feelings, and physical distress to more extreme cues such as avoiding all trauma-related situations. Persons with PTSD are at higher risk for suicide and intentional self-harm.

PTSD can happen to anyone. It is not a sign of weakness. [1] And it can happen to non-military folks as well, especially first-responders, including police officers, firefighters, EMTs, and hospital emergency personnel.

And let me repeat, PTSD can happen to anyone. PTSD is not a sign of weakness or moral failure or questionable character. This is not merely my opinion. This is a fact.

I began to learn more about PTSD and the parallel condition of moral injury when my friend the Rev. Dr. Rita Nakashima Brock, the founding co-director of The Soul Repair Center at Brite Divinity School, in Fort Worth, Texas, and her co-author, Dr. Gabriella Lettini, published their book *Soul Repair: Recovering from Moral Injury after War*. From Rita I learned about the amazing opportunities available to religious communities to participate in veteran recovery.

Dr. Brock is the daughter of a Korean War veteran and stepdaughter of a World War II and Vietnam War veteran and she began to be acutely aware of the challenging predicament faced all too frequently by American veterans. Over the past two decades, suicides by veterans have escalated dramatically even though increased research and treatment options for PTSD have been available for them. New studies suggest that a different hidden wound of war — moral injury — may be a significant factor in veteran suicides.

As Rita explains: "Moral injury is a negative self-judgment based on having transgressed core moral beliefs and values. . . . Its symptoms include shame, survivor guilt, depression, despair, addiction, distrust, anger, a need to make amends, and the loss of a desire to live."[2] In addition to therapy, it requires caring people who offer compassionate support for recovery.[3]

The military man, the Roman centurion in Matthew's gospel, makes a simple request: "But only say the word and my servant will be healed."

Our brothers and sisters enduring PTSD and moral injury wait silently, sometimes agonizingly, yearning for a healing word of hope and encouragement. We are the hands and feet and caring presence of Jesus to these current-day centurions. And the words yearned for by our brothers and sisters shall come from our tongues.

So, what shall we say? What word, or what words, can we utter that can provide healing?

I want to suggest a five-finger exercise that we can employ whenever we run into anyone — friend, family member, anyone — needing healing from PTSD and moral injury.

1. *Listen and hear.* Listen in the silence. Listen in the awkwardness. Listen for opportunities for support and connections with other veterans, other folks who have had similar experiences. Listen with "patience with their silence and with the confusion, grief, anger, and shame it carries."[4]

2. *Love.* Love without judgment or judgmentalism. Love them toward their own self-forgiveness. Say your love: "I love you" and "You are lovable."

3. *Live with hopefulness.* Live with hope and anticipation of their embrace of our common humanness. Week after week, Christ reaches out to each and every one of us — in all of our brokenness, with all of our dirt and grime, all of our mistakes, big and small, all of our shortcomings, incidental and catastrophic, and repeats, "It is all right — believe it or not — to be people."[5]

4. *Learn.* Learn how we are all called to grow toward wholeness, day by day, breath by breath. God is not finished with any one of us. We are all works in progress, under construction. And in that process, there is great joy.

5. *Let the community of faith — let Overland Park Christian Church — have faith for those whose faith has waned or withered and wilted into almost nothing.* It's interesting to me that the last word that Jesus offers the centurion in Matthew's gospel account is "Go; let it be done for you according to your faith." This, too, may be a word we can offer our modern centurions, all those enduring through PTSD and moral injury. We, too, can help our brothers and sisters "Go." Go to groups of other veterans. Go to a therapist's office for a listening ear. Go to a recovery group. And, alternatively, we can say, let it be done according to our faith. You say, Mr./Ms. Centurion, that you don't have much faith? No worries. We'll have faith for you until

your faith returns. We can say, let the healing be done according to the faith of Overland Park Christian Church, a body of believers that will maintain faith for those whose faith has waned or withered and wilted.

I don't offer this five-finger exercise as a panacea or cure-all but as words that might have some healing properties in them. If we will listen, and love, and live with hopefulness, and learn, and let OPCC carry the faith of others, perhaps we will be better able to welcome home the men and women who are sent off to war. Perhaps we can bring them home truly to peace. Perhaps this is one of the things that we in the community of faith can do to help anyone touched by PTSD or moral injury come all the way home.

Amen.

NOTES

1. According to the APA and the US Department of Veterans Affairs.
   See https://www.ptsd.va.gov/understand/common/common _adults.asp
2. Nakashima Brock, Col. Herman Keizer, Jr., and Dr. Gabriella Lettini, "Moral Injury: The Crucial Missing Piece in Understanding Soldier Suicides," *The Huffington Post*, July 23, 2012, updated Sept.2, 2012, (https://www.huffpost.com/entry/moral-injury-the-crucial-missing-piece-in-understanding-soldier-suicides_b_1686674)
3. Shared by Dr. Brock in numerous workshops I've attended.
4. Rita Nakashima Brock and Gabriella Lettini, *Soul Repair: Recovering from Moral Injury after War* (Boston: Beacon Press, 2012), p. 128.'
5. Here I've adapted a phrase from Annie Dillard's *Teaching a Stone to Talk* (New York: Harper & Row, 1982). See especially p. 38.

45

RACIAL JUSTICE

Text: Micah 6:8

Good evening, and thank you! I want to thank my friend and colleague Rabbi Alan Londy for his gracious invitation and kind regard to even think of me to fill this esteemed pulpit for this Shabbat service. I also want to thank the members and lay leaders of this congregation who have also offered such tender care and a sense of warmth and hospitality, not only to me, but to all guests here on this occasion.

I'm also thankful for the topic your rabbi invited me—or I should say *instructed* me—to focus upon for our common consideration this evening.

Even though racial justice may seem to some folks to be a daunting theme, and even though there is so much about which we could be understandably despairing in connection with that theme, it is a timely topic, ripe on the vine of a powerful consummation.

Such a topic as racial justice is altogether appropriate and timely, given that we have assembled a mere four days after the national Martin Luther King holiday, and given all that has gone on in the world:

- the series of events that have fomented around Ferguson, Missouri, over the course of the last seven months;
- the debut of the movie *Selma*;
- the fiftieth anniversary of the event that the movie celebrates—the march by Dr. King, SCLC, and John Lewis, along with Rabbi Abraham Joshua Heschel and other Jewish leaders for the sake of voting rights for all Americans.

And it is not merely because we abide in the shadow of Dr. King's legacy that we gather and focus upon the theme of racial justice. Rather, I am here with you to remember what has transpired, and to note what is going on presently, and to point to all that is yet to be.

This evening I'd like to draw your attention to one of the truly premier texts of the entire Hebrew Bible, Micah 6:8: "God has shown you, O humanity, what is good; and what does the Lord require of you but to do justice, to love kindness, and to walk humbly with your God."

"Right religion" is how Joseph Parker once described this text, before which "all controversy, all resentful intellectualism, all selfish calculation . . . . must fall."[1]

Note with me, first of all, that the Lord calls for doing justice:

- Not merely feeling that justice would be a good thing to do, a fine ideal, a lofty goal, a fetching notion, a wonderful principle, or a wondrous abstraction.

- Nor is it merely a collection of mellifluous words, however eloquent they might fall upon the ear. These are not empty phrases describing what we think we might do one day.
- Rather, we are mandated by God to do justice. By . . . the Shaper of the Shema, the Signal Artist at Sinai, the Deliverer of Daniel, the Justifier of Job, the Foundation of the World, the One who listens to every cry of every hurting and wounded and disinherited, disenfranchised, discussed and cussed child of God who ever yearned for a listening ear in the middle of the night!

The Lord of all says . . . do justice. Do justice in the way that the poet and justice advocate Marge Piercy describes in her poem "To Be of Use":

The people I love . . .
jump into work head first. . . .

The pitcher cries for water to carry
and a person for work that is real.[2]

Now, please note that justice is never justice if it becomes reptilian, cold and calculating and humorless. Justice, to be a justice that really lasts and has generative power, is always tempered with compassion.

Doing justice sometimes requires balancing the scales of what's right and what's wrong, and making sure everyone gets a fair shake, or to use Walter Brueggemann's haunting clarification, "to sort out what belongs to whom and to return it to them."[3]

To do justice in a human and humane fashion means, to paraphrase Paul Tillich, mastering two truisms: *Justice without love is legalism. Love without justice is sentimentality.*

It also means that we are to engage with honest assessments of the past and encounters with what may prove to be uncomfortable truths. I once had a fundamental encounter with an exceedingly uncomfortable truth.

When I was twelve years old our family lived in Brownsville, Texas. Oscar Galvan was my best friend then. Ours was the only Anglo family in the neighborhood. Many of my first vocabulary words were Spanish since the vast majority of the culture that surrounded us was Hispanic. Oscar Galvan, four houses down the block, was Hispanic. But still he accepted me. One bright summer day, as we participated in one of our favored childhood pastimes—lying comfortably on the St. Augustine grass and gazing up to the sky to trace shapes in the clouds—Oscar asked me, out of the blue, "Will you still be my friend next year, when we get to Stell Junior High School?"

I was dumbfounded by such a question. "Of course I will," I replied. "Why would you ever think I wouldn't'?"

"Well," Oscar pondered deeply, "you know what they do with us over there, don't you?"

"No," I said with shock, hardly able to imagine what he was talking about.

"See, you're Anglo and I'm Mexican," Oscar said, "and when we get into junior high school, they start to divide us up, and I just wondered if you'd still be my friend."

"Of course, I will, Oscar, I'll be your very best friend," I declared with boldness.

But Oscar knew something about dominant American culture that I hadn't yet figured out. In my naiveté I had promised more than I could deliver. A short year after we had our friendship discussion, Oscar was but a faint remembrance of a distant summer, and we were no longer best friends.

(I should add that, fortunately, four decades after the painful leave-taking in our relationship, Oscar and I reconnected over a fine Tex-Mex dinner in Austin, Texas, talking late into the evening, and renewed our friendship with gladness and deep gratitude. And the relationship abided, due largely, I believe, to Oscar's generous spirit.)

Before we depart, I need to say something about strategic, visionary hopefulness. Allow me to share two stories with you.

First story. When the faith-based organization MORE2 (Metro Organization for Racial & Economic Equity) came into being in 2004, it had eleven congregations (it has grown to include more than two dozen congregations now). At the beginning, it was determined that one of our chief values was living-wage jobs. In the summer of 2005, there was a $5 billion building boom going on in the construction business in greater Kansas City, with most of the projects being publicly funded—local, state and federal. Because of the public funding, most of those projects required a certain percentage of minority and women workers—both in the workforce and in the sub-contractors engaged in the projects. A thorough survey done by *The Kansas City Star* revealed that none of the projects were anywhere close to meeting the targeted MBE/WBE goals or the workforce numbers for the projects. In response, MORE2 created The Jericho Table to bring down the walls separating the construction jobs and the qualified minority and women workers in Kansas City. Major construction companies like JE Dunn, Turner, Walton, Straub, and Huber were all represented, as were minority construction workers and unions, with the MORE2 leadership conducting and leading the meetings of The Jericho Table.

One of the projects was the ICON Bridge project, which would eventually be known as the Kit Bond Bridge, replacing the old Paseo Bridge. MORE2 helped to write the request for proposal (RFP) for that project and included a thirty percent MBE/WBE sub-contractors provision and a thirty percent minority and women workforce provision. We tapped into a Highway Fund allowance for one-half of one percent of the $250 million project to go toward training for minorities and women through the Full Employment Council. The project was completed with all those strategically envisioned goals fulfilled or exceeded! Which meant that justice was done and a whole new group of minority and women construction workers had real careers in the construction industry. Strategic, visionary hopefulness!

Second story. In 1926, Mordecai Wyatt Johnson became the first African American president of Howard University. Mordecai Johnson would go on to lure Dr. Howard Thurman and his wife Sue Bailey Thurman to join the faculty and then, nearly a decade later, to encourage them to go on a Pilgrimage of Friendship to India, where they would be among the first four African Americans to meet and have deep discussions with Mohandas K. Gandhi. Thurman would then bear the tenets of nonviolence to the United States, where he would convey the great Mahatma's strategy to generations of adherents who would lead the civil rights struggle toward its fulfillment.

When he began, however, Mordecai Johnson had another primary concern: raising the standards of the law school, which was then little more than a night school. Supreme Court Associate Justice Louis D. Brandeis counseled Johnson, emphasizing that the foundation for overcoming racial discrimination was embedded in the Constitution. "What was needed," Brandeis averred, "was for lawyers to be prepared to base their arguments before the Court precisely upon the guarantees in the document."[4]

Agreeing with Brandeis' thesis and taking his counsel to heart, Mordecai Johnson secured Charles Hamilton Houston as vice-dean of the Howard University School of Law in 1929, and things got moving. An initial class of thirty students was eventually enrolled in Howard University's now accredited full-time program with an intensified civil rights curriculum. Johnson and Houston were bound and determined to train top-notch, world-class lawyers who would lead the fight against racial injustice. Among the first eight students who graduated in 1933 was a young man named Thurgood Marshall.[5]

The rest, as they say, is history. Marshall would go on to lead the successful Brown v. Board of Education case that abolished legal segregation in public education in the United States. Eventually, he became the first African American appointed to the Supreme Court.

Mordecai Johnson and Charles Hamilton Houston were not the only ones to lead America toward the dismantling of institutional prejudice in the twentieth century, but their strategic, visionary hopefulness contributed mightily to the transformation of American culture and the promise of American democracy for one and all. *Strategic, visionary hopefulness* — this is what is required to make for greater racial justice for one and all.

I close with two quotations from my friend Seymour who dropped by my office this afternoon to see what I was up to.

When I told Seymour I was looking forward to being with the great folks of the New Reform Temple, he said, "Well, remind them of what my grandpa used to tell me."

"What's that, Seymour? What did your grandpa always used to say?" I asked him.

He replied, "We ain't what we ought to be, and we ain't what we want to be, but thank God Almighty we ain't what we was."

Then there was one more thing Seymour and I discussed. It had to do with what kind of city Kansas City is, and what kind of city we want to be known as.

And I leave you, my friends with the question that Seymour and I settled on as an ultimately worthy question for any congregation and city concerned about racial justice.

"So," Seymour said, "when you think of Paris, you think of croissants and cafes and the Eiffel tower. When you think of London, it's fish and chips and London Bridge and Big Ben. When you think of Australia, it's kangaroos, billabongs, and the Sydney Opera House."

Could it be that when you and I and others think of Kansas City, we think of barbecue, and jazz, and . . . a people and a place and an entire community committed to racial justice?

Could it be?
Could it be?
Will it be?
Let it be so!
Amen.

NOTES

1. Joseph Parker, *The People's Bible: Discourses Upon Holy Scripture*, (New York: Funk & Wagnalls, 1892), vol. 17, p. 289.
    See also, https://archive.org/details/peoplesbibledisc17park/page/288/mode/2up
2. Marge Piercy, *To Be of Use* (Garden City, New Jersey: Doubleday and Company, Inc., 1973), pp. 49-50.
3. Walter Brueggemann, Sharon Parks, and Thomas H. Groome, *To Act Justly, Love Tenderly, Walk Humbly: An Agenda for Ministers* (Eugene, Oregon: Wipf & Stock Publishers, 1997), p. 5.
4. See https://www.encyclopedia.com/people/social-sciences-and-law/political-science-biographies/mordecai-wyatt-johnson and Richard I. McKinney, *Mordecai: The Man and His Message: The Story of Mordecai Wyatt Johnson* (Washington, D.C.: Howard University Press, 1997), pp. 70-71.
5. See Richard I. McKinney, *Mordecai: The Man and His Message: The Story of Mordecai Wyatt Johnson*, pp. 70-74.

46

ON ENTERTAINING ANGELS UNAWARES
Text: Hebrews 13:2

Good morning! And thank you! Thank you for the hospitality and graciousness which you've extended to me this morning, and all along the path to this gathering. I'm especially grateful to Sue Trowbridge and your senior minister, Dr. Kendyl Gibbons, who tendered the generous invitation to me to attempt to fill this esteemed pulpit. I'm also grateful to Anthony Edwards and Diana Hughes for their accommodating and welcoming spirits. And my, my, my, what a group of gifted musicians and singers you are blessed with here at All Souls. Also, it nearly goes without saying that I'm delighted to see so many All Souls friends this morning. It's good to recall the years of commitments we've shared through community involvement, not the least of which have been the empowering justice endeavors set to our hands through MORE[2] (Metro Organization for Racial and Economic Equity).

Speaking of justice, I know that you all have wrestled mightily and are still wrestling fervently with the state of our country since a certain election took place back in November.

It seems we are living in the strangest political climate any of us have ever seen.

Time will likely confirm that the current occupant of the White House has the highest "Transactional Quotient" in the history of the Presidency. It seems that all matters — political, financial, social, and relational — are, at their foundation, basically transactional from some folks' perspectives. That is, all things, all groups, all connections, all relationships are to be understood as transactions of a "deal" nature. Recall how we heard ad nauseam during the presidential campaign about making the "best deals." Deals, deals, deals, we were reminded again and again, were the *sine qua non* of what it meant to be a leader. And nearly always, the deals imagined had to do with money and material worth. Deals — this for that, tit for tat, quid pro quo — were (and now are) part of the "deal" with America.

But values like loyalty, trust, love, fidelity, truthfulness are not subject — finally and foundationally — to deal-making. (Are these really values any longer if they can be bought or sold or traded like one commodity among other commodities?) To live a truly ethical, a soundly moral, and an utmost human life, we are called to embody our values in our very essence, in our character, not to trade them in for "a better deal."

In the face of all we confront as a nation, as a community, and as individuals, allow me to offer a hope-filled word of support to you all (and maybe to remind myself). While it is small comfort, there is some reassurance in knowing that we've had bad leaders and leaders who have acted badly before. A brief representative list would surely include the following:

- Don't ask Native Americans to honor any monument celebrating President Andrew Jackson, whose racist actions resulted in the Trail of Tears and its horrific displacement and cultural annihilation.
- Remember President Andrew Johnson, whose recklessness and alcoholism nearly undid various accomplishments of Abraham Lincoln, some of the noblest and most transformative our country has ever known.
- Remember, too, that President James Buchanan was the one who insinuated support for the Dred Scott decision, one of the Supreme Court's most ignoble moments.
- Recall that President Franklin Delano Roosevelt turned away the M.S. St. Louis, a transatlantic ocean liner full of Jewish immigrants seeking asylum from Nazi Germany in 1939. Recall, as well, his endorsement and signing of Executive Order 9066, mandating the imprisonment of some 120,000 U.S. citizens of Japanese ancestry in internment camps from 1942 until the end of the World War II in 1945.
- And of course, how could any of us ever forget President Richard Nixon's paranoia and criminal actions in the shame-filled Watergate scandal that led to the biggest constitutional crisis in modern U.S. history.

So, be encouraged! Oh, yes, we've elected bad leaders and leaders who've acted badly before. And because we've prevailed before, I believe we can prevail again. Once more, vigilance is in order!

I.

This morning, at this sacred desk, for just a few moments, I'd like to address the theme *"On Entertaining Angels Unawares."*

I use this title to launch some serious questions: How do we treat strangers? How do we deal with "the other"? What's the role of hospitality in the life of a faith community? In light of what is going on in the United States, around the world, and here in Kansas City, this is an engaging and challenging theme to consider as we each seek to fulfill the dual responsibilities of living our faith and expressing our citizenship.

The focus of this sermon is prompted by two sources. First, the scriptural text of Hebrews 13:2. It is one of the most famous and most succinct mandates in the New Testament: "Do not neglect to show hospitality to strangers, for thereby some have entertained angels unawares."

Of course, it has parallels in the Hebrew Bible. In the book of Deuteronomy (10:17–19), the people are commanded, "For the Lord your God is . . . mighty and awesome, executing justice for the orphan and the widow, and loving strangers, providing them food and clothing. And you also shall love the stranger, for you were strangers in the land of Egypt."

The book of Psalms (146:9) also extols the worth and value of the stranger, saying, "The Lord watches over the strangers; [the Lord] upholds the orphan and the widow."

Catholicism is replete with religious orders, the Benedictines chief among them, who specialize in practicing hospitality as a premier virtue.

Rumi, the mystic founder of Sufism and the most widely read poet in the English language, said we are all called to express hospitality to one another, for no one is a stranger when we know that we are all signing the same song.

In Islam, hospitality is expressed when guests are served with cheerfulness and grace. Muhammad himself declared that hospitality was a sure sign of one's faith and was to be extended to one and all regardless of their religious beliefs.

Now, Howard Thurman would remind us that something — a mandate, an edict, a charge — is in a religion because it's true and not that something is true because it's in that religion. In other words, hospitality is a universally charged value.

In religion after religion, and in one sacred text after another, showing and sharing hospitality is deemed and esteemed as being the essential core of what it means to stand at the intersection of Humanity Highway and Divinity Drive.

We can all think of myriad reasons for this mandate, both inside and outside our faith experiences.

Hospitality, as my grandmother taught me, and maybe as your parents and grandparents taught you, too, is simply the decent thing to do. Hospitality, like honesty, is the best policy.

For others of us, hospitality is what we do to others because it has been done to us, and we wish to pay it forward. Is this the reason that some of you are here this morning, because this congregation, at a crucial juncture in your life's journey, proffered life-blessing, soul-enriching hospitality to you? Are you here because in ways that are nearly unspeakably mysterious to you, you feel compelled to learn more about that hospitality and to share it with others so that their lives can be blessed and their souls can be enriched as well? I suspect so.

Or it could be that you know what happens to a congregation when such hospitality is not shared.

II.

Fred Craddock tells the story of a church in East Tennessee that made a rule that only property owners could be members of the church. The town was bustling with newcomers, some from way up North and most from faraway, exotic places. And many of these foreign invaders were mere renters wherever they lived. So, a rule was put into effect: only property owners could become members of that particular church. After a while, the parking lot grew sparser and sparser, less and less populated by fewer and fewer vehicles. Eventually the church closed. But barely a generation later—not quite twenty years—the church was reopened, and the pastor who had fought against the property-owner rule (but who had obviously lost) went back for a visit. The parking lot was jam-packed. Totally full. And there was barely a place to find inside. Finally, they did find a place and sat and marveled at the transformation. It certainly was a new day. No property-owner membership policy was in effect, that was for sure.

There was every sort of folks imaginable in the place. Both the obviously rich and the abjectly poor were represented. And dress code? Forget it. Every fashion possible was represented. There had been some changes, however, in the arrangement of the house of worship. Where the communion table had once stood, a new piece of furniture had been set. It was a salad bar, for the church had been turned into a barbecue restaurant where, it said, above the door and emblazoned in bright neon, "All You Can Eat, All Are Welcome!"[1]

The members of that church possessed no sense of hospitality, and that congregation died. The barbecue joint practiced open-ended hospitality and thrived.

Now before any one of us becomes too moralistic about the call to hospitality, let's admit that there's some wisdom in a cautionary approach to strangers.

From an early age, we teach our children, "Don't talk with strangers."

When I was in college, it was easy to hitch-hike. Did it twice, in fact. From Fort Worth to Los Angeles, and back. And from Fort Worth to San Francisco and back. But I wouldn't counsel that now. Sometimes strangers aren't just strange, they're dangerous!

But look what has been wrought when we make a personal caution into a social ethic. We then abide, in Parker Palmer's words, "In the Company of Strangers," in which there is instilled in every pore of the body politic an infectious suspicion about those who are different, odd, strangers to us.[2]

III.

Now it's time for a brief confession about the second origin of this sermonic word.

Beyond the scriptural word from the book of Hebrews, there is another source of inspiration for this sermon as well. Simply put, I owe a debt of gratitude to Steve Bannon. Or perhaps I should say I owe this sermon to the *Washington Post*, which reported about Steve Bannon. For it was this disreputable character—with the beguiling-ness of Rasputin and the nefarious flair of a pitiless propagandist—who uttered a challenging and chilling question two years ago, when he was chairman of Breitbart, the alt-right so-called news program. Bannon's words had to do with what would become the present "Muslim ban" executive order regarding the exclusion from the U.S. of folks from seven (and now six) Muslim majority countries. In the course of his interview with Congressman Ryan Zinke (R-Mont.), Rep. Zinke said he "opposed [then] President Obama's plan to resettle some Syrian refugees in the United States. 'We need to put a stop on refugees until we can vet,' Zinke said. [But] Bannon cut him off. 'Why even let 'em in?' he asked." [3]

That challenging and chilling question could be applied not only to Syrian refugees and other people from Muslim-majority countries but also to Latinos whose entrance into the U.S. the current administration would likewise like to limit in radical fashion.

To that question— "Why let 'em in?" —allow me to offer a response:

WHY LET 'EM IN? . . . because Albert Einstein was not only the greatest physicist of the 20th century but also a German immigrant to the U.S. Without Einstein, we'd have to erase from the American scene any vestige of the theory of relativity, and the laws of thermodynamics, and the theory of black holes, and one of the most heralded campaigns for peace our nation has ever seen.

WHY LET 'EM IN? . . . because Ieoh Ming Pei was not only one of America's most famous architects but also a Chinese immigrant to the U.S. Without I.M. Pei, we'd likely have no East Wing of the National Gallery of Art in Washington, D.C., nor the John F. Kennedy Memorial Library in Boston, nor the Rock and Roll Hall of Fame in Cleveland.

WHY LET 'EM IN? . . . because Elie Wiesel was not only the recipient of the 1986 Nobel Peace Prize and one of the greatest champions for human dignity the world has ever seen but also a Romanian immigrant to the U.S. Without Wiesel, we wouldn't have the powerful impetus to remember the Holocaust and thereby to resist all instances of genocide and fascism whenever they raise their evil, ugly heads.

WHY LET 'EM IN? . . . because Jerry Yang, was not only the founder of Yahoo but also a Chinese immigrant to the U.S. Without Yang, we'd likely not have one of the most trafficked internet sites in the world. Without Yang, Stanford University would be $75 million poorer and not have the state-of-the-art Environment and Energy Building.

WHY LET 'EM IN? . . . because Joseph Pulitzer was not only the owner of The St. Louis Post-Dispatch and The New York World newspapers which exposed corruption and tax evaders and the leader of the campaign to build a pedestal for the Statue of Liberty so it could be shipped from France. He was also a Hungarian immigrant to the U.S. Without Mr. Pulitzer or the standards he set for journalistic excellence or his visionary legacy, there would be no Pulitzer Prizes.

WHY LET 'EM IN? . . . because Irving Berlin was not only a composer of some of America's most beloved music, including "White Christmas," "There's No Business Like Show Business," "Always," and "God Bless America," but he was also a Russian immigrant to the U.S.

WHY LET 'EM IN? . . . because not only did John Muir's writing lead to the creation of Yosemite National Park and the founding of the Sierra Club, not only did his leadership help to establish Grand Canyon, Sequoia, Petrified Forest, and Mount Rainier national parks, but he was also an immigrant to the U.S. from Scotland.

WHY LET 'EM IN? . . . because Felix Frankfurter was not only a leading constitutional scholar from Harvard who advised President Roosevelt about the agencies of the New Deal and eventually an eminent member of the U.S. Supreme Court, but he was also an Austrian immigrant to the U.S.

WHY LET 'EM IN? . . . because basketball Hall-of-Famer Hakeem Olajuwon is a Nigerian immigrant to the U.S.

WHY LET 'EM IN? . . . because Oscar-winning director Ang Lee is a Taiwanese immigrant to the U.S.

WHY LET 'EM IN? . . . because former Secretary of State Madeleine Albright is a Czechoslovakian immigrant to the U.S.

WHY LET 'EM IN? . . . because rock music superstar Dave Matthews is a South African immigrant to the U.S.

WHY LET 'EM IN? . . . because esteemed novelist and Presidential Medal of Freedom recipient Isabel Allende is a Chilean immigrant to the U.S.

WHY LET 'EM IN? . . . because Boys Town founder Father Flanagan was an Irish immigrant to the U.S.

WHY LET 'EM IN? . . . because Bob Hope was a British immigrant to the U.S.

Why let 'em in, indeed! "Do not neglect to show hospitality to strangers, for thereby some have entertained angels unawares."

And here's another, more important reason you are called to show hospitality to strangers and let 'em in: It's who you are, here at the corner of Walnut and 45th Streets, and wherever else you gather to express your faith and values. It's who you are. And everyone can behold it in . . . your . . . name: All Souls!

You're not a church of "The Few-The Proud-The Brave" Souls.

Nor a church of "First-Come-First-Serve" Souls.

Nor a church of "Perfect-People" Souls.

Nor a church of "A-List" Souls.

No, you are named the All Souls Unitarian Universalist Church. All Souls is a place and a people where Maya Angelou's poetic wisdom is lived out consistently and courageously every day: "We are more alike, my friends,/Than we are unalike./ We are more alike, my friends,/ Than we are unalike."[4]

IV.

Before I go, allow me one final valediction, a "five-finger exercise," if you will, that I'd suggest for your consideration, as we wade together through the morass of misdirection and the politics of improvisational contradiction and propagandistic bullying, as we try to disentangle fact from fiction about Russia's possible tampering with our electoral process and all the rest:

1. Let us support and defend immigrants and their children against deportation, slandering, and dehumanization.

2. Let us champion diversity for all people and vociferously resist xenophobic intolerance of others because of racial, religious, national origin, gender-identity, sexual orientation, or any other differences.

3.   Let us hope for a transformation in our nation, away from nationalistic tribalism and toward a vigorous embrace of collective insight and religious pluralism that has been a hallmark of the United States when we've been at our best. This is truly the American way.

4.   Let us be vigilant against the demagoguery, bigotry, , and chaotic confusion sewn by those consorting to undermine our trust in each other, our trust in a free press, and our trust in the progress made thus far beyond the abject racism, sexism, and divisiveness of bygone eras.

5.   Let us register as many voters as we can wherever we are, and let us promote voter education and citizenship involvement with and among one and all.

No amount of additional vetting (beyond the average of two years of review and screening that already takes place for those seeking to immigrate to this country) and no amount of demonizing of or bloviating about "strangers" should cause us to forget the clarion call of hospitality contained in Emma Lazarus' sonnet *"The New Colossus."* Inscribed on a bronze plaque on the pedestal for the Statue of Liberty are these immortal words:

Give me your tired, your poor,
Your huddled masses yearning to breathe free,
The wretched refuse of your teeming shore.
Send these, the homeless, tempest-tost to me,
I lift my lamp beside the golden door.

This is what it means to be exquisitely faithful. This is the best way to express and to fulfill our citizenship. Amen.

NOTES
1. See Fred B. Craddock, *Craddock Stories* (St. Louis: Chalice Press, 2001), p. 28-29.
2. Parker Palmer, *The Company of Strangers* (New York: Crossroad, 1981).
3. "'Why even let 'em in?' Understanding Bannon's worldview and the policies that follow," by Frances Stead Sellers and David A. Farenthold, *Washington Post*, January 31, 2017. (https://www.washingtonpost.com/politics/bannon-explained-his-worldview-well-before-it-became-official-us-policy/2017/01/31/2f4102ac-e7ca-11e6-80c2-30e57e57e05d_story.html?utm_term=.49f184b7f483)
4. Maya Angelou, *The Complete Collected Poems* (New York: Random House, 1994), p. 225.

SIGNAL MOMENTS

47

LIFE IS TO BE CELEBRATED
Texts: Psalm 118:24, 26 – 27, 29 and Philippians 4:4 – 9

This morning we begin a new sermon series, *One More Thing!* This series is an important one to me and, as others have told me, to our family of faith, since it will be the last four sermons I offer as Community's senior minister. These four messages will seek to sum up some of the hallmark themes that have marked our time together as people and pastor over the last thirty years. Each Sunday and each sermon will be precious beyond description to me and, I hope and trust, useful to Community's members and friends.

It is a supreme joy to share this message with you this morning, for if there's anything I am convinced of — by virtue of God's assurances through faith and through the testimony of the Biblical witness and through the manifold graces of the community known as the Church (in all of its bungling and beautiful glory) — it is this thesis: "Life Is Meant to Be Celebrated."

I.

Over the course of my ministry, in congregations both small and large, among all sorts of Christians and amidst all kinds of life situations, it has become crystal clear that not all people hold to the notion that life is to be celebrated. Not all people believe in rejoicing. And they don't necessarily recommend it to their friends. Some folks believe life is merely to be tolerated.

These sorts of folks would side with some interpreters of Paul who say that the word we translate as "rejoice" in the fourth chapter of Philippians is better understood as meaning "farewell." "Don't get too excited about what Paul is saying here," they urge. "This is just a goodbye scene, nothing more."

But they couldn't be more wrong in such an interpretation.

The apostle Paul is writing to his most beloved congregation, one that he helped to found in one of his first missionary journeys. He could be writing from prison, very likely, toward the end of his life. He's summing up his hopes and dreams for the Philippians, and he offers a remarkable closing word of benediction upon them. "Finally," Paul says — and you know whenever Paul says "finally," this is the time for his closing word of benediction upon the Philippians — "beloved, whatever is true, whatever is honorable, whatever is just, whatever is pure, whatever is pleasing, whatever is commendable, if there is any excellence and if there is anything worthy of praise, think about these things."[1]

But before he gets to the benediction, he bids the Philippians to "Rejoice!"

As I've said, some folks just can't handle rejoicing or celebrating at all, and would agree with Henry David Thoreau who declared that "The mass of [humanity] lead lives of quiet desperation."

II.

Other folks hold fast to the notion that life is to be modulated, to be lived cautiously, always on an even keel.

A dear friend doesn't like too many highs or too many lows in his life.

Doesn't want to experience any kind of roller-coaster-like existence.

Doesn't like his food too spicy.

Doesn't drive over the speed limit except for an occasional tap on the gas pedal to go a little over 55 for about two minutes.

Likes his music to be rock and roll but not raucous rock and roll.

Likes his work load to be full but not too full.

Likes the church he attends to be challenging but not overly so.

Likes his Kaufman Stadium hot dog with mustard and relish but would never choose a Sheboygan brat and would never, never, never, ever add sauerkraut to it.

All in all, according to my friend, life should be modulated.

III.

Some folks believe life is merely to be adjudicated.

That is, they believe that life, real life, life at its foundational base, is a vale of tears in which we are called to determine the moralistic right things to do and to strive thereafter always to do the right, without humor or flair or any obstacle getting in our way. For such folks, life is a hard road, fraught with difficulties and dangers to one's moral life, and there is not much time for nor much purpose in pursuing anything like pleasure in life. Life is a grim task of seeing if our lives match up with the shoulds and shouldn'ts, the dos and don'ts that must rule our existence. Do you know some folks like that? Most of us have tipped in that direction at least on occasion.

On *Religion on the Line*, we hear rather frequently from listeners for whom this is the dominant motif in their life. They usually are trying to impress upon us three co-hosts that theirs is the only religious interpretation of a Biblical text or that their theological position is correct and on the mark. Their primary focus—at nearly every turn, so far as I have been able to determine—is to avoid hell. It's not that heaven is so beautiful and fetching and ultimately preferable, but rather that they are fascinated with hellishness. (By the way, as most of you who have listened to the show on occasion know, these folks are convinced that the theology we co-hosts express is rife with hellishness.)

I've often wondered if these folks are related to Thomas Hobbes, whose philosophical treatise *Leviathan* described the limits of human life as "solitary, poor, nasty, brutish and short."[2]

For these folks, hellishness is the extreme dragon of the human drama, and we are in constant danger of being dragged down into it.

IV.

But Paul says forget toleration, modulation, and adjudication and focus instead on celebration!

And what constitutes celebration for Paul? And what would it mean for you and me to wake up each morning and seek out rejoicing moments in need of celebrating.

I think it first means for us to assume that God is benevolent and gracious and intends us to receive everything we truly need in life. In other words, we can trust that God is a God of abundance. And we need not live anything but a handed-over live, making our requests known to God, and God's peace will eventually shower down on us.

I think the second thing we can do is to know that there is an abundant array of good qualities and positive dynamics available to us all, at all times. This is surely one of the most important implications when Paul declares that they should be imitators of his, focusing on what is true, honorable, pleasing, commendable, if there is any excellence, anything worthy of praise. All of which is to say that the best of our human journey occurs at the intersection of Humanity Highway and Divinity Drive. When we allow the possibilities for such an intersection to be constructed, or better yet, when we actively, purposefully pursue the construction of such an intersection, an empowering process abounds. And hearts are glad. And, to quote Tony Campolo, "It's party time!"

Which brings me to the main point about this main point about this one more thing: What about the party? Or better yet, what about the parties we are to engage in?

Celebrations naturally flow with success. They renew and expand our esteem for others and ourselves. Through celebrating a personal achievement, an organizational milestone, or significant life event, we finalize it. This is why every birthday is important, as well as every anniversary, every special attainment.

We bring the achievements, milestones, and events of our lives to full completion through celebration. And when that happens, they become a part of our self-image and expand our esteem. Nothing succeeds like success.

It has been a privilege to be a pastor here, where we celebrate our members' attainments and achievements with flair and flourish. Whether it was a particular member's milestone of fifty years of membership or a special wedding anniversary or a child's birth or a Sunday School teacher's years of continuous service, celebration has been a key punctuation point at Community. And in each celebration, there has always been an impetus for further achievement and attainment, further points of inspiration for the doing of our faith commitments.

Personal achievements, milestones and significant events left uncelebrated remain open and incomplete. When this is the case, we may end up feeling that what we achieved wasn't worth our effort, and therefore we may not be re-energized for the next step on our journey. We may even slip into a negative spiral.

But rewards and celebration revitalize us and keep us in a positive spiral as we move step by step to fulfill our personal and congregational mission. And as we do so, the experience of celebration affirms our competency, stimulates creativity, and expands our horizons.

So, are you ready to party? If you're not, get ready. It's the way of the gospel.

NOTES
1. Philippians 4:8
2. Thomas Hobbes, *Leviathan* (London: Penguin Classics, 2017), Ch. 13, p. 73.

48

DON'T FORGET TO REMEMBER

Text: Deuteronomy 6:4–2

Many thanks for your welcome and hospitality on this most unusual of Sunday mornings for you and for me.

I want to say a special thank you to Dr. Gentle for his graciousness and the generous invitation to be with you this morning. And I want to offer a huge word of gratitude to my niece, whom you may know as Kathryn Blaisdell, but whom I call Katie. It's always a special treat to be with her and an extra-special one to share worship with her in her "home" church.

This is a return trip for me to this honored pulpit. But I must say this is probably the most memorable visit.

I've been remembering and wondering whether Washington has seen a more dramatic week of concentrated seismic and meteorological events. Earthquake on the front end of the week and hurricane Irene on the tail end! Such events give new meaning to what was said by two well-wishers in Kansas City who encouraged me to come up here and give an "earth-shaking word" and to "preach up a storm." But make note that the earthquake and the hurricane happened prior to my arrival to this admired pulpit and *not* after I preached.

Please do receive my sincere thanks for this opportunity to be with you and know that we at Community Christian Church are sincerely and prayerfully concerned for the family of faith here at National City as you and the rest of the folks on the east coast proceed to recover from the earthquake and hurricane Irene. This is a week to remember indeed, for a long, long time.

Of course, this morning we all are remembering Dr. Martin Luther King Jr.'s life and legacy. The official dedication of the Martin Luther King Jr. Memorial that was set for today will be rescheduled. But we can still join with Dr. King's brothers, the Alpha Phi Alpha fraternity, along with innumerable others in the news media and on the internet, in treasuring Dr. King's exemplary significance.

To do such remembering is exceedingly appropriate for this or any other sanctuary. Remembering is an absolutely essential element of worship. There's nothing coincidental or casual about the time-honored words imprinted on countless communion tables across the land: "DO THIS IN REMEMBRANCE OF ME." We cannot worship without remembering.

Remembering is one of the key features of our humanness. Not the remembering of instinct or of habit, though those are good things in themselves. What I mean is the remembering that goes with marking life as holy and worthy and deserving of celebration.

I'm remembering. You're remembering. We all are engaged in remembering. And this is good.

In the book of Deuteronomy, we learn that memory is not only a good but also a sacred task.

From this morning's scripture reading, you have heard one of the greatest texts within the Hebrew Bible, one that is echoed in each of the New Testament gospels in one way or another.

In Matthew's and Mark's gospels it is referenced as the key to inheriting eternal life. In Luke's gospel it's the introduction to the Good Samaritan parable.

"Shema" is what this text is called, for *shema* is the Hebrew word for "hear." "Hear, O Israel, the Lord is our God, the Lord alone." "Shema, O Israel." "Shema."

And then come the instructions for sacred rituals of remembering: keep them in your heart, recite them to your children, have some conversation about them at home at the kitchen table, and when you're away from home, and when you lie down and when your rise, tie them to your hands and put them on your forehead and place them on the entrance-ways to your homes.

It's all about memory. And what are we to remember? Remember that the first and most important aspect of your life is to love God.

The Shema is a mark of the Israelites' movement from a nomadic life to a settled life, from impermanence to stability, from wandering with no direction home to being at home in a geographical locale that will become familiar and dear and cherished.[1] And the key to that movement is remembering to "love God with all your heart and with all your soul and with all your might."

When I was becoming a Horned Frog at the beloved Purple Mountain of Texas Christian University in Fort Worth, Texas, I had the privilege of taking a course from David Vanderwerken on William Faulkner. We read all of Faulkner's novels and short stories. In one of my favorite Faulkner novels, *Light in August*, in the sixth chapter, Faulkner offers an arresting opening line: "Memory believes before knowing remembers."[2] We Faulkner devotees went around for weeks stroking our chins and muttering "Memory believes before knowing remembers. Memory believes before knowing remembers." We had no idea what that actually meant! Now, some decades after those halcyon days, I think I finally figured it out. What did Faulkner mean by "Memory believes before knowing remembers"? I think he meant that remembering is an essential task, a sacred, life-giving undertaking, that remembering is a key to it all. To life, to relationships, to faith. Remember.

Now, the Israelites—and we, too—could relegate God and God's provisions to a bygone time. It's easy to do that, you know, to cast God only into the past, to long nostalgically for a time, as a defeatist might say, when God really was God and not just an absentee landlord.

Some people believe that remembering is a call to live in the past, in the proverbial good old days.

But allow me to ask, do any of us truly prefer the good old days when outhouses were the norm? Do any of us really want to return to the world as it was during World War II? Speak with any veteran from World War II—if they will speak at all about what costly experiences they endured — and I doubt if you will find any of them preferring to turn back the hands of time to the battles of the Allied troops against the Axis forces in Europe or the chaotic climes of the South Pacific?

My question about nostalgia is also this: When do we stop regressing into the distant past when things were supposedly really good? 1980? 1960? 1944? Anybody want to choose 1929? Shall we go back to 1860? 1492? What shall it be? No, none of those times. Our remembering shouldn't cast us into some idealized past but rather should compel us to move into the future.

Which is what the Martin Luther King Jr. Memorial is all about, too. As you all know, the King Memorial was unveiled on the Washington Mall in Washington, D.C., and was scheduled for dedication 48 years to this very day and hour after the high drama of the March on Washington and Dr. King's divinely touched "I Have a Dream" oration.

Those of you who've already seen it, either in person or in photographs, will attest to its magisterial character. The thirty-foot-tall sculpture, rendered by Chinese artist Lei Yixin, depicts Dr. King gazing out on the world with a countenance of fierce intensity and arms folded in bold determination.

Referencing one of his greatest rhetorical flourishes, there is chiseled into the memorial's side the memorable phrase, "Out of the mountain of despair, a stone of hope."

There is also a simple, singularly beautiful aspect of the memorial that deserves noting. What's so wondrous about the memorial is its seeming incompleteness. Dr. King is not standing clear of the granite, but rather is emerging from it, not yet completely free of it. It's as if the sculptor Yexin wanted to dramatize the indisputable fact that while Dr. King's dream is indelibly, undeniably etched in the American consciousness, the fulfillment of the dream is set to our hands. As Dr. King famously proclaimed, "Until all are free, I am not free."

Dr. King, and all people who admire his example, would have us heed the high calling of our prophetic role as people of faith, to "keep on walking, keep on talking, walking up the King's Highway," until, one day, Dr. King's dream is fulfilled and perhaps, perchance — could you, would we, ever dare to dream! — he would walk right out of that statue and shake your hand!

Our remembering should also compel us to realize that we are called to live in the only place and only time we have, here and now, and to recognize the most useful asset at our disposal, the best gift we have received, the greatest power we possess is this: God's presence in the here and now.

As Carl Jung put it in an adage inscribed above the front door of his home, *Vocatus, atque non vocatus, deus aderit.* "Bidden or unbidden, God is here."

A year ago last spring, on a bright Saturday afternoon, at Somerset Vineyard, near Louisburg, Kansas, I was privileged to officiate at the wedding of one of Community's members, Deidre Kalman, whom I had baptized as a youth, and her fiancée, Wade Walker. An unanticipated gift graced the day celebrating Deidre's and Wade's union.

In the beauty of the bucolic setting, the wedding party proceeded down the hillside to the place of the ceremony by a shimmering lake. Everyone was beautiful — attendants, mothers, flower girl, friends. And, of course, the bride and groom. And then I spoke the words I came to say, "Dearly Beloved, we are gathered together in the presence of God, and in the face of this company, to witness and to bless the joining of this woman and this man in holy matrimony."

Very quickly I came to the conclusion of the opening welcome, "So Deidre and Wade are here, and we are, for we would be no place else on the face of the earth. And Another is here as well, God is here . . ." and before I could get out the rest of the phrase ("to witness and to bless and to make yet holier still this holy matrimony"), little Christina Johnson, the petite three-year-old flower girl, shot a startled glance at her mother and shouted out "God is here, Mama! God is here!"

Talking with Christina's mother after the ceremony, while also telling Christina my thanks for the best seven-word sermon I had heard in a long time, I found out that Christina's father had died before she was born, killed in action in Iraq. "But," I said with what was surely a quizzical look on my face, "there doesn't seem to be a hole in her life."

"No, there isn't," her mother said to me, "God has filled that hole. It's a God-shaped hole now."

Despite what was surely an existential deficit, Christina and her mother spoke to God every night in their prayers, and she practiced, daily, the presence of God.

"God is here, Mama! God is here!" In honor of those who have gone before us and as we strive to love God with all our hearts and all our souls and all our might, will you say that phrase with me? "God is here, Mama! God is here!"

As with the Israelites who recite the Shema, as with Jesus who called all of us his followers to remember, as with the civil rights movement led by one now beautifully memorialized on the Washington Mall, may we take care not to forget, God is here! God is here! God is here!

Amen.

NOTES

1. *The Interpreter's Bible* (New York: Abingdon Press, 1953),vol. 1, p. 375.
2. William Faulkner, *Light in August* (New York: Vintage International, 1990), p. 119.

49

INGREDIENTS FOR A WORTHY RELIGION
Text: James 1:22 – 27

To start off the New Year we begin a brand new sermon series, *You've Got Mail!*, based on shorter letters in the New Testament. While some people may be familiar with the hallmark gospel texts (Matthew, Mark, Luke and John) and with some of the more prominent letters by the apostle Paul (I & II Corinthians, Romans, Philippians, for example), the shorter letters sometimes go begging for attention.

So, over the course of the months of January and February, we'll explore the sheer power of the shorter letters, including Paul's correspondence with Timothy and the Thessalonians, as well as his seeming "text message" to Philemon. We'll also examine a letter by Peter and the one-chapter-long letter by Jude. I hope and trust this series will lead us all to a better appreciation of the great graces available throughout the New Testament.

I.

This first message in the new series centers on the book of James. There is in James' a fervent focus on the practical dimensions of the Christian faith, which is also balanced by an equal emphasis on the "enough-ness" of God's grace.

James is among seven books in the New Testament that are called the "catholic" (meaning universal) epistles. The general grouping of the books of the New Testament goes as follow: the Gospels and the book of Acts, written by gospeler Luke, then apostle Paul's letters to the churches, which are followed by Paul's letters to persons (Timothy, Titus, and Philemon), and then the letters not written by Paul but adjudged by the Church to be important enough to be included in what we call the New Testament today. This latter group is where James belongs. These letters are given their names—James, I and II Peter, I, II, and III John—after the person who is presumed to have written them.

Now, just because James is little and comes so late in the arrangement of the books of the New Testament, do not underestimate its enduring capacity to stimulate faith.

James is a peculiar and a much-disputed and much-appreciated letter. If you were to look at the "postmarks" on James' letter—garnered from the rounds it made among the congregations in the Church's first few centuries of existence—you'd behold a fairly maltreated piece of mail, tattered at the corners and punched by every postal station imaginable.

II.

In the Early Church Fathers' reading of the book of James, they didn't find much to be quotable. Tertullian, one of the most loquacious of the fathers, would quote portions of the New Testament 7,258 times in his theological treatises. But never once did he quote James. The great Jerome gave a begrudging seal of approval for James, saying it was "OK," but he was still uncertain about James' authorship. It would take Augustine, finally, in the fourth century, to vouch that this was not only an important letter but also an authentic letter written by James, brother of Jesus, head of the church in Jerusalem after Jesus' resurrection.[1]

Syrian Church — There are on this letter seven centuries of postmarks from the Syrian churches, for it wasn't until the eighth century that the Syrian church finally accepted it as scripture.[2]

Greek Church — On James' envelope there are also "postmarks" from the churches where Greek culture had an impact. But it would take Athanasius's Easter letter (written from a post in Egypt) to put to rest James' dependability.[3]

Martin Luther — There is a peculiar postmark from Germany, handwritten it seems, from one Martin Luther, who, in the process of his reforming ways, described James as "an epistle of straw," and even went so far as to write on its envelope, "Return to Sender, who is Satan who resides in Rome."[4]

Still, ultimately, James has come to us as part of the Bible, tattered corners and all, disputations and all, not only as a besmirched and much-traveled piece of hard-copy mail, but also as a missive of massive importance for you and me. To mix our metaphors a bit and to emphasize the e-mail reference of our sermon series title, James has finally arrived in your faith's e-mail in-box with the announcement that "You've Got Mail!" As you attempt to open it, may you see it is a much-forwarded communication, sent by one friend to another to another, so much so that you nearly give up before you finally arrive at the letter's contents. But arrive you do, and then you behold:

- A lot of imperatives (60+) in the 108 verses of James.
- Only one reference to Christ (which is among the features of the letter to which Luther objected).
- A tone of urgency that seems to imply the author's assumption about a forthcoming return of Christ, what some in the Church have described as "The Second Coming."
- The recipients of the letter are obviously poor.[5]
- The instructions are firm and forceful regarding how James believes Christians are supposed to live. There isn't much nuance in James; he really proclaims with conviction and means to convert all of us readers with as much moral suasion as we can stand: *This is the right way! Follow it!*

III.

One of the more important messages we can gather from this mail from James is the key ingredients for any religion worth having. And those ingredients are found in our text for the morning.

(1) Be doers of the word, and not merely hearers who deceive themselves. In other words, your faith is to have integrity between what you hear in worship and what you do in response in the world. In still other words, don't be hypocrites, hearing the faith and perhaps even saying it, but never enacting it your actual life.

William Barclay put it this way: "That which is heard in the holy place is to be lived in the market place."[6]

My dear friend Rabbi Michael Zedek put it this way, after the fashion of the famed rabbi of London, Leo Baeck, who said, "More important than the sermon the rabbi gives is the sermon the rabbi lives."

And William Willimon, when commenting on this text, asks "[W]hat will we do with that which we have said, sung, and heard [in worship]?" Then he reminds us Christians of the normal interchange between preacher and a member at the door after the service. "'Pastor, that was a wonderful sermon,' said the parishioner . . . . 'That remains to be seen,' said the preacher."[7]

I can easily see why James puts this imperative so prominently, toward to beginning of his letter, since it is hypocrisy that harms a religion's reputation and a believer's integrity more than nearly anything else. I've listened to countless tales of folks who have been bruised by the lack of integrity and sometimes abject hypocrisy of what they heard in the churches of their youth (things like love and caring and compassion) and then what they beheld as that church's inactions (inactions like indifference and judgmentalism) beyond Sunday.

(2) Bridle [your] tongues. Of all the books in the New Testament, James is the most pointed in highlighting the harm and hurt that loose lips can do in human relations. False witness, uninformed commentary, and worst of all, gossip — these are weapons of pernicious destruction in human affairs. In the movie *Doubt*, Father Flynn preaches powerfully about the ill effects of gossip by likening gossip to the release of pillow feathers in the wind. Father Flynn must have read the book of James.

But note with me that there are also two other unavoidably beautiful and powerful declarations for any religion that is worthy, according to James: "Religion that is pure and undefiled before God . . . is this: to care for orphans and widows in their distress, and to keep oneself unstained by the world."

(3) Care for orphans and widows. This is a fundamental way of caring for the most vulnerable members of the community. For James and the community he led, this would amount to a social security system, since orphans and widows had no one to provide for their long-term care and overall well-being. By caring for orphans and widows one helps to preserve not only their dignity and human regard but their actual health and survival.

I'm glad to say that Community has been doing this in some significant new ways over the last several months. First, we've begun providing meals of support and caring love for those who experience the loss of a loved one. Regardless of your situation or need, even if you're one of the top chefs in Kansas City, you will receive a meal each week for six weeks after your beloved dies. And regarding those who might be called orphans, we have Jean Sailors and the hundred Community folks who responded to the recent challenge by Cornerstones of Care to provide gifts for children and youth who otherwise would have had little to celebrate at Christmas time if it were not for your generosity.

(4) Keep oneself unstained by the world. This has to mean not disengaged, but untarnished. Not unentangled, but unsullied. Not untouched, but uncorrupted. For James is a highly practical set of instructions about matters that are truly "worldly."

Eugene Peterson puts it just right when, in *The Message*, he renders verse 27: "Real religion, the kind that passes muster before God the Father, is this: Reach out to the homeless and loveless in their plight, and guard against corruption from the godless world."[8]

Guard against corruption from the godless world—yes, that's it. To guard against the corruptions of despair and cynicism and fearfulness and hopeless skepticism that seeps still so deeply into our culture.

In an effort to reinforce what James implores here about "keep[ing] oneself unstained," (or, as Peterson has it, "guard[ing] against corruption"), allow me to remind you of the Ignatius Imperative. The Rule of Ignatius, the founder of the Jesuits, reminds all of the priests in the Jesuit order, and indeed all Christians, to exhaust all possible positive interpretations of every person, place, thing, deed, or statement before going negative. One of the principal ways we can keep ourselves unstained and uncorrupted by the world is to resist the cynicism that has saturated into far too many facets of our lives. The Ignatius Imperative can empower us in that resistance. Such cynicism can be called truly "godless" because it eventually abandons all hope. The Ignatius Imperative leads to hope and life.

I knew another man named James who lived out this principle of James the epistle writer. James Stell was an embodiment of the Ignatius Imperative. When he worshiped at Community, he'd normally sit in the balcony or to the side, at the end of an aisle by himself. He loved his family immensely, proud of his two daughters and sons-in-law, prouder still of his grandchildren. He cared for his wife. He was at peace in his faith. In all my encounters with James, including when he was battling cancer, I never knew James to complain. Not once. Nor did I ever hear him disparage another person. Not once. He never went negative. James Stell knew the Ignatius Imperative. James Stell surely must have read James the epistle writer in his journey in faith.

IV.

I'm normally loath to suggest New Year's resolutions for myself or anyone else, since most resolutions are so easily dismissed as overly idealistic or too saccharine to be taken seriously. Still, in these uncertain times, and with an ear toward what James has declared in his mail to our time, it does seem useful to share among ourselves those notions I believe might be helpful. Thus, the following *"Ten Suggestions to Start Off the New Year"*:

1) Trust the regular discipline of prayer to surprise you with new information about yourself and new insights about the life you share within the family of faith. Countless testimonies reveal that prayer is one of the most soul-widening, mind-expanding, heart-deepening events you can ever experience.

2) Learn how to handle one new piece of technology this year. It helps no one to abide as an "electronics dinosaur." Besides, learning new skills is sheer fun.

3) Share meals with your loved ones as often as you can. Eating with others satisfies the soul as well as the stomach.

4) Carve out some silence for yourself every day. (In a time in history overly saturated with information and a culture glutted with the ding-dong din of hyper-entertainment, a little peace and quiet can do wonders for your overall disposition and relationships with others.)

5) Acquire at least one new favorite song in the next six months. The soundtracks of our lives are always needing new tunes.

6) Speak to every child you meet. Treasurable encounters with genius await anyone who will speak and, more importantly, listen to the children in our midst.

7) Practice regular worship, weekly if not more frequently, in and out of town, as one of your personal foundations for living a life of excellence. Worship is at the heart of what it means to be people of faith, as we express our deepest longings, our highest hopes, our most persistent questions, and our most fervent dreams. The expression of gratitude and the exhilaration of joy, coupled with the shared enjoyment of grace and forgiveness, are essential elements of both worship and exemplary human living.

8) Smile and laugh more. Smiling and laughing keep the energy vampires away.

9) Burn the candles, use the nice sheets, buy the expensive greeting card. Don't save them for special occasions. Today is special.

10) No matter how you feel, wake up, get up, dress up and show up. You are an important child of God with great graces that only you can share.

I offer these not as resolutions for a new year but as echoes of what the epistle of James holds forth for us all regarding the ingredients of a worthy religion.

May these be the elements of a faith of integrity that strengthens the control of our tongues, inspires compassion for the vulnerable, and keeps us moving toward the positive in all aspects of our live, individually and collectively.

Amen. And again, Happy New Year! I love you and may God bless everyone, everywhere.

NOTES

1. William Barclay, *The Letters of James and Peter* (Philadelphia: Westminster, 1960), pp. 3-4.
2. Barclay, p. 4.
3. Barclay, p. 6.
4. The "epistle of straw" is, by now, common knowledge in the history of the controversies surrounding James. The reference to Luther's attribution of "satanic" authorship comes by way of a lecture by Dr. Jack Forstman at Vanderbilt Divinity School.
5. James 2:2-6; see also *The New Interpreter's Bible* (Nashville: Abingdon, 1995), vol. 10, p. 377.
6. Barclay, p. 69.
7. (http://www.chapel.duke.edu/worship/sunday/)
8. See https://www.biblegateway.com/passage/?search=James%201&version=MSG

50

FAITH ISN'T CERTAINTY
Text: Mark 9:14 – 24

Lent is a time for deepening faith. I hope and trust you're experiencing such a deepening. I hope and trust that you're experiencing the Lenten season as a blessing for your faith, that your prayers are becoming deeper, that your study times are taking on new urgency, that you're being quickened to greater service, that your worship is becoming more energized.

Today we come to one of the most important aspects of what we believe as Christians and how we embody that belief in the twenty-first century. The theme for this Sunday in our Lenten *CREDO* sermon series is the relationship between faith and doubt. Faith is a presupposition of the classical creeds of the church. That we believe in Christ, that we hold basic tenets of faith about God and the reality of God's love and grace, are assumed by most folks who are part of Christian congregations.

But this morning we're homing in on the basic tension that also abides in our hearts and minds as part of the Christian faith tradition, as part of the "Christian *Matrix*," to use a reference to one of the better movie series related to faith and mystery and belief.

A significant part of the deepening of faith has to do with engaging new questions, teasing out new answers to old questions and often replacing time-worn and tattered answers with fresh ones. The questions remain, and that's a good thing.

Dealing with questions that life presents to faith was put into a classical formula in the fifth century by Augustine, the Bishop of Hippo in North Africa. Eventually it came to be known as *fides quaerens intellectum*. In English that translates to "faith seeking understanding." "For there are some things which we do not believe unless we understand them, and there are other things which we do not understand unless we believe them."[1]

Later on, in the thirteenth century, Thomas Aquinas would reverse that phrasing to read "understanding seeking faith."

Six hundred years later, Paul Tillich would declare that doubt is always an essential part of seeking to understand what faith is all about.[2] "Doubt isn't the opposite of faith; it is an element of faith," he said. And he would go on to describe the methodological, skeptical, and existential sorts of doubting within human experience.

One of his students, Frederick Buechner, picked up on this note as he took Tillich's classes at Union Theological Seminary in New York City. Buechner would go on to write novels and literary and faith-related essays, composing some of the most daringly positive descriptions of doubt's essential connection to faith. He said, "If you don't have any doubts, you are either kidding yourself or asleep. Doubts are the ants in the pants of faith. They keep it awake and moving."[3]

Now, there are some believers, some theologians, some denominations that would hold that doubt has no place in the Christian faith. Certainty, they would contend, is what the Christian way promises and delivers. To raise the specter of doubt is to cast suspicion on the whole enterprise of believing. Some folks in this camp would go so far as to condemn my sermon title this morning, so sure are they that faith casts away all doubts.

But there are more than a few dangers when it comes to casting out all doubts from faith:

- To maintain that faith always leads to certainty in all matters pertaining to God results in confusion. Certainty runs counter to our experience of all of God's mysterious, wondrous ways.
- It takes away all the fun why questions, as well as all the vexing ones, too. In other words, certainty is boringly dependable but also deadening, as far as an interesting life goes.
- Certainty in religion also almost always leads to some sort of violence—physical, emotional, relational, political. Nazi Germany was founded on Hitler's certainty.

Fred Phelps and his sad family members have made a pathetic, sick career of certainty. And the basis for suicide bombers around the globe, including those that have attacked the U.S., is always the certainty of their positions.

When we are honest about our faith, however, we know that somehow certainty and faith don't really go together, but faith and doubt do.

Anne Lamott puts it bluntly:

The opposite of faith is not doubt: It is certainty. It is madness. You can tell you have created God in your own image when it turns out that he or she hates all the same people you do. The first holy truth in God 101 is that men and women of true faith have always had to accept the mystery of God's identity and love and ways. I hate that, but it's the truth. [4]

She also said, "Certainty is missing the point entirely. Faith includes noticing the mess, and emptiness and discomfort, and letting it be there until some light returns. Faith also means reaching deeply within for the sense one was born with, the sense to go for a walk."[5] Faith and doubt go together, in other words, really, hand in hand.

Regarding faith and doubt, the ninth chapter of Mark's gospel contains one of the greatest nameless characters in the entirety of Holy Writ. Though Matthew and Luke have the semblance of this story of the healing of a boy— suffering apparently from epileptic seizures—Mark alone gives voice to one of the most profound utterances that faithful people can ever make: "I believe, help my unbelief." This utterance gives us our cue this morning about the true nature of faith.

The scene in Mark is a big affair. Jesus has come down from the mount of transfiguration and happens upon a dispute going on between his disciples and the scribes. Before Jesus can determine what the argument is all about, the crowd rushes toward him, and a voice from the back plaintively describes the situation: "Teacher, I brought you my son, who is possessed by a spirit that has robbed him of speech. Whenever it seizes him, it throws him to the ground. He foams at the mouth, gnashes his teeth and becomes rigid. I asked your disciples to drive out the spirit, but they could not" (vv. 17-18). In today's scientifically dominated culture, we would diagnose the boy as having some sort of epilepsy. In Jesus' day, the likely cause for the boy's condition would be understood to be a demonic presence. In fact, when the boy is brought near to Jesus so he can see him, Mark says that a "spirit" sees Jesus and immediately convulses the boy, causing him to fall on the ground, roll about and foam at the mouth. The poor father, delirious with loving worry and worrisome love, cries out to Jesus, "This has been going on forever. If you are able to do something to help my boy, please do it now."

To which Jesus takes offense because the man said "if you are able." "If? Come on now, you have no idea who you are dealing with. All things can be done for the one who believes." Then comes the father's desperate, divinely prompted, tender declaration. Douglas John Hall says, "No Biblical verse is more existentially meaningful . . . than this prayer."[6] "I believe, help my unbelief," says the loving father.

Hall is right. It's hard to imagine a more commendable, succinct way of showing your faith. He simply declares that he believes. His statement echoes what the Epistle to the Hebrews declares: "Now faith is the substance of things hoped for, the evidence of things not seen" (Hebrews 11:1). The father is offering an honest summation of his faith, however limited it may be.

The father shows his humility by being honest and forthright about the limits of his belief. He doesn't believe everything. He knows himself well enough to ask for help. He's like the driver who's become humble and mature enough to ask directions when he's lost.

In 1903, a young poet, Franz Xavier Kappus began writing letters to the great German poet Rilke. The correspondence would last over five years. Rilke eventually published his half of the correspondence in what has now become a classic text, *Letters to a Young Poet*. Of all the advice and counsel Rilke gave to Kappus, one of the most profound pieces was "be patient towards all that is unsolved in your heart and . . . try to love the questions themselves . . . . [Y]ou will [then] live into the answers."[7]

"O the depth of the riches and wisdom and knowledge of God! How unsearchable are his judgments and how inscrutable his ways!"(Romans 11:33)

Mother Teresa was, for all intents and purposes, a person of absolute faith, wasn't she? The energy and inspiration for Mother Teresa's extraordinary capacity for loving others, she said, again and again, derived from prayer. For her, the best life possible is a life lived in a disciplined rhythm of prayer and service. Prayer, she counseled, was the best activity in which we can discover God's exceeding love for each one of us individually and for the world as a whole. Mother Teresa was a person of seemingly absolute faith.

And yet, since her death, Mother Teresa has given another distinct gift to the world through the revelations about the extended season of despair in her spiritual life. In *Mother Teresa: Come Be My Light*, a collection of her letters to her spiritual advisors, directors, and confessors, she expressed that she felt as if God were absent from her, except in fleeting moments, during the last fifty years of her life as a nun. [8]

Some people were deeply disturbed by these disclosures. Some Christian fundamentalists pointed to the revelations of her despair as evidence of her not truly being a Christian. Some said she was damned to hell despite her countless good works. Others said they were offended that anyone would reveal anything negative like doubt in connection to Mother Teresa. But the doubting side of Mother Teresa's journey as a Christian is really a blessed bequest.

Like all of us, if and when we are radically honest, Mother Teresa knew hesitation in her hopefulness, reluctance in her trust, and an absence of absolute certainty.

Indeed, there was within Mother Teresa's experience of despair a deep, resonating bond with the one she followed as the Savior of her life: "My God, my God, why have you forsaken me?"[9] That she had such tormenting years of struggle and yet still acted in the spirit of God's love on behalf of the poorest of the poor is one of the main reasons she is a premier great soul, and an inspiring exemplar.

Before I close, I want to give you three pieces of homework.

(1) Like the father who so graphically loved his son did, declare your beliefs as much as you know them to be true. Be ready to say what you believe, and be forthright and straightforward about them. As he was, be humble and bold in your declaration, all at the same time.

(2) As the pleading father and as Mother Teresa did, petition God for help with your unbelief. Make an appointment with any one of us on the ministerial staff. We are here for you. My times of counseling and listening to people stretching and going deeper have nearly doubled this Lenten season. It is always an honor to be with people in their spiritual transformations. But also make an appointment with God on a regular basis, on your calendar, your iPhone or Blackberry, whatever device you use, electronic or hard paper copy: "God, 3:00 p.m., Wednesday." And then show up for that appointment. You will be surprised, at first, at how God will come to meet you. And if God doesn't seem to meet you in exactly the way you desire, the discipline of your showing up will direct your path in good ways, as it did with Mother Teresa, to do good service to people in need.

(3) Shape your prayers as thanksgiving prayers for God's presence with you, even when you don't feel it. Express your gratitude with the following prayer: *Gracious God, there's a common bond between the beseeching father in Mark's gospel and the young poet friend of Rilke and Mother Teresa and all other fellow strugglers and me: I don't always trust that You are there. Sometimes I can't see any evidence whatsoever that*

You even care. Yet, like Mother Teresa did — and like the beseeching father and the young poet and my fellow strugglers — I will keep on saying the words and keeping my appointments with You and showing up and acting in love toward others. And in doing those actions, I am trusting that I will eventually have a sure sense of Your presence, through Jesus Christ. Amen.

NOTES

1. Augustine, *An Augustine Synthesis*, arranged by Erich Przywara (Eugene, Oregon: Wipf & Stock, 2014), p. 59.
2. Paul Tillich, *The Dynamics of Faith* (New York: Harper & Row, 1957)
3. Frederick Buechner, *Wishful Thinking: A Theological ABC* (New York: Harper and Row, 1973), p. 20.
4. Anne Lamott, "God Doesn't Take Sides," Salon.com, April 27, 2005.
    https://www.salon.com/2005/04/27/gods_warning_signs/
5. Anne Lamott, "Advent 2003," Salon.com, Dec. 6, 2003.
    https://www.salon.com/2003/12/05/advent/
6. Douglas John Hall, *Thinking the Faith: Christian Theology in a North American Context* (Minneapolis: Fortress Press, 1991), p. 250.
7. Quoted in William Sloane Coffin, *Letters to A Young Doubter* (Louisville: Westminster John Knox, 2005), p. ix.
8. Brian Kolodiejchuk, ed., *Mother Teresa: Come Be My Light: The Private Writings of the Saint of Calcutta*, compiled and edited by (New York: Doubleday, 2007).
9. Matthew 27:46.

51

LIFE'S TOO SHORT FOR ANYTHING BUT LOVE
Text: I Corinthians 13:1–7

I'm deeply thankful for the welcome and the hospitality from you. And how blessed and honored I am to be invited by my friend Donna Porter to attempt to fill this pulpit with a word.

It is a rich blessing to see friends from Kansas City! When I see your faces, I am reminded of Psalm 139: Whither shall I go from thy spirit? or whither shall I flee from thy presence? If I ascend [into a pulpit in Kansas City], thou art there! If I take the wings of the morning, [and hie myself unto the mountainous heights of New Mexico], thou art there.

Thanks to you all for welcoming me back. I'll keep coming back until I get it right.

About getting it right, I was recently reminded of the peculiar relationship between those who give sermons and those who hear them and of the nuances in certain compliments for a sermon.

The story is told about a woman who came up to her pastor one Sunday after the sermon, and said, "Pastor, that sermon was like the peace of God and the love of God combined."

The pastor said, "Well, thank you. That is one of the best compliments I've ever been given."

"Yes," the woman said, "it was like the peace of God because it surpassed all understanding, and it was like the love of God because it endured forever."

This morning I am compelled by an urgency to say something of substance and sustenance about the gospel. This urgency emanates from Paul's correspondence with the cantankerous, rascal Corinthians.

In Paul's first letter to the Corinthians, he writes out of a deep knowledge of who they are and what they have experienced, and from a posture of extremely high hopes for what they might become as Christians.

In essence he reminds them of their bottom line.

The Corinthian Christians had been acting like babies in the faith, exhibiting extreme immaturity, showing that they were out of sync with how Jesus would have them act. And so, the bottom line for them was what? Their bottom line was to get their spirits right, to feed on the right cuisine and to quit their out-of-sync-ness. At first, they had been infants in Christ, Paul says, and so he fed them only milk, baby food for their faith.

Further into the letter, Paul declares that the bottom line now includes some "meat," that is, some spiritual sustenance fit for mature Christians. They were to exercise the great gifts God had placed within each of them.

Then, after he describes the multitude of gifts that had been poured into the cantankerous Corinthians, he declares: "And I will show you a still more excellent way."

And this "still more excellent way" is the ultimate bottom line for every Christian and for the Church as a whole. You heard it just a few minutes ago, the "meaty," complex, textured, layered, and nuanced treatment of love in the thirteenth chapter of I Corinthians. This is a bottom line that goes beyond the "milk" he mentioned feeding the Corinthians in the third chapter.

This "still more excellent way" is such a good word for us this morning.

There are among us this morning those who have known tremendous loss. And yet you survived.

There are among us this morning those who have known the death of a parent at too early of an age. And yet you survived.

There are among us this morning those who have endured great impediments to a healthy life, those who have known pain and suffering in body, mind, and soul. And yet you survived.

There are among us this morning those who have known the heartache that comes from radically disruptive transitions—on the job, in your community, in our churches. And yet you survived.

There are among us this morning those who have wrestled with questions of faith—during sleepless nights and days suffused with torment and anguish—all the while echoing the steadfast stance of Frederick Buechner, who declared "If there is no room for doubt, there is no room for me." And yet you survived.

How and why did you survive? Because of love!

Love is the sine qua non of faith, the indispensable condition, the essential element, without which a Christian—without which the Church—cannot exist.

There is no baseball game without a baseball diamond.

There is no electricity without electrons.

There is no surgery without a surgeon.

There is no art without an artist.

And there is no Christian faith without love.

What makes Love the real bottom line for those of us in the faith? I'm glad you asked that question!

I.

First and foremost, this love flows from God. It is God who is described first in all these words in the thirteenth chapter of Corinthians.

We may read them at weddings as the basic, ideal elements in a model marriage, and they are that. But, first and foremost, they are the powerful descriptions of the love that comes to us from God's own heart.

Listen! "Love is patient; love is kind; love is not envious or boastful or arrogant or rude. It does not insist on its own way; it is not irritable or resentful; it does not rejoice in wrongdoing, but rejoices in the truth."

And you thought you had to do all that by yourself! These are the qualities of God, first!

II.

Next, this Love binds members one to another and builds bridges with the community in which the church is situated.

Love is the message that needs to be spoken and shared with all, and especially, as Howard Thurman put it so wisely, with those "whose backs are against the wall." For one and all, love is the most powerful force we can ever know. Love surrounds a church, I believe, if that church attempts to surround everyone they know with love.

As an example of this dynamic, allow me to point to Community Christian Church. If you've ever been to Community, you've noticed — or if you ever come to visit, you will notice — that it is an unusual looking church. With its Frank Lloyd Wright designed architecture, with its bright white walls on every side, it is sort of a sitting target, a kind of ground zero for anyone with a mind to vandalize it with graffiti. Yet, in all my knowledge and within my entire tenure of more than thirty years as a pastor at Community, only once did we ever experience anyone spray-painting any message on our gunite walls. I believe that fortunate status was due to the fact that we tried to love everyone we encountered, inside and outside the church walls, including our immediate neighborhood. Love surrounded — and continued to surround Community — as we attempted to surround everyone we knew with love.

Now, I said only once did we ever suffer the indignity of graffiti, and that was an instance of anti-Semitic hatred on the night before we were to open our doors to a Jewish congregation for a community dialogue about the movie *The Passion of the Christ*. (Sometimes, as you seek to do what is right and good in the community and try to love your neighbors, the ones who don't believe in love may push back.)

But, as you extend yourself in love to others, a miracle occurs. You begin to be less fearful.

This love is so powerful in the Church that "[i]t bears all things, believes all things, hopes all things, endures all things." If you've got love — love of God, love of one another, love of neighbor, no matter who they are — at your core, you then can take on any challenge, face any danger, overcome any obstacle.

III.

Love is what fuels the Church's ministries, and love deserves to be celebrated every chance you get.

The Christian faith is founded on a powerful thesis: Life is meant to be celebrated and not merely tolerated!

Is there an anniversary going on—between a couple, in your community, here at Idlewild? Then celebrate it in love.

Of course, you are passing a significant congregational milestone this year—seventy-seven years of ascending to this beautiful place! How long has the chapel been of use to you and your family? Then observe and celebrate to a fare-thee-well all those years in this chapel. Celebrate it with love!

Celebrating your life together in community reinforces the sense of comfort and strength and confidence you have one with another. And as you experience more comfort and strength and confidence together, you have yet even more and more experiences to celebrate. Celebration is part of the success cycle of any community worthy of the name.

If you keep the flame of love lit on the altar of your soul, then all will eventually be well. And you will have kept faithful to the indispensable condition, the essential element of the gospel of God, that without which you have nothing, but with which you have everything you will ever need.

IV.

Love is the ultimate spiritual food upon which the mature faithful and any worthy community feasts.

Love is the final bottom line—God's supreme trump card—by which all things are measured.

Love—which is what God in Christ came to impart to us—is the premier way for all our relationships to become fulfilled. As a wise church elder once eloquently declared to me in a moment of private counsel, "If you ain't got love, you ain't got nothin'."

But if you got love, if you live in love, by love, with love, you can overcome anything that may come your way.

Another way of putting this is "Life's too short for anything but love," which is how I once put it in a reflection right after I had an AMI, Acute Myocardial Infarction, which is the name the doctor gave the one hundred percent blockage I was experiencing in one of the vessels leading into my heart. It's otherwise known as a heart attack.

Ever since that existential speed bump, the precious nature of each new day has become progressively clear to me and the miraculous character of each moment of earthly existence has been made increasingly plain. All of which gave me pause to compose a catalogue of reinforced priority values.

Life's too short for instant coffee.
Life's too short for anything but honesty.
Life's too short for anything but wooden bats in baseball.
Life's too short to wallow in guilt.
Life's too short to hang on to a grudge.
Life's too short to ignore autumn leaves.
Life's too short for not forgiving others.
Life's too short to be a victim.
Life's too short to disregard even one full moon.
Life's too short not to have poetry in your life.

Life's too short not to play with your grandchildren.
Life's too short for processed cheese.
Life's too short to live without courtesy.
Life's too short not to pet a cat whose back rises to your touch.
Life's too short to be cynical for even a nanosecond.
Life's too short not to stand up to a bully.
Life's too short to ignore a snow rainbow.
Life's too short not to savor a peach.
Life's too short to be a coward.
Life's too short not to stand up for justice for all people.
Life's too short not to exercise your citizenship every Election Day.
Life's too short to color with only four crayons in the 64-crayon pack.
Life's too short not to make new friends.
Life's too short not to pray.
Life's too short for anything but at least fifteen percent tips.
Life's too short to refuse a hug.
Life's too short to neglect your birthday.
Life's too short to show anything but kindness toward a stranger.
Life's too short to be unmerciful.
Life's too short to be ungrateful for each new day.
Life's too short for anything but love.

For indeed, as Paul said so definitively, "And now faith, hope, and love abide, these three; but the greatest of these is love."

And I know this to be an incontrovertible truth: You will experience the greatest growth in grace you've ever seen, as you focus on "the greatest of these."

Amen.

52

SURROUNDED

Text: Hebrews 12:1 – 2

One of my preaching heroes, and a spiritual giant of the first rank, has said that the ultimate work of God's grace is to make us gracious. More and more, I am finding that axiom to be an irrefutable truth.

This morning I come to you as one who is grateful nearly beyond the power of language to convey. I say "nearly" because I must try, in some small way, to tell you my thanks. In the place that witnessed my stumbling maturation through the wild ways of adolescence toward young adulthood, I am quick to say thanks.

Thanks to Rev. Dave Everton for his gracious invitation to come and preach here, on the heels of the occasion of the Sam Rayburn High School Choir Reunion, which was held just this past Friday night.

Thanks to David Snyder for initiating the idea of this guest pulpit moment even being possible and for his warm hospitality.

Thanks to Dale and Carol Adams for their generous hospitality.

And I am grateful, abidingly grateful to this congregation, far more than you can ever imagine.

It has been ten years since I most recently traipsed through here one hot August day. It has been nearly twenty years since I was present in Pasadena for a hilarious twentieth high school reunion. And it has been nearly forty years since I last worshiped with this family of faith. On this Father's Day in the year 2010, it gives me great satisfaction to say thanks to you – all of you, fathers and mothers, men and women – for lovingly "fathering" me when I was in my high school years. By your caring actions, I have incurred a debt I can never repay. My only option is to live my life and share my faith so that others may also know God's great love through the salvific ways of Jesus Christ. This is a momentous occasion for me, and I thank you for it.

I am currently on sabbatical for three months – away from my duties at Community Christian Church in Kansas City, Missouri. After the May 2 celebration of my twenty-fifth anniversary at the corner of 46th and Main in Kansas City, I was granted time to get away and refresh and enjoy and revel in some research.

As I have traversed more than 3,172 miles across twelve states in my trusty Jeep, I have been anticipating this moment with great eagerness.

Now, given the miles traveled and the distance away from Kansas City, you would think I would have a lot of time in solitude, in a kind of sacred, spiritual singularity. Alone. But you would be amiss in that assumption. Quite the opposite has occurred.

Instead of singularity and solitude, I have been . . . surrounded.

On the way to this appointed moment, I have been surrounded by the sounds of Alison Krauss and Union Station and Rascal Flats and Willis Alan Ramsey and Willie Nelson, as my Jeep became a musical cocoon.

I have been surrounded by the visual feast of the countrysides and cityscapes of the South and the Southwest in all their verdant beauty.

I have been surrounded by the sound of my wife Priscilla's voice on my cell phone as she gave updates on our cat Cleo, her continuous battles with the rabbits tormenting her tomato patch, and the height of the grass, which will require the immediate attention of my lawnmower when I return home next Tuesday.

I have been surrounded by memories of this church and the diligence and devotion of Sunday-school teachers like Jack and Maureen Sullivan and youth group sponsors like the Praytors, the Millers, the Duffs, and more. And I shall remain eternally grateful for the great graces of Roy and Annetta Daniel — Annetta for her comforting ways and Roy for his encouragement of so many of us in our faith journeys, whether as clergy or lay persons, but always as Christians making a difference in the world. I continuously feel surrounded by memories of Roy Daniel, whose official retirement from the ministry, by the way, was held at Community in Kansas City. As I drove by the old First Christian building on Wafer the other day, I recalled two lessons Roy taught me:

(1) Work for what you want to achieve, which he made real for me, for instance, when he had me scrub the floors of the sanctuary to earn a scholarship to attend the International Affairs Seminar in Washington, D.C. and New York.

(2) It is always easier to ask for forgiveness than it is to ask for permission. Roy lived out that proposition to the utmost degree!

So, as you can see, I have been surrounded. But, let me be quick to say, no more surrounded than you have been, than you are, than we all are, if we are awake and aware and alive in our Christian journeys.

The book of Hebrews gives us this insight in a peculiar and powerful way in one of its most memorable passages.

Hebrews is actually a book of sermons, bedazzling in its beauty, rich in its metaphors. A preacher could easily preach three months of sermons on nearly any of its chapters. Its plentitude of themes and its high and soaring poetry are the stuff of which heartfelt, passionate sermons are made.

In the extraordinarily fertile twelfth chapter and its gems of wisdom and meaning, we read, "Therefore, since we are surrounded by so great a cloud of witnesses, let us also lay aside every weight, and sin which clings so closely, and let us run with perseverance the race that is set before us, looking to Jesus the pioneer and perfecter of our faith, who for the joy that was set before him endured the cross, despising the shame, and is seated at the right hand of the throne of God."

The analogy is to the kind of foot races that predominated in the time of the early church. Throughout the Roman Empire, there were races in arenas, in towns and villages, in public areas. The readers of and listeners to the epistle to the Hebrews would know such a reference and would be energetically connected to the scene: "let us run with perseverance the race that is set before us."

First, you have to put off anything weighing you down.

And then there's the goal: "looking to Jesus the pioneer and perfecter of our faith."

Telescope with me just a bit further and consider the opening phrase, which contains another metaphor referring to the race: "so great a cloud of witnesses." Here is a cloud of witnesses, a cheering throng encouraging you on, a huge posse of prompters and prodders, people serving as witnesses of your life and your efforts in the race of faith.

But look with me once more in telescopic fashion and consider the importance of one little word that commences the passage.

The runner is there, shedding everything that would keep the runner from running toward victory. In this case, it's not merely heavy sandals or a fifteen-pound tunic. Rather it's the weighty matter of sin and sin's dragging effects.

And the crowd is there. In fact, it's a "cloud of witnesses." Now, behold the size and the situation of the witnesses as the dynamics of the crowd and the race and the runner are captured in one little word: "surrounded."

Surrounded. Surrounded. Such a strong word. And such a right word to be associated with those who would witness one's efforts in life and faith. But what does it mean?

Could it mean that the runner of the race of faith is to be mindful of the moral gaze of those who have gone before?

In our family, my mother had a guilt-producing, heart-chastening phrase she employed in order to discipline us, or, more accurately, me. When I would do something off-center from proper behavior, she'd say "The Hills don't do that sort of thing!" And she normally said it with an arched eyebrow to emphasize the point.

"The Hills." Meaning? Meaning . . . we were surrounded by the righteous eyes of our family. who would never do (or get caught doing) what I had been doing. Surrounded. Have you ever been surrounded like that? And is this what the writer to the Hebrews meant, and means, to know that countless righteousness-seeking eyes were gazing upon the runner?

Or could it be that the Hebrews writer meant to convey how the King James Version has the translation, existentially "encompassed"? On all sides, at every turn, a colossal stadium of folks watching your every move, ready to cheer you to victory and nothing less. That's a bit intimidating when you think of it.

I have a friend who hates Easter. "They're all there, all of them!" he says, in a kind of incensed fury that reminds you of Lewis Black at his most perturbed. "I resent it," he says. He says, "They show up for just one Sunday a year and expect me to like it that they're there!" "Yes," I responded. "They're there! That's the point, don't you think? Can't you rejoice in that? "I ask him. "I suppose, but they're all looking at me for something, and it's a lot of pressure. I mean, this may be my only shot," he said. It took me a while to really empathize with him, since I love Easter more than almost any other day on the Christian calendar.

And I treasure it when everyone shows up. It's like a royal family reunion of those seeking a word about hope and goodness. And I really thought he had it wrong. It wasn't, and it never is, about him or me, or any other preacher or church leader. No one can really mess up Easter. The gospel has a power of its own. Love — divine, eternal love, made manifest in our oh-so-human lives — conquers death, and that's what we are to celebrate on resurrection morning.

But my friend feels encompassed, encircled, penned in, on display on Easter Sunday, and certainly under pressure. His sense of being surrounded is a debilitating, throttling, choking kind of experience. Under pressure. The kind of pressure you would feel if a dark cloud of eyes were looking at you for a superior performance.

Or the word "surrounded" could mean fenced in, besieged, blockaded — surrounded in such a way that you can do nothing but what the crowd wants you to do. No volition. No alternatives. Caught, in other words — able to do nothing else but a task that has been arbitrarily set to your hands.

Last October, Priscilla and I celebrated our twentieth anniversary by enjoying the low-country beauty and bounty of Savannah, Georgia. And yes, we did make it to The Lady and Son's for dinner one evening. This is the now-famous restaurant of Paula Deen, whose thick Georgia accent and foot-high lemon meringue pies have become legendary. She's more than merely the Martha-Stewart-south-of-the-Mason-Dixon-line. She's a veritable industry unto herself.

What most folks don't know, unless they're among the legions of her devoted cookbook readers (and I'm not and thus didn't know), is that for most of her life, Paula Dean has suffered from agoraphobia. She has battled a stifling fear of open places. Like they used to say in Koine Greek during the early days of the Church, she has a fear of the *agora*, the open place, usually the market-place, where — you guessed it! — "a cloud of witnesses" seemingly can behold your every move. Paula Deen would not resonate positively with that word, surrounded. And she has countless friends who know exactly how she feels.

In the face of all these less-than-positive perspectives on the phrase, "since we are surrounded by so great a cloud of witnesses," allow me to offer what I think is the foundational meaning behind the word "surrounded" in the twelfth chapter of Hebrews: proudly, lovingly embraced.

It goes like this: "Therefore, since we are proudly, lovingly embraced by such a throng of folks who care for us, let us run the faith-race."

Carlyle Marney emphasized this angle when he described "the cloud of witnesses" as a balcony full of family members and friends, who look down from their balcony perch at the performance of your life upon earth's stage, ready for your every utterance in the grand drama of life, ever eager to cheer you on with "Bravo!" and "Encore!"

I now have a new image to remind me of the loving, proud embrace of those who witness the life we share in the Christian faith race.

In the middle of Savannah, in Savannah's historic district, on the eastern edge of Monterrey Square, laid out by James Oglethorpe in 1733, there sits the current sanctuary of Temple Mickve Israel. Founded as a congregation

277 years ago, with a building that dates back to 1878, the people of Mickve Israel have instituted a special remembrance feature on the walls of their hallowed place of worship. Large brass memorial plaques adorn the walls of the sanctuary, and these plaques are inscribed with the names of the members who have died in the course of the history of the congregation. Seemingly innumerable names, countless plaques, treasured names. Like Reform Jewish congregations all over the U.S. and throughout the world, during the Kaddish portion of their weekly Shabbat services, the names of those who died in years past during that particular week are spoken aloud. And not only that, at Mickve Israel, they are symbolized on their plaques.

When I went into the Mickve Israel sanctuary to pray, I noticed that certain little lights were lit up on the plaques. Each wall of plaques had a few lights lit up on it. I looked closer and saw there was a small, discreet lightbulb by each name. A few names lit up, and then many dark. And then the awareness hit me, which I confirmed later with the receptionist at the temple door. The lights were turned on for those who had died during that particular week in years past. The next week, different names would be lit up, and the week after that still other different names. In the course of a year, the name of every deceased member of Mickve Israel would be spoken and every light would blink on.

And I, what did I think? It was so very natural, so easy, in the middle of the Mickve Israel sanctuary, to think of a treasured verse of scripture: "Since we are surrounded by so great a cloud of witnesses."

Surrounded by the illuminating blessings of precious memories.

Surrounded by the witness of life and light and grace and care and untold faithful efforts.

Surrounded by the loving embrace, the embracing love of those who have gone before.

Surrounded by those who called us into faith, those who made it possible — teachers, vacation Bible-school leaders, youth-group sponsors — those who provided examples for living and encouragement for growth.

Surrounded by pastors and ministers and church members who invited us into a heart-felt, mind-stretching, soul-deepening journey.

I felt what surely the members of Mickve Israel have felt for 277 years: Surrounded! Proudly, lovingly embraced!

Now you may not have such plaques here in the sanctuary, but you do have illuminations that can remind you that you are surrounded by a great cloud of witnesses.

You have windows in this building through which the light of the waiting world shines through. I want to suggest to you this morning that the windows and the light shining through the windows of this building, each and every time you gather here, represent the great cloud of witnesses who are proudly, lovingly embracing you in the grand race of faith. In other words, you are always, and especially here, surrounded!

Surrounded by the encouraging gazes of former Sunday-school teachers and youth-group leaders and parents and pastors.

Surrounded by the wider reaches of the Christian Church (Disciples of Christ).

Surrounded by the great array of great souls who have gone before all of us: Albert Schweitzer and Flannery O'Connor and Bill Wilson, the founder of A.A., and Millard Fuller, the founder of Habitat of Humanity, and Madeleine L'Engle and Cesar Chavez and Rosa Parks and Gardner C. Taylor and Martin Luther and Martin Luther King and Mother Teresa and so many more. All of these, and myriad other saints, surround us with their lovingly proud embraces.

This magisterium of the ages includes the beholding, witnessing encouragement of every person who has followed after the carpenter from Nazareth, the rabbi known as the Master Teacher, the one whom they and we have proclaimed (and will continue to proclaim) as "the light of the world."

So, whenever you come into this place, I invite you to say a word. Say it with a deep gratitude for the proud, loving embrace in which you have been enfolded. Whenever you come to this table, whenever you dedicate a baby, whenever you lay to rest one of First Christian's saints, whenever you witness a couple pledging their troth to one another in a wedding ceremony, say it. Say it as prayer, as thanksgiving, as praise, as exaltation: "Surrounded. Surrounded. Surrounded."

When I return to Kansas City after this portion of the sabbatical, there will surely be some inquiries about my itinerary, where I've been, what I've seen, how I've experienced the time away. When folks ask "How was it, what was it like?" I already have in my mind how I will respond. I will simply say, "It was beautiful, almost more than I ever imagined or hoped for. I suppose the best word I can use to describe what it was like is . . . surrounded." Amen.

TIMES AND PLACES

Every actual sermon has a time and place in which it is preached. As I have said before, there really are no effective sermons which are "timeless" or "for all humanity." Sermons have impact when they are locatable in time and in connection with a particular congregation or a specific event. Naturally, sermons may touch upon what folks call timeless truths, eternal verities, and deathless dreams. But, because sermons are proffered as part of time-specific gatherings, they exist for a moment. Thus, the following times and places for the sermons in this volume may be of interest to the reader.

Most of the sermons in this collection were first offered at Community Christian Church, in Kansas City, Missouri, where I enjoyed the extreme privilege and high honor of serving for more than thirty years. Some have found "legs" and have traveled to multiple venues. Those sermons are "Holy Hiding," "Buck O'Neil: Loving You," "I and Thou," "My God, My God, Why Have You Forsaken Me?," "Father, Forgive Them, For They Know Not What They Do," "Hands on the Table," "Remember the Dream," "Healing a Violent World," "Racial Justice," "On Entertaining Angels Unawares," "Don't Forget to Remember," "Ingredients for a Worthy Religion," "Life's Too Short for Anything but Love," and "Surrounded." The times and places indicated for these particular sermons are either the earliest or the most recent dates and locations.

1 – On Seeing the Elephant and Hearing the Owl
Sunday morning, January 23, 2011, Community Christian Church, Kansas City, Missouri

2 – Taking Love Seriously
Sunday morning, October 31, 2010, Community Christian Church, Kansas City, Missouri

3 – Letting Go of Anxiety
Sunday morning, January 2, 2011, Community Christian Church, Kansas City, Missouri

4 – Overcoming the Hell of Hatred
Sunday morning, March 27, 2011, Community Christian Church, Kansas City, Missouri

5 – Three Stages of Forgiveness
Sunday morning, August 14, 2011, Community Christian Church, Kansas City, Missouri

6 – God Wants You to Laugh
Sunday morning, September 26, 2010, Community Christian Church, Kansas City, Missouri

7 – What Do You Do with Psalm 137 (and Other Troubling Bible Passages)?
Sunday morning, May 22, 2011, Community Christian Church, Kansas City, Missouri

8 – The Better Angels of Our Nature: Abraham Lincoln
Sunday morning, September 14, 2008, Community Christian Church, Kansas City, Missouri

9 – The Strength of Meekness
Sunday morning, February 6, 2011, Community Christian Church, Kansas City, MO

10 – A Word about Water
Sunday morning, April 28, 2013, Community Christian Church, Kansas City, MO

11 – Have Mercy!
Sunday morning, February 20, 2011, Community Christian Church, Kansas City, MO

12 – Everyone's a Theologian
Sunday morning, March 13, 2011, Community Christian Church, Kansas City, MO

13 – When Religion Is Sick
Sunday morning, September 19, 2010, Community Christian Church, Kansas City, MO

14 – Vessels of Grace
Sunday morning, November 7, 2010, Community Christian Church, Kansas City, MO

15 – The Blessedness of the Body
Sunday morning, January 8, 2012, Community Christian Church, Kansas City, MO

16 – Buck O'Neil—Loving You
Sunday morning, June 23, 2019, Shawnee Community Christian Church, Shawnee, KS

17 – New Year's Resolutions That Matter
Sunday morning, January 1, 2012, Community Christian Church, Kansas City, MO

18 – Holy Hiding
Shrove Tuesday, February 5, 2008, Christ UMC, Independence, MO

19 – Humble Ashes and Crazy Hope
Ash Wednesday, February 25, 2009, Community Christian Church, Kansas City, MO

20 – I and Thou
Ash Wednesday, February 17, 2010, Community Christian Church, Kansas City, MO

21 – Ashes to Ashes, Heart to Heart
Ash Wednesday, March 9, 2011, Community Christian Church, Kansas City, MO

22 – Strong at the Broken Places
Ash Wednesday, February 22, 2012, Community Christian Church, Kansas City, MO

23 – Where Your Treasure Is
Ash Wednesday, March 5, 2014, Community Christian Church, Kansas City, MO

24 – Cardiac Care
Ash Wednesday, February 18, 2015, Community Christian Church, Kansas City, MO

25 – In the Beginning . . . Light!
Sunday morning, February 26, 2012, Community Christian Church, Kansas City, MO

26 – Wanna Get Away?
Sunday morning, September 14, 2008, Community Christian Church, Kansas City, MO

27 – Hands on the Table
Maundy Thursday evening, April 5, 2007, Colonial United Church of Christ, Prairie Village, KS

28 – My God, My God, Why Have You Forsaken Me?
Good Friday, March 30, 2018, Friendship Baptist Church, Kansas City, MO

29 – Father, Forgive Them, For They Know Not What They Do
Good Friday, April 10, 2020, Friendship Baptist Church (Virtual), Kansas City, MO

30 – Love Always Resurrects!
Easter Sunday, April 24, 2010, Brush Creek Amphitheater and Community Christian Church, Kansas City, MO

31 – ADVENT: Time for Testimony
Monday evening, December 3, 2007, Ecumenical Advent Service, Westwood Christian Church, Westwood, KS

32 – Shepherds: Waking Up to A Precious Gift
Sunday morning, November 30, 2018 Community Christian Church, Kansas City, MO

33 – What the Magi Saw
Wednesday evening, December 15, 2010, Community Christian Church, Kansas City, MO

34 – Joy?
Sunday morning, December 16, 2012, Community Christian Church, Kansas City, MO

35 – A Christmas of Firsts
Wednesday evening, December 17, 2008, Community Christian Church, Kansas City, MO

36 – The Angels' Journey of Love
Christmas Eve, December 24, 2007, Community Christian Church, Kansas City, MO

37 – Mysterious Stranger in the Straw
Christmas Eve, December 24, 2007, Community Christian Church, Kansas City, MO

38 – The First Christmases
Christmas Eve, December 24, 2011, Community Christian Church, Kansas City, MO

39 – The Ultimate Christmas Star
Christmas Eve, December 24, 2014, Community Christian Church, Kansas City, MO

40 – You Have Found Favor with God
Christmas Eve, December 24, 2012, Community Christian Church, Kansas City, MO

41 – A Time for Singing
Sunday morning, December 25, 2011, Community Christian Church, Kansas City, MO

42 – Remember the Dream!
Sunday morning, January 25, 2009, St. James UMC, Kansas City, MO

43 – Healing a Violent World
Sunday morning, January 20, 2013, Community Christian Church, Kansas City, MO
Sunday morning, January 27, 2013, St. James UMC, Kansas City, MO

44 – But Only Say the Word
Sunday morning, February 23, 2020, Overland Park Christian Church, Overland Park, KS

45 – Racial Justice
Friday evening, January 23, 2015, The New Reform Temple, Kansas City, MO

46 – On Entertaining Angels Unawares
Sunday morning, March 12, 2017, All Souls Unitarian Universalist Church, Kansas City, MO

47 – Life Is to Be Celebrated
Sunday morning, June 7, 2015, Community Christian Church, Kansas City, MO

48 – Don't Forget to Remember
Sunday morning, August 28, 2011, National City Christian Church, Washington, D.C.

49 – Ingredients of a Worthy Religion
Sunday morning, January 4, 2009, Community Christian Church, Kansas City, MO

50 – Faith Isn't Certainty
Sunday morning, March 20, 2011, Community Christian Church, Kansas City, MO

51 – Life's Too Short for Anything But Love
Sunday morning, July 22, 2018, Idlewild Community, Eagle Nest, NM

52 – Surrounded
Sunday morning, June 27, 2010, First Christian Church, Pasadena, TX

ABOUT THE AUTHOR

Robert Lee Hill served for more than thirty years at the Community Christian Church (Disciples of Christ) in Kansas City, Missouri, before being named Minister Emeritus in 2015. He works now as a nonfiction writer, poet, and community consultant for non-profit organizations focusing on social justice issues, particularly the increase of community engagement regarding quality education for all students in public schools, empowering citizens through voter registration, and quality health care for all.

Before his time in Kansas City, he served for four and a half years as Special Projects Director and Co-Director of Project Return, Inc., a non-profit agency working with ex-prisoners and their families in Nashville, Tennessee. Much prior to that, after his first year in college, he was drafted as a Conscientious Objector and spent two transformative years as a Youth and Family Worker at All Peoples Christian Church in South Central Los Angeles, where he would eventually be ordained.

He holds a B.A. degree from Texas Christian University, an M.Div. degree from Vanderbilt University Divinity School, and a D.D. degree from Christian Theological Seminary.

Since 1993, he has been co-host of the renowned Sunday morning radio show *Religion on the Line* on KCMO-Talk Radio 710 AM/103.7 FM.

He has written or edited ten previous books, including *All You Need Is (More) Love, Life's Too Short for Anything But Love, The Color of Sabbath,* and a volume of poems, *Hard to Tell.*

His papers and letters are archived at the State Historical Society of Missouri—Kansas City Research Center.